Trade, Aid and Security

Trade, Aid and Security

An Agenda for Peace and Development

Edited by
**Oli Brown, Mark Halle, Sonia Peña Moreno
and Sebastian Winkler**

London • Sterling, VA

First published by Earthscan in the UK and USA in 2007

ISBN-13: 978-1-84407-419-8 (paperback)
ISBN-13: 978-1-84407-420-4 (hardback)

Typeset by JS Typesetting Ltd, Porthcawl, Mid Glamorgan
Printed and bound in the UK by Cromwell Press, Trowbridge
Cover design by Susanne Harris
Front cover image 'After the War, Angola 2002' by Amelia Bookstein
Back cover image 'Carrying Water, Thyolo, Malawi 2002' by Amelia Bookstein

For a full list of publications please contact:

Earthscan
8–12 Camden High Street
London, NW1 0JH, UK
Tel: +44 (0)20 7387 8558
Fax: +44 (0)20 7387 8998
Email: earthinfo@earthscan.co.uk
Web: **www.earthscan.co.uk**

22883 Quicksilver Drive, Sterling, VA 20166-2012, USA

Earthscan is an imprint of James and James (Science Publishers) Ltd and publishes in
association with the International Institute for Environment and Development

A catalogue record for this book is available from the British Library

Library of Congress Cataloging-in-Publication Data
Trade, aid, and security : an agenda for peace and development / edited by
Oli Brown ... [et al.].
    p. cm.
  ISBN-13: 978-1-84407-420-4 (hardback)
  ISBN-10: 1-84407-420-X (hardback)
  ISBN-13: 978-1-84407-419-8 (pbk.)
  ISBN-10: 1-84407-419-6 (pbk.)
 1. Peace–Economic aspects. 2. Economic development–International
cooperation. 3. International trade–Political aspects. 4. Economic
assistance–International cooperation. 5. Security, International–Economic
aspects. I. Brown, Oli.
  JZ5538.T73 2007
  338.9–dc22

                                                        2006100474

This publication is printed on FSC certified totally chlorine-free paper.
FSC (the Forest Stewardship Council) is an international network to
promote responsible management of the world's forests.

Contents

List of Tables and Boxes

Tables

Boxes

The World Conservation Union and the International Institute for Sustainable Development

The World Conservation Union

Founded in 1948, The World Conservation Union (IUCN) brings together states, government agencies and a diverse range of non-governmental organizations (NGOs) in a unique world partnership: over 1000 members in all, spread across some 140 countries.

As a union, IUCN seeks to influence, encourage and assist societies throughout the world to conserve the integrity and diversity of nature and to ensure that any use of natural resources is equitable and ecologically sustainable.

IUCN builds on the strengths of its members, networks and partners to enhance their capacity and to support global alliances to safeguard natural resources at local, regional and global levels.

International Institute for Sustainable Development

The International Institute for Sustainable Development (IISD), based in Winnipeg, Canada, contributes to sustainable development by advancing policy recommendations on international trade and investment, economic policy, climate change and energy, measurement and assessment, and sustainable natural resources management. Through the internet, we report on international negotiations and share knowledge gained through collaborative projects with global partners, resulting in more rigorous research, capacity building in developing countries and better dialogue between north and south.

IISD's vision is better living for all – sustainably; its mission is to champion innovation, enabling societies to live sustainably. IISD is registered as a charitable organization in Canada and has 501(c)(3) status in the US. IISD receives core operating support from the Government of Canada, provided through the Canadian International Development Agency (CIDA), the International

Development Research Centre (IDRC) and Environment Canada, and from the Province of Manitoba. The Institute receives project funding from numerous governments inside and outside Canada, United Nations' agencies, foundations and the private sector. Visit www.iisd.org for more information.

List of Contributors

Richard Auty is Emeritus Professor of Economic Geography at Lancaster University. He previously taught at Dartmouth College and was a visiting fellow at the Institute of Development Studies (Sussex), Harvard Institute for International Development, Resources for the Future and the Woodrow Wilson School, Princeton.

Lloyd Axworthy is President and Vice Chancellor of the University of Winnipeg. Formerly Director and CEO of the Liu Institute for Global Issues at the University of British Columbia, and Canada's Foreign Minister from 1995 to 2000, Lloyd Axworthy's political career spanned 27 years, 6 of which he served in the Manitoba Legislative Assembly and 21 in the Federal Parliament. In 1997 he was nominated for the Nobel Peace Prize for his work on banning land mines.

Karen Ballentine is an independent consultant on the political economy of armed conflict. In 2004–05, she was Senior Consultant for the Fafo Institute for Applied International Studies. From 2000 to 2003, she directed the Economic Agendas in Civil Wars Program at the International Peace Academy.

Duncan Brack is an Associate Fellow of the Energy, Environment and Development Programme at Chatham House (the Royal Institute of International Affairs) in London in the UK, where he works mainly on illegal trade in natural resources. From 1998 to 2003, he was Head of the Programme, and from 1995 to 1998 a Senior Research Fellow at Chatham House, working on trade and environment issues.

Oli Brown is the coordinator of IISD–IUCN's Trade, Aid and Security initiative. After two years in Nepal managing education and conservation projects, Oli worked as a trade policy researcher for Oxfam GB. He has completed consultancies for the United Nations Development Programme (UNDP), New Zealand's International Aid and Development Agency (NZAID) and International Alert and has worked on a wide range of trade, environment and sustainable development issues.

Mark Curtis is currently an independent author, journalist and consultant. He is a former Research Fellow at Chatham House (the Royal Institute of International Affairs) and was until recently Director of the World Development Movement.

Mark Halle directs IISD's global programme on trade and investment as well as its European office in Geneva, Switzerland. He serves as a Senior Advisor to IUCN and runs the trade activities of the International Institute for Environment and Development's (IIED) Regional and International Networking Group. He is founder and former Chairman of the Board of the International Centre for Trade and Sustainable Development.

Gavin Hayman is an investigator and campaigner with Global Witness based in London, UK. He has contributed substantially to Global Witness' work on oil, gas and mining, and the linkages between natural resources and conflict.

Philippe Le Billon is Assistant Professor at the University of British Columbia, Department of Geography and Liu Institute for Global Issues. Holding an MBA and DPhil in Geography, he previously worked with the Overseas Development Institute and the International Institute for Strategic Studies on humanitarian and resource management issues.

Sonia Peña Moreno works at the Policy, Biodiversity and International Agreements Unit of IUCN. Her work as Policy Officer is related to issues of environmental governance, IUCN's general policy and environmental policy at the multilateral level.

Ian Smillie is an Ottawa-based development consultant and writer. He serves as Research Coordinator on Partnership Africa Canada's 'Diamonds and Human Security Project' and is an NGO participant in the intergovernmental 'Kimberley Process', which is developing a global certification system for rough diamonds.

Sebastian Winkler is Senior European Policy Officer and Head of the Countdown 2010 Secretariat at IUCN.

Acknowledgements

This book is the culmination of a four-year research collaboration between the IISD and the IUCN. It could not have been completed without the help and support of many valued colleagues and friends.

From the beginning, the direction and scope of our research has been guided by a dedicated and talented advisory group who have given generously of their time and experience. Without their input this project would have been much diminished. Chaired by the Honourable Lloyd Axworthy, the group included Duncan Brack, Gavin Hayman, Mark Beaumont Taylor, Valerie de Campos Mello, Christian Friis Bach, Georg Frerks, Ian Smillie, Leiv Lunde and Syed Mansoob Murshed. We are greatly indebted to them all.

We are also deeply grateful to our contributing authors, whose professionalism, insights and patience made the development of this book an inspiring and educational experience. In addition many reviewers helped to polish the chapters: among them Jessie Banfield, Don Hubert, Aaron Cosbey and Adam Barbolet. Special thanks must also go to Jason Switzer for his central role in developing these ideas and nurturing the project through its early years.

We are indebted to Rob West and the excellent team at Earthscan for seeing this volume through to completion, and to Stu Slayen and Deborah Murith for helping to smooth the publication process. Meanwhile the management skills of Clarita Martinet-Fay helped to keep this project on-track through the years and we owe a huge debt of thanks to Alec Crawford for his tireless editorial efforts to bring this volume together.

Warm thanks to David Runnalls, William Glanville and Martha Chouchena-Rojas, respectively President and vice-President of IISD, and Head of the Policy, Biodiversity and International Agreements Unit at IUCN, for their consistent moral and intellectual support for this project. Last, but certainly not least, we would like to acknowledge our donors, the Norwegian Agency for Development Cooperation (NORAD) and the Italian Ministry of Foreign Affairs (Directorate General for Development Cooperation – DGCS), who have generously supported the Trade, Aid and Security initiative from its inception.

Oli Brown
Mark Halle
Sonia Peña Moreno
Sebastian Winkler

Foreword

Lloyd Axworthy

Common risks threaten the security of individuals, regardless of their nationality. Old notions of national security predicated on the defence of state borders make little sense when the threats posed by violence and conflict, international networks of terrorists and criminals, pandemics and natural disasters require a new approach to protecting people.

The idea of 'human security' emerged as the Cold War ended and the inadequacies of the nation state system to meet the demands of globalization came into focus. The watchword for the human security idea was the principle of 'responsibility to protect' (R2P). If a state legitimately protects its citizens then it is in full right to exercise its sovereign power. If it fails to do so, or in fact is the perpetrator of a serious attack on the rights of its citizens, then the international community must assume the function. Under R2P, there shall be no more Rwanda and Srebrenica, or indeed Darfur.

This has an important bearing on development policy because peace and security are essential preconditions for sustainable development. Progress is impossible in the midst of conflict and insecurity; institutions cannot function, people cannot plan for the future and education and sanitation take a backseat to day-to-day survival. It is no coincidence that those countries that are the furthest away from achieving the Millennium Development Goals (MDGs) are those that continue to suffer political and economic instability.

As a Special United Nations (UN) Envoy for Ethiopia and Eritrea I saw just how intimate is the connection. The failure of the two governments to engage in any effort to resolve their border dispute and the corollary failure of the international community to seriously address the issue had a major impact on the well-being of the people in the two countries. A World Bank study concluded that millions were inflicted with enduring poverty because of a 'security' issue. Yet governmental aid agencies, the UN Millennium Development Goals Secretariat and a variety of multilateral agencies, while calling for more money to alleviate the poverty of the region, would not consider the security element as a necessary condition needing resolution.

At the UN's World Summit in September 2005, world leaders accepted the idea of a responsibility to protect; a definition of sovereignty that is centred not on the prerogatives of the state but on its primary responsibility to protect its citizens. It is a principle that needs to be incorporated as part of any aid and trade strategy.

This historic commitment came out of the work of the International Commission on Intervention and State Sovereignty, established by Canada in 2000 at the request of the Secretary General. Their 2001 report stated: 'Such a responsibility implies an evaluation of the issue from the perspective of the victim, not the intervener; if a state cannot provide protection or is the author of the crime, then it forfeits its sovereign right and the international community steps in, not just to protect, but to prevent and rebuild.'

As the latter part of this passage makes clear, the responsibility to prevent and rebuild are crucial components of the responsibility to protect principle. Prevention will always be a less costly alternative to war.

As Canadian foreign minister between 1996 and 2000 I saw that international responses to crises were (and still are) overwhelmingly reactive – we were constantly trying to put out the fires. It became obvious to me that the 'fires' are more common because the international system does not lend itself to conflict prevention.

The idea of R2P has come a long way. But I'd suggest that we need to take the idea even further. Rather than focusing our attention solely on reactive responses to conflict, we must also consider how current policies can systematically undermine peace and development.

Trade and aid policies are two of the areas that most require our attention. The direction and priorities of trade and aid policies, largely decided by the developed world, can have profound impacts on the economies and stability of the developing world – in both positive and negative ways.

In theory at least, if trade and aid policies are carefully designed and implemented, they should encourage peace and security. Trade can establish incentives for peace by building a sense of interdependence and community. Trade can also be a powerful driver of economic growth and stability, reducing poverty and providing non-military means to resolve disputes. There's some truth in the old saying that countries (and regions) that trade tend not to fight.

Likewise, aid can help tackle the underlying causes of conflict by reducing inequalities, tackling poverty, providing basic services and promoting sustainable livelihoods. Aid can also help to improve domestic governance and help countries bounce back from economic shocks.

However, it is increasingly clear that international trade does not automatically reinforce stability or security. Nor is aid, as currently constructed, successfully achieving its aim of poverty alleviation. The reality is that badly designed trade and aid policies are too often increasing the likelihood and longevity of violent conflict.

In practice, the rules that govern international trade are fundamentally unfair, biased towards rich countries and their corporations. Current trade policy in Organisation for Economic Co-operation and Development (OECD) countries denies vital market access to the developing world's products, particularly their agricultural goods. Escalating tariffs, complex regulations and perverse domestic subsidies in the developed world continue to inhibit the efforts of developing countries to diversify their economies.

At the same time, developing countries are being pushed to adopt uncompromising market liberalization, which can reduce government revenues and undermine employment, increasing the prospects for political instability and competition over scarce resources.

In essence, the poorly designed and unfair trade policies of the developed world are stunting economic growth in the developing world and leaving many countries locked into notoriously volatile commodity markets. A reliance on the export of natural resources tends to lead to weaker institutions, economic dependence and political instability. Coupled with poorly governed international markets for natural resources, faltering economic growth and unpredictable government revenues, this has proven to be an explosive combination time and again around the world.

Likewise, aid has not always been an entirely positive force. Critics of development assistance have long argued that aid can make a bad situation worse, that it can ignore signs of trouble, that in supporting bad governments it can help set the stage for conflict, and that in ignoring security considerations it contributes to poverty.

In essence, trade, aid and security are all mutually reliant; if aid policy is going to be effective at lifting people out of poverty it must be conducted in a secure environment free from the existence or threat of violent conflict. Aid should also help countries and communities access the very real benefits of fair international trade. And countries will only be able to gain from international trade if they have the capacity to negotiate even-handed trade agreements.

We need to go beyond R2P. The international community also has, I would suggest, a solemn 'responsibility to prevent' the outbreak of conflict. The extent to which we are helping to promote stability and avoid armed conflict is crucially dependent on the structural conditions established by our trade and aid policies. If we're serious about reducing armed conflict around the world we must first – and at the very least – ensure that our trade and aid policies 'do no harm'.

Clearly, trade and aid policies are not the sole sources of violent conflict: identity, ideology and history are all important factors. The point is simply that peace-building is not just about sending battalions of peacekeeping troops in blue helmets. Peace-building and conflict prevention must also be about tackling the underlying causes of conflict – fixing the system that is permitting the fires.

This book is about fixing that system. Written by leading experts, and benefiting greatly from the guidance of a committed and talented advisory committee, it develops our understanding of the complex links between trade, aid and security. It focuses on what should be our end objectives: ensuring trade and aid policies are conflict-sensitive, fostering responsible business conduct, reducing the trade in 'conflict resources', promoting good governance and helping countries to manage more effectively the revenues they receive from natural resources and aid. Most importantly, it suggests practical solutions that the international community and domestic policy makers can adopt to achieve these goals.

We have an opportunity to carry forward the momentum generated by the R2P movement and reform the elements of trade and aid policy that undermine peace and stability around the world. Now that would be a tremendous contribution to human security.

Lloyd Axworthy is President of the University of Winnipeg and former foreign minister of Canada. He also chaired the advisory committee of the IISD–IUCN Trade, Aid and Security initiative.

List of Acronyms and Abbreviations

ACP	Africa, Caribbean and Pacific
AGOA	African Growth and Opportunity Agreement
ASCM	Agreement on Subsidies and Countervailing Measures
ASM	artisanal and small-scale mining
ATCA	Alien Torts Claims Act
BP	British Petroleum
CCAMLR	Convention on the Conservation of Antarctic Marine Living Resources
CERF	Central Emergency Response Fund
CFF	Compensatory Finance Facility
CIDA	Canadian International Development Agency
CITES	Convention on International Trade in Endangered Species of Wild Fauna and Flora
CPET	Central Point of Expertise on Timber
CPN	Communist Party of Nepal
CSA	Canadian Standards Association
CSR	corporate social responsibility
DAC	Development Assistance Committee (OECD)
DFID	Department for International Development (UK)
DRC	Democratic Republic of the Congo
EBA	Everything But Arms
EC	European Commission
ECA	export credit agency
ECHO	European Commission's Humanitarian Aid Office
EITI	Extractive Industries Transparency Initiative
EPA	Economic Partnership Agreement
EU	European Union
FAO	Food and Agricultural Organization
FATF	Financial Action Task Force
FDI	foreign direct investment
FIS	Front Islamique du Salut of Algeria
FLEGT	Forest Law Enforcement, Governance and Trade
FLN	Front de Libération Nationale of Algeria
FSC	Forest Stewardship Council

G8	Group of eight
GATT	General Agreement on Tariffs and Trade
GDI	gross domestic income
GDP	gross domestic product
GNI	gross national income
GNP	gross national product
GRRT	Guide on Resource Revenue Transparency
GSP	Generalized System of Preferences
HIPC	heavily indebted poor countries
IDS	Institute of Development Studies (UK)
IFC	International Finance Corporation
IFI	International Financial Institution
IIED	International Institute for Environment and Development
IISD	International Institute for Sustainable Development
IMF	International Monetary Fund
IPO	Initial Public Offering
IUU	illegal, unregulated and unreported fishing
IUCN	World Conservation Union, formerly the International Union for the Conservation of Nature
KPCS	Kimberley Process Certification Scheme
LDC	Least Developed Country
MCA	Millennium Challenge Account
MDG	Millennium Development Goals
MEA	Multilateral Environmental Agreement
MFDC	Movement of the Democratic Forces of Casamance
MIGA	Multilateral Investment Guarantee Agency
MSC	Marine Stewardship Council
NAFTA	North America Free Trade Agreement
NATO	North Atlantic Treaty Organization
NEPAD	New Partnership for Africa's Development
NGO	non-governmental organization
NZAID	New Zealand's International Aid and Development Agency
OCHA	Office for the Coordination of Humanitarian Assistance (UN)
ODA	overseas development aid
OECD	Organisation for Economic Co-operation and Development
OPEC	Organization of the Petroleum Exporting Countries
PNG	Papua New Guinea
PRSP	poverty reduction strategy paper
PWYP	Publish What You Pay
R2P	responsibility to protect
ROSC	Reports on the Observance of Standards and Codes
RTA	regional trade agreement
RUF	Revolutionary United Front (Sierra Leone)
SDT	special and differential treatment
SSM	special safeguard mechanism
TNC	Transnational Corporation

UN	United Nations
UNCTAD	United Nations Conference on Trade and Development
UNDP	United Nations Development Programme
UNESCO	United Nations Educational, Scientific and Cultural Organization
UNHCR	United Nations High Commissioner for Refugees
UNITA	União Nacional para a Independência Total de Angola
UNRISD	United Nations Research Institute for Social Development
USAID	United States Agency for International Development
VP	Voluntary Principles
WTO	World Trade Organization
WWF	World Wildlife Fund

Introduction

Trade, Aid and Security: An Agenda for Peace and Development

Duncan Brack

The battle for peace has to be fought on two fronts. The first front is the security front, where victory spells freedom from fear. The second is the economic and social front, where victory means freedom from want. Only victory on both fronts can assure the world of an enduring peace.

These words, spoken by US Secretary of State Edwin Stettinius during the founding conference of the UN, remain as true today as they did when he uttered them in 1945 (UNDP, 2005, p168). And yet more than 60 years later, victory has not been won on either front. Far too many of the world's peoples live in fear and in want – and, as Stettinius recognized, the one feeds on the other.

Over the six decades that separate us from the foundation of the UN, the landscape of global security has changed beyond all recognition. The ending of World War II – still in progress during the conference – did not bring an end to conflict. Nationalist insurgencies fought colonial powers, usually with success, only to find that independence often released ethnic tensions and civil wars within the new states. The armed truce established by the global superpowers ensured that there was no return to global conflict, but proxy wars fought by their clients erupted throughout the developing world. The ending of the Cold War may have brought some relief from the threat of nuclear confrontation, but it has now given way to the global war on terror, and a widespread perception that the world is becoming not more but less safe.

The 'war on terror', however, has not replaced more conventional wars; since 1990, more than 3 million people have died in armed conflicts, and many more as a result of famine and disease associated with war (in contrast, perhaps 20,000 have died as result of terrorist incidents since 1998). Compared to the ColdWar period, however, the nature of these wars has changed fundamentally: conflict is now much more strongly associated with poverty. From 1946 to 1989, low-income countries accounted for just over one third of all conflicts, but during the period 1990–2003, low-income developing countries constituted more than half of all the countries and territories experiencing violent conflict. Nearly 40 per cent of the world's recent conflicts, including several of the bloodiest and longest, have been in Africa. And even though the number of conflicts has fallen since 1990, today's wars last longer, and their impact on development is accordingly more severe (UNDP, 2005, pp151–154).

Despite this changing pattern of security and conflict, the international institutions erected in the aftermath of World War II, in response to the threats posed by conflicts *between* states, have remained largely unchanged in their architecture and outlook. Yet nowadays most conflicts are not between but *within* states – poor states – and most victims are not soldiers but civilians. It ought to be even more difficult today than it was in Stettinius' time to consider peace and development – freedom from fear and freedom from want – as separate and unconnected objectives, yet that is largely what today's global and national institutions still do. Aid policy and trade policy – the crucial tools to unlock development – are seldom looked at from the perspective of promoting security, and security is not generally seen as a precondition for development.

The need to see these objectives – trade, aid and security – as interlocking components of the overriding objectives of peace and development is the point of this book. Our chapter authors, all leading experts in their fields, demonstrate how current approaches to aid and trade, although they have had some successes, have all too often failed to eradicate poverty, insecurity and conflict – and even, in some cases, have actually made them worse. We focus on the poorest countries, and in particular on those most highly dependent on the extraction of natural resources, such as timber, oil or gems; often these countries are poor and conflict-ridden precisely because they are reliant on natural resources. And the revenues that flow from the markets of the west and the newly industrializing countries, hungry for the natural resources poor countries produce, often both stimulate wars and pay for them.

This is a key moment for the exploration of these trade–aid–security linkages. After years of decline, aid spending has finally turned up again, even though much of the increase over the last two years has been devoted to one country, Iraq. The failure of the reconstruction effort in Iraq is a stark reminder of the way in which development both relies on peace and security and is an essential precondition for it. At the same time Liberia and, perhaps, the Democratic Republic of the Congo (DRC), provide more positive examples of the use of aid in post-conflict reconstruction.

No country, however, has ever been lifted out of poverty through development aid alone. Developing countries need the access to international markets and foreign investment that allows their economies to develop and diversify. So the dismantling of trade barriers to poor-country exports is a crucial part of the equation. Yet with the World Trade Organization (WTO) Doha Round of negotiations somewhere, in the words of Indian trade minister Kamal Nath, 'between intensive care and the crematorium', there seems little hope of further progress on that front. In any case, some time ago it became impossible to present Doha as the 'development round' it was originally supposed to be.

This faltering progress on aid and trade takes place against the background of a mounting threat to security and development everywhere – the impact of environmental degradation, and in particular of catastrophic climate change. The hundreds of thousands who marched to 'make poverty history' during the Group of eight (G8) summit in 2005 chose the wrong target. Unless radical action is taken soon, climate change (mitigation of which was the other G8 priority) will undo all the benefits of greater aid and debt relief, and more. Ecosystem collapse risks fatally undermining development and therefore security and therefore peace.

So the need for action is urgent. And although conflict may now be more strongly associated with poor countries than in previous decades, its impacts affect us all, wherever we live. The moral responsibility to address suffering, the shared interest in peace and global security and the awareness of the consequences of conflict, including the spread of disease and famine, growing environmental degradation and the escalation in the numbers of refugees, provide more than enough justification for taking this urgent action, now.

Security and development

Why does development depend so crucially upon peace and security? For most of the post-war period, the debate about 'security' focused on military threats to sovereign states. However, as the UN High-Level Panel on Threats, Challenges and Change argued in 2004, this is no longer an adequate definition. The panel identified a much broader range of issues as threats to security: violence within states, including civil wars, large-scale human rights abuses and genocide; poverty, infectious disease and environmental degradation; nuclear, radiological, chemical and biological weapons; terrorism; and transnational organized crime.

Against this broader background, the link between peace and development becomes obvious. Sustainable development requires, above all, change and innovation in the way in which economic activities are carried out. It requires long-term investment in new technologies and new ways of doing things. It requires the provision of resources for basic needs and for social and economic infrastructure. It requires good governance, including respect for the rule of law and basic human rights, and effective, responsive and incorrupt democratic institutions. None of these requirements for achieving sustainable development are rendered more possible by insecurity.

'Failed states', such as Somalia, provide a grim reminder of what the absence of security means for sustainable development. Societies faced with conflict or the threat of conflict invest in military resources at the expense of social and economic investments. Powerful military elites threaten democracy and the rule of law, and tend to generate corruption. In periods of uncertainty and instability, it becomes rational to avoid long-term investments, and concentrate on shorter-term survival, or on investing in other, more stable, countries. Most obviously, conflict itself leads to loss of life, consumes wealth and resources and causes environmental damage: as the World Bank described it, it is 'development in reverse' (World Bank, 2003, pix).

These arguments were recognized in the Plan of Implementation of the World Summit on Sustainable Development, agreed at Johannesburg in 2002, which listed peace and security, along with many other issues, as underlying prerequisites for sustainable development.[1] As the summary of the debate at one of the round tables put it, 'A number of participants pointed out that peace and security are essential preconditions for economic growth and development as well as protection of the environment. Sustainable development is impossible in regions and countries marked by conflicts, upheavals and wars' (UN, 2002, p123).

And sustainable development itself is an effective counter to conflict and insecurity. Figures derived from World Bank econometric models show a striking relationship between the wealth of a nation and its chances of having a civil war. A country with a gross domestic product (GDP) of $250 per capita has a predicted probability of war beginning at some point over the following five years of 15 per cent, all else being equal. [NB: Throughout this book, '$' denotes US dollars.] This probability reduces by half for a country with GDP of $600 per capita, and by half again, to less than 4 per cent, for a country with $1250 per head; countries with GDP of over $5000 per capita have a less than 1 per cent chance of experiencing civil conflict (Humphreys, 2003, p2).[2] 'Civil war thus reflects not just a problem *for* development, but a failure *of* development' (World Bank, 2003, pix).

The promotion of sustainable development, then, is vital to the realization of peace and security. This is particularly important in the case of countries highly dependent on the exploitation of natural resources – including minerals, fossil fuels, timber and agricultural commodities – which are peculiarly vulnerable to instability and conflict.

Development, natural resources and security

Why should this be so? There are two sets of reasons, as a series of World Bank studies concluded in 2003. 'Developing countries face substantially higher risks of violent conflict and poor governance if they are highly dependent on primary commodities... Revenues from the legal or illegal exploitation of natural resources have financed devastating conflicts in a large number of countries... Even where countries initially manage to avoid violent conflict, large rents from natural resources can weaken state structures and make governments less accountable, often leading to the emergence of secessionist rebellions and all-out civil war' (Bannon and Collier, 2003, pix).

Natural resources pay for wars

Most obviously, natural resources can act as a source of the financing that is necessary to sustain armed forces and fight wars – particularly civil wars, where insurgent organizations do not benefit from the tax revenues enjoyed by governments. Unless the rebels are financed from outside the country – and this is now much less likely than it was at the height of the Cold War – they must generate income by operating business activities alongside their military operations. Since rebel groups tend to be based in rural areas, extortion rackets aimed at the exploitation of primary commodities with high economic rents are an obvious activity; often this can escalate into complete control of commodity extraction and trade.

In Cambodia, for example, after Chinese support dried up in the late 1980s, the Khmer Rouge turned to logging and gem-mining to fund their war against the Vietnamese-supported government. Timber and diamonds paid for Charles Taylor's wars in Liberia and Sierra Leone. Even the humble cashew nut helped generate revenues that funded conflict in Senegal. The most extreme example is the brutal series of civil wars and foreign incursions in DRC, a country enormously rich in diamonds, timber and coltan.

Conflict may sometimes be triggered by the expectation of future control of resources. Studies show that violent secessionist movements are statistically more likely if the country has valuable natural resources; this not only provides the revenue needed to arm the groups but may also help to foster the belief that the area in which the resources are located can survive and prosper as an independent entity. The existence of natural gas reserves in Aceh province in Indonesia, for example – according to some estimates, the most extensive in the world – helped to stimulate a secessionist movement that signed a peace agreement with the central government only after the devastating effects of the Indian Ocean tsunami in 2004.

Natural resources are rarely, of course, the sole source of conflict: identity (including ethnicity and religion), ideology, poor governance and corruption are all important factors, and may frequently lead to conflict even where there is no particular abundance of natural resources. Nevertheless, where it exists, resource wealth can often underpin and lengthen those conflicts that do arise from other causes. And conflicts themselves can often increase the rate of natural resource extraction, as other forms of income generation – manufacturing, tourism, and so on – contract and become less valuable.

These linkages between natural resources and conflict are never, however, inevitable. 'For every resource-rich country that has suffered from violent conflict', observed Michael Ross, 'two or three have avoided it' (Ross, 2003, p19). The challenge for aid and trade policy-makers is therefore to devise ways in which to break the links, and ensure that natural resources can be exploited without stimulating or funding conflict. This is the theme of two chapters in this book: Chapter 2, which demonstrates how aid can be designed to be conflict sensitive, and Chapter 4, which examines the series of ways in which conflict resources can be excluded from external markets, thus ending their function as a generator of war finance.

Natural resources generate instability: The 'natural resource curse'

The second reason why natural resources are often associated with conflict is less direct than the first, but no less important. As we have seen, poor countries are more prone to instability and conflict than richer ones; and countries that rely on natural resource exploitation are frequently poor.

Intuitively, this seems wrong; an abundance of natural resources ought to be a blessing for a country and its population, providing a ready source of employment, export earnings and wealth. Yet this is not borne out by experience. Twelve out of the world's 20 most mineral-dependent states are classified as highly indebted poor countries, and five of them have experienced civil wars since 1990. Three of the world's six most oil-dependent states are similarly classified, and five out of the top 20 suffered civil wars in the 1990s.

Why should resource wealth cause poverty? Governments reliant on profits (or rents) from natural resource exploitation generally do a much worse job of building stable political institutions than do those reliant on general taxation, and are much less responsive to public opinion. The presidency of Mobutu Sese Seko in resource-rich Zaire (now DRC) from 1965 to 1997 earned a reputation as one of the world's foremost examples of kleptocracy, generating more than $5 billion in personal fortune for Mobutu and his family while his people starved and the country's infrastructure collapsed.

Similarly, governments reliant on income from resources rather than people tend not to bother to invest in basic services such as health care and, critically, education. They often fail to diversify their economies into other activities, which may lead directly to economic crises if the terms of trade become adverse – which can often happen for volatile primary commodities. In 1989, for example, after the export quota system of the International Coffee Agreement broke down, world coffee prices fell sharply. Rwanda, a major coffee producer, saw its export earnings halve in three years, with severe impacts on rural livelihoods, and an accompanying growth in support in coffee-growing areas for the rebel Rwandan Patriotic Front (Gasana, 2002).

Governance suffers from the corruption engendered by large flows of revenues, and from the ways in which governments fearing dissent often use resource-derived revenues to dispense patronage and bolster internal security. In Angola, for example, over $1 billion of oil revenues per year – about a quarter of the state's yearly income – have gone unaccounted for since 1996 (Global Witness, 2004, p4).

There may also be local grievances arising from the activities of the extractive industries, which frequently cause major disruption to local communities and local environments. On a wider scale, the distribution of the benefits from natural resource extraction may increase inequalities – even in the absence of widespread corruption – and engender dissatisfaction and instability. In 1988, unhappiness over the perceived unfairness of the distribution of the earnings from the Panguna copper and gold mine in Bougainville Island, Papua New Guinea (which had generated nearly half of PNG's export earnings in the previous 20 years), combined with resentment at the mine's environmental impact, led to a secessionist conflict that is estimated to have claimed 10,000 lives.

In addition to resource *abundance* leading to conflict, resource *scarcity* can do the same. The rapid growth in population in recent decades has been accompanied by a dramatic increase in the exploitation of natural resources to meet their needs. This has been accompanied in turn by environmental degradation and resource shortages, including land erosion, desertification and degradation, water shortages, deforestation, agricultural failures and exhaustion of fisheries. All these factors of course contribute to poverty and economic failure, which may then contribute to conflict as a reaction to perceived failures of governance, such as some communities being favoured at the expense of others. They may also lead directly to conflicts over the control of what resources remain, not simply out of a desire to seize revenues, but as a matter of economic survival. 'Water wars' have been predicted for some time, and oil wars, of course, may already have taken place.

As above, it is never inevitable that resource-rich countries will be poor and unstable. Botswana, for example, rich in diamonds, copper and nickel, has nevertheless been consistently among the fastest growing and least violent countries in Africa; but it is the exception, not the rule. Once again, the challenge for policy makers is to ensure that aid and trade policies help countries manage the revenues from natural resources intelligently and sustainably. This is the theme of several chapters of the book. Chapter 1 argues for the reform of international trade policy to recognize the value of security, Chapter 3 deals in detail with the theme of governance, Chapter 5 looks at the behaviour of extractive companies in fragile and war-torn states, and Chapter 6 deals with the key problem of managing revenue flows.

It should be clear, then, that trade and aid policies are critical to efforts to avoid or ameliorate conflict over the exploitation of natural resources. If poorly designed and applied, however, they can also sometimes exacerbate it. The next two sections look in more detail at the trade and aid policy context.

Trade

The rapid expansion of international trade and investment has been one of the defining characteristics of the world economy since 1945, and a key factor in the complex of processes known as 'globalization'. For example, international merchandise trade (primary commodities and manufactured products) has grown almost 30-fold in volume since 1950. In 1973 less than a twentieth of world product was traded; now the proportion is one-fifth (Maddison, 2001).

Trade and security

The links between international trade and security have been recognized for centuries. As the French philosopher Montesquieu put it in 1749, 'wherever there is commerce, manners are gentle' (Humphreys, 2003, p8). At the most basic level, trade promotes prosperity and reduces poverty. More than that, however, free trade has also been seen as the agency that would foster internationalism and end war. 'For the disbanding of great armies and the promotion of peace,' wrote John Bright, one of the leaders of the Anti-Corn Law League in 1840s Britain, 'I rely on the abolition of tariffs, on the brotherhood of the nations resulting from free trade in the products of industry' (Sturgis, 1969). Trade was believed to promote interdependence and a sense of international community, building links between peoples and nations and rendering conflict less likely. In more recent times this has been supported by empirical research, showing that states that trade with each other are indeed less likely to fight each other (Humphreys, 2003, p8).

These arguments were forgotten, or ignored, during the disastrous trade wars of the 1930s, but the end of World War II saw a revival of the belief in the political as well as the economic benefits of trade. The establishment of new international institutions – the UN, the World Bank, the International Monetary Fund (IMF) – brought with it the hope of effective regulation of international economics and an equitable international system to govern the relationships of nations. These organizations were supposed to be accompanied by an international trade organization, but the proposal was vetoed by the US, and its creation, in the form of the WTO, took a further 40 years (its 'provisional' substitute, the General Agreement on Tariffs and Trade (GATT), operating in the meantime).

Similarly, the creation of the European Economic Community in 1958 owed much to the belief of its founding fathers in the building of a community of nations through trade. The economic links created by the Community not only helped to integrate western Europe in economic terms but also laid the foundations for the closer monetary and political linkages now embodied in the European Union (EU). Perhaps most importantly, and in contrast to other regional agreements, the EU and its predecessors have provided a means of redistributing income from rich to poor countries, an effective compensation mechanism for the losers from trade liberalization. In security terms, the results have been striking: whereas in the 75-year period from 1870 to 1945, western Europe was afflicted by three major wars, two of them becoming global in reach, in the 50 years since the creation of the Community, no armed conflicts have taken place between these states.

These arguments are relevant to developed and developing countries alike, and have underpinned the establishment of a plethora of regional economic agreements and institutions, though none have proceeded as far as the EU in political as well as economic integration. As well as forging direct links between countries, trade creates a situation of mutual dependence that conflict may menace. Trade liberalization can also help to expose and reduce inequitable privileges, elite rent-seeking, and corruption.

Furthermore, international institutions provide forums for international dispute resolution, and may enable the use of alternative forms of pressure to military force, including trade sanctions, financial coercion and diplomatic and public pressure. As one member of the European Parliament put it in 2004, 'if Slovakia had not been joining the EU, its persecution of the Hungarian-speaking minority under the Meciar government could not have been stopped. Soon, neighbouring Hungary would no doubt have been forced by its public opinion to intervene. All the makings of a Balkan-style crisis were there. Economic integration gives each member state an unprecedented stake in good neighbourliness' (Huhne, 2004).

Similarly, international trade may help to enhance security within as well as between states. The economic prosperity that should result can help to reduce poverty-driven conflicts. Resource wealth can in the right circumstances be translated into capital for more broadly based development and distribution. Finances can be harnessed to improve the protection and sustainable exploitation of the natural resource base and compensate those who lose out from the process of trade liberalization.[3]

Trade and insecurity

It should be noted that while in theory, and frequently in practice, trade does bring all these benefits, there can be major negative impacts too. The process of trade liberalization has been deeply uneven, benefiting rich economies more than the poorest, and the gains from trade have not been distributed evenly throughout the global economy. Industrialized countries still maintain higher trade barriers against many developing-country exports than they do against each others'. The world's poorest countries saw their share in world trade drop from 0.6 per cent in 1980 to 0.4 per cent in 2000 (UNCTAD, 1999).

Many of the problems caused by dependency on natural resources come from the volatility of resource revenues. For the last century, international prices for primary commodities, including oil and minerals, have been far more volatile than prices for manufactured goods, and since 1970 this volatility has grown worse. Throughout the 1980s the average price of commodities (excluding oil) fell by 5 per cent a year in real terms, so that in 1990 commodity prices were 45 per cent below their 1980 levels and 10 per cent lower in real terms than in the middle of the Great Depression in 1932 (South Centre, 1996). They then stabilized somewhat in the 1990s and began an upward turn again towards the end of the decade, on the back of booming demand, mainly in China and India.

Despite this recent improvement, studies suggest that it is the volatility of the revenue flows that matters, whether they vary up or down, rather than their absolute levels. Revenue shocks from fluctuations in export earnings tend to promote corruption, weaken state institutions and create a host of budget and management problems. In theory, governments ought to be able to buffer their economies against market shocks by setting up stabilization funds, but experience with such mechanisms has not been encouraging, with the funds often being poorly managed and ending up doing more harm than good. International commodity agreements and cartels, common in the 1960s and 1970s, have now almost all collapsed, with the major exception of the Organization of the Petroleum Exporting Countries (OPEC). The impact of the ending of the International Coffee Agreement's export quota system on global coffee prices and on rural poverty and unrest in Rwanda has been noted above; over the last 30 years, coffee prices have swung from a little over $0.40 a pound to over $3, an almost eight-fold variation.[4]

Another possible counter to this problem is economic diversification; an obvious first step is to develop downstream industries to process and add value to raw materials. Yet this strategy often fails to work in practice. One reason is that industrialized states still place higher tariffs on processed goods than on raw materials, in order to protect their own industrial sectors from competition. Mean tariffs levied by the OECD states on copper and copper products in 2001, for example, varied from zero for copper ores and concentrates to 4.12 per cent for tubes and pipes of refined copper; for aluminium, from zero for ores and concentrates to 6.13 per cent for wire (UNCTAD–TRAINS, 2001). Subsidies are also still common, particularly in the agricultural sector, where farm lobbies in the US, EU and Japan exert a political influence out of all proportion to their economic significance.

Many developing countries have nevertheless succeeded in diversifying away from reliance on primary commodities, but it is never an easy process. When international demand for raw materials is high, their prices tend to rise, and commodity-exporting countries experience a growth in their export earnings. In turn, however, this pushes up the value of their currencies, making their exports relatively more expensive. Any other industrial sectors they may have, such as manufacturing, then find it more difficult to export, and even in the domestic market their products may be undercut by cheaper imports. This can lead to the so-called 'hollowing-out' of the economy, where resource extraction becomes the only internationally competitive sector; this is often known as the 'Dutch disease' after the experience of The Netherlands following the discovery of gas reserves in the North Sea in the 1960s. When commodity prices fall again, the manufacturing sector may have shrunk too much to generate the export earnings and employment needed to compensate, and government revenue may be taken up with more urgent needs such as addressing unemployment and maintaining basic services.

Trade may also contribute directly to conflict and insecurity by providing export and earnings opportunities for groups engaged in conflict – as we saw above. Export markets very seldom discriminate between products produced under the rule of legitimate governments and those whose revenues fund armed groups – or between products produced and exported in accordance with national laws, and those which are illegal. In recent years a number of international initiatives, including the Kimberley Process on conflict diamonds, and the EU's Forest Law Enforcement, Governance and Trade initiative (FLEGT) on illegal timber, have been launched to try and provide means through which conflict-related or illegal resources can be excluded from consumer markets.

It should be clear, however, that international trade has the potential to assist countries to escape from poverty. Aid cannot do this by itself; developing countries need the access to international markets and foreign investment that allows their economies to develop and diversify. It was for this reason that the WTO's Doha Round of trade negotiations, which started in 2001, was labelled the 'development round', supposedly focusing on direct benefits to the poorest countries. Yet even if the Round had succeeded, and trade barriers against developing countries had been reduced, many poor countries lack the capacity to benefit fully from trade and investment liberalization.

Economies opened up abruptly to trade can suffer severe consequences, including major impacts on particular sectors and regions and a loss of government revenue from lower import and export duties (on which poor countries, lacking efficient income tax systems, are often highly dependent). The de-regulation and privatization that often accompanies trade and investment liberalization opens developing country economies to new stresses and new requirements for government regulation and enforcement for which they are often not well suited. Transnational corporations, particularly those in the extractive industries, can often prove resistant to regulation by their host-state governments, with negative social and environmental consequences. So while in the long term trade liberalization will generally have positive consequences, in the short term it may engender increased inequality, hardship and instability, undermining government authority and leading to a greater possibility of conflict. The latest set of proposals in the Doha Round when it was suspended in July 2006, while attractive, on balance, to medium-income developing countries with large export sectors, offered very little to the poorest countries and in many cases would have made their situation worse.

Aid

It has been commonplace in recent years to write off official development assistance, or 'aid', as increasingly irrelevant. Overseas development aid (ODA) fell steadily in real terms throughout the 1990s. Although it rose again after 2001, and in 2004 reached $79.5 billion, this still represents just 0.26 per cent of OECD countries' gross national product (GNP), and in any case a significant proportion of the increase was accounted for by aid to Iraq. Only five donor countries have ever reached the UN's target of 0.7 per cent of GNP devoted to international development aid.

In contrast, flows of foreign direct investment (FDI) have grown substantially in recent decades, and for the developing world as a whole have been worth about 10 times as much as overseas aid (though in recent years, with the end of the wave of 1990s privatizations, FDI has fallen). Yet this has been very heavily skewed towards the richer developing countries; in recent years China has been overwhelmingly the most important destination, and throughout the 1990s the top 10 developing-country recipients together received more than 70 per cent of total flows to the developing world. For the 37 countries in the 'low human development' category of the UN's Human Development Index, in 2003 FDI was greater than overseas aid for just five of them; on average for this group, aid was worth almost seven times as much as FDI (UNDP, 2005).

Aid and security

For the poorest countries, then, aid still has a vital role to play. Poor countries enjoy least access to FDI primarily because of structural problems in their economies: a shortage of skills needed to convert the capital, political risk and restrictions on capital inflows. Aid can help in tackling all of these problems, and thereby enabling poor countries to benefit from inward investment.

Similarly, as we have seen, many poor countries lack the capacity fully to benefit from trade liberalization, which needs effective governance structures such as a lack of corruption, trade-friendly customs agencies, an independent judiciary, a tax system that does not need to rely on import and export duties, and so on. Once again, aid can assist a country in preparing for the opening up of its markets, in diversifying its economy, and in improving infrastructure, including transport, power and telecommunications. This can in turn help to lower business costs and improve the international competitiveness of activities that do not rely on high location-specific rents for their profitability.

Crucially, aid can also assist in supporting good governance, including developing efficient and incorrupt bureaucracies, improving the democratic nature of institutions of government, and introducing policies designed to ensure that local communities benefit from economic activity such as mineral or fossil fuel extraction. An important element is revenue transparency, which can help to build the legitimacy of governments and reduce support for rebel movements where this feeds on perceived corruption or misappropriation of revenues. Independent monitoring, supported by donor governments, is likely to be an important element in this, as is support for the development of civil society groups that can use the information thus made available.

Finally, aid can be specifically used to prevent conflict and to improve post-conflict recovery. Neither of these areas has been extensively studied, but World Bank research shows that the returns on aid in countries emerging from large-scale civil war can be particularly high. Supporting social policies, particularly health services, and regenerating local economies and social structures through community-led initiatives should therefore have a high priority (Humphreys, 2003, p19).

Aid and insecurity

If used properly, then, aid should be able to weaken or remove the underlying causes of conflict and insecurity. Yet often it can be misused. Aid has been accused of contributing to the conflict dynamic in Sudan, of propping up the Mobutu regime in Zaire and the Marcos regime in the Philippines, and of financing socially divisive resettlement and transmigration schemes throughout Asia and Latin America. Aid can also be appropriated by armed groups; in Sudan, for example, rebel movements have looted and taxed aid deliveries, and established 'humanitarian' front organizations to interface directly with the aid community (Halle et al, 2002).

As we have seen, many countries that are highly dependent on natural resources are likely to be among the poorest developing countries, and are accordingly more dependent on aid than the average. Given the potential volatility and lack of control over aid flows by the domestic government, this can sometimes exaggerate, rather than reduce, the instabilities associated with natural resources.

Indeed, there is a strong parallel between revenues from aid disbursements and those from export earnings from natural resources. Both can contribute to instability for much the same reasons: corruption, mismanagement and volatility. In less than two months in 1998–99, for example, Malawi received $150 million in balance-of-payments support, more that twice the total of aid disbursements in the preceding 18 months, equivalent to 11 per cent of GDP (Bulir and Hamann, 2001). Similarly, aid can be cut off just when it is most needed, for example after unforeseen economic shocks.

Conditionality of aid, having fallen from favour in the 1980s, seems to be making a comeback, this time linked to good governance. At the UN Financing for Development Conference in Monterrey in 2002, the US proposed a 'Millennium Challenge Account' linking greater contributions from developed nations to greater responsibility from developing nations. Development assistance would be provided to those countries 'that rule justly, invest in their people, and encourage economic freedom'.[5] The US subsequently established the Millennium Challenge Corporation to administer the system, and has pledged significant funding for it.

Some types of conditionality may be justifiable. Yet aid is still often used as a weapon of foreign policy by donors, irrespective of its impact on poor people – the mass withdrawal of aid from the Palestinian Authority after the election of a Hamas-led government in January 2006 being just one example. Similarly, aid can be used to impose donor-country moral positions regardless of the development consequences, as seen in the US refusal to support family planning policies.

Most commonly now, the conditions imposed on their economies by the international financial institutions often exacerbate instability in poor countries. The structural adjustment policies promoted by the IMF and World Bank, and the liberalizing approach of the WTO, though they may well have positive impacts in the long term, often entail significant economic, social and environmental shocks in the short term, including loss of government revenues, cuts in government services, increased price competition in domestic markets and rising unemployment. All these can undermine government authority and increase support for insurgencies and rebel movements. The World Development Movement's publication *States of Unrest*, for example, catalogued protests against the impact of IMF and World Bank policies in 25 countries in 2003, charting 111 separate incidents of civil unrest involving millions of people (World Development Movement, 2003).

And sometimes conditionality objectives may be established and then never followed through. Following the end of the civil war in Cambodia, donors and the new government agreed a programme of forest policy reform, which included the presence of the non-governmental organization (NGO) Global Witness as an independent monitor. Despite the imposition of a moratorium on cutting in forest concessions in January 2002, uncontrolled logging continued, and overall, the forestry sector remained characterized by lack of transparency, poor governance and corruption; Global Witness personnel carrying out their monitoring functions were subjected to threats and intimidation. Donors did not, however, exert any pressure on the Cambodian government to carry out its original commitments, with the result that the forest policy reform programme has largely failed.

Using trade and aid policy to build security

Trade and aid policy, then, are particularly important to the linkages between natural resource dependency and conflict. Used intelligently, they can break the links. Trade policy can assist countries to diversify away from over-reliance on a small number of natural resource exports, reducing the economy's vulnerability to external shocks, generating prosperity and reducing the likelihood of conflict. Aid can play a supportive role in helping to prepare countries for this process of opening up to investment and trade. It can be specifically applied to improve the management of natural resources, prevent conflict and increase the chances of recovery after conflict.

Applied insensitively, however, trade policy can increase inequality and weaken government structures, causing instability and increasing the chance of conflict. Trade can open up markets to conflict resources, funding rebellions and prolonging wars. Aid can also increase instability and contribute to corruption, mismanagement and failures of governance. Withdrawn too soon, or used in the wrong way, it can hinder recovery from conflict.

The chapters that follow develop these key themes and demonstrate just how crucial is the application of trade and aid policy to security and the ending of conflict, to the achievement of Stettinius' goals of freedom from fear and freedom from want. They present case studies of how trade and aid policy have so far often been misused, and show not only *why* they must be changed but *how* they can be. Together they form an agenda for action.

Chapter 1 looks at how trade policies can be designed to reduce, rather than increase, the likelihood or longevity of conflict. As above, it demonstrates how the current system of international trade is fundamentally unfair and biased towards rich countries and the corporations based in those states. The chapter argues for an approach to trade policy that recognizes the value of security – including improving market access for poor country exports, increasing support for developing country efforts to diversity their economies, and allowing poor countries greater trade policy flexibility.

Chapter 2 examines how aid policies can be constructed to be 'conflict-sensitive'. It looks at how aid policy comprehensively failed to be so designed and applied in Rwanda, and may be failing again in Nigeria and Bangladesh. It provides a comprehensive critique of the current approaches of delivering aid, and sets out a series of potential reforms, highlighting the importance of governance, including human rights, economic governance, democracy, justice and the role of civil society. The chapter looks in more detail at the 'natural resource curse' and how conflict-sensitive aid policy can be used to tackle it. It argues for a more systematic approach to humanitarian assistance, and for better linkages between relief and development. It deals with the responsibilities of the donors, first in how the conditions they attach to their aid are negotiated, and then in the developed world's failure, to date, to fulfil its commitments to the Millennium Development Goals (MDGs).

Chapter 3 returns to the underlying theme of governance, and its linkages to both trade and aid policy. As the chapter observes, good governance has become an explicit objective of both aid and trade policies. The chapter examines the concept of 'good governance' – covering factors such as a focus on poverty reduction in government programmes, a commitment to good financial management, and respect for human rights – and how it might be quantified. It looks both at 'carrots' – conditionality in aid disbursements and incentives in trade deals – and 'sticks' – the use of economic sanctions and the withdrawal of aid – and at capacity building and trade integration as instruments for promoting good governance, and concludes with recommendations for improving their application.

Chapter 4 turns back to trade, and the fact that the process of trade liberalization has expanded exports of undesirable products – conflict resources and illegal products – along with exports of legitimate goods. It takes a closer look at the concept of 'conflict resources', where the extraction of natural resources such as timber, coltan or diamonds has been linked to the initiation, or the prolongation, of armed conflict. It examines critically the record of UN sanctions in isolating the countries that have promoted such exports from world trade, and proposes a series of reforms designed to make such sanctions operate more effectively. Finally, it looks at schemes designed to exclude particular types of products (rather than countries) from world markets – including systems in operation or being developed for diamonds, timber, wildlife and fish – and examines a number of other measures, including government procurement policy and voluntary certification schemes, for building protected markets for exports that are conflict-free, legal or sustainable.

Chapter 5 looks at the extractive companies and financial institutions which are the central agents of global trade and investment, and in particular their activities in fragile and war-torn states. These are often problematic – not only because they may violate established norms, as some do, but because they often operate beyond the reach of current normative and regulatory frameworks. The chapter identifies the underlying problem of the global marketplace for natural resources being shaped by an incentive structure highly permissive of aggressive, often predatory, resource exploitation, even in otherwise high-risk settings. Failures of governance at both host-state and global levels are a common problem. The chapter identifies three major approaches in the emerging spectrum of regulatory responses – voluntary self-regulation by companies, mandatory regulation by states, and mixed forms that supplement regulation with market rewards – and presents a series of recommendations for improving their effectiveness.

Finally, Chapter 6 looks at the key problem of managing revenue flows – both from natural resources and from aid programmes. As argued above, in some cases, because of mismanagement, or just wide fluctuations in their magnitude, these revenue flows can trigger economic growth collapses, feed grievances, and sustain repressive regimes or armed groups. Examples of unsuccessful revenue deployment, such as Algeria and Iraq, are contrasted with more successful cases such as Botswana and Mozambique. The chapter identifies the three key policy priorities: creating an enabling environment within which the private sector can invest efficiently, stabilizing revenue flows from natural resources and aid to ensure that such flows do not out-strip domestic absorptive capacity, and controlling corrupt rent-seeking and ensuring that an increasing proportion of revenue goes toward increasing the capacity of the poorest to participate in economic development. The chapter presents recommendations for the improvement of revenue management, in terms of transparency, accountability, revenue sharing and income stabilization.

Notes

1   'Peace, security, stability and respect for human rights and fundamental freedoms, including the right to development, as well as respect for cultural diversity, are essential for achieving sustainable development and ensuring that sustainable development benefits all.' Para 138: 'Good governance is essential for sustainable development. Sound economic policies, solid democratic institutions responsive to the needs of the people and improved infrastructure are the basis for sustained economic growth, poverty eradication, and employment creation. Freedom, peace and security, domestic stability, respect for human rights, including the right to development, and the rule of law, gender equality, market-oriented policies, and an overall commitment to just and democratic societies are also essential and mutually reinforcing.'

2   Humphreys used the Collier–Hoeffler model to make his calculations, found in Collier, P. and Hoeffler, A. (2002) 'On the incidence of civil war in Africa', *Journal of Conflict Resolution*, vol 46, no 1, pp13–28.

3   The question of whether domestic trade (trade within a country) can also bring the benefits of international trade is an important one, particularly when considering the links with civil war, but in fact almost no research has been carried out on this topic.

4   International Coffee Organization composite indicator price; see www.ico.org/asp/display10.asp. Over the period 1976–2006, the lowest figure was ¢41.17, in

September 2001, and the highest ¢314.96, in April 1977; the latest (June 2006) figure was ¢86.04.

5   See the Millennium Challenge Corporation at www.mca.gov.

References

Bannon, I. and Collier, P. (eds) (2003) *Natural Resources and Violent Conflict: Options and Actions*, Washington DC, World Bank

Bulir, A. and Hamann, A. (2001) 'How volatile and unpredictable are aid flows and what are the policy implications?' IMF Working Paper WP/01/167, Washington DC, IMF

Gasana, J. (2002) 'Natural resource scarcity and violence in Rwanda', in Matthew, R., Halle, M. and Switzer, J. (eds) *Conserving the Peace: Resources, Livelihoods and Security*, Winnipeg and Gland, IISD and IUCN

Global Witness (2004) *Time for Transparency: Coming Clean on Oil, Mining and Gas Revenues*, London, Global Witness

Halle, M., Switzer, J. and Winkler, S. (2002) *Trade, Aid and Security: Elements of a Positive Paradigm*, Geneva, IISD and IUCN

Huhne, C. (2004) Member of European Parliament, Speech from 3 September 2004

Humphreys, M. (2003) *Economics and Violent Conflict*, Cambridge, MA, Harvard University

Maddison, A. (2001) *Monitoring The World Economy: A Millennial Perspective*, Paris, OECD

Ross, M. (2003) 'The natural resource curse: How wealth can make you poor', in Bannon, I and Collier, P. (eds) *Natural Resources and Violent Conflict: Options and Actions*, Washington DC, World Bank

South Centre (1996) *Financial Flows to Developing Countries: An Overview*, Geneva, South Centre

Sturgis, J. L. (1969) *John Bright and the Empire*, London, University of London

UNCTAD (1999) *The Least Developed Countries Report 1999*, Geneva, UNCTAD

UNCTAD–TRAINS database, 1 June 2001

UNDP (2005) *Human Development Report 2005*, New York, United Nations

United Nations (2002) 'Chair's summary of discussion at Round table 2' *Report of the World Summit on Sustainable Development*, New York, UN

World Bank (2003) *Breaking the Conflict Trap: Civil War and Development Policy*, Washington DC, World Bank/OUP

World Development Movement (2003) *States of Unrest III: Resistance to IMF and World Bank Policies in Poor Countries*, London, World Development Movement

Chapter 1

Designing Conflict-sensitive Trade Policy

Mark Curtis

Introduction

Designing trade policies that do not increase the likelihood or longevity of conflict is a critical task for the international community. Trade policies that limit market access, increase the volatility of commodity prices, unfairly subsidize developed country exports and constrain the trade policy flexibility of the developing world affect those countries' stability and security as well as their overall economic well-being.

In short, the current system of international trade is fundamentally unfair and biased towards rich countries and the corporations based in those states. Restrictions on market access and continuing domestic subsidies by rich countries consign many developing countries to reliance on the export of primary commodities. Over the past five decades these commodities have suffered from declining and volatile prices – a trend that is strongly correlated with political instability and conflict.

At the same time, developing countries are being pushed to adapt to an increasingly liberalized global trading system, from which many barely benefit and some are losing out, often reducing government revenues and undermining livelihoods – serving to increase the prospects for political instability and competition over scarce resources.

This chapter outlines some of the ways in which trade policy affects conflict and recommends how trade policies could be more conflict sensitive. It is noticeable that in much of the discussion on global trade policy, the potential impact of trade on conflict has featured very little. This was the case even in the run-up to the WTO ministerial in Hong Kong, and is surprising given that both advocates and critics of trade liberalization often argue that the impact of trade liberalization is large, and also that many of the countries and regions worst affected by conflict are also at the centre of debates on trade liberalization. In short, conflict-sensitive trade policy is a relatively new area of analysis that has not received sufficient attention on the part of the international community.

Policies in these areas therefore need to be very carefully considered, indeed changed, by OECD states as well as international institutions such as the WTO. For this to occur there needs to be a clear understanding of the links between trade policy and conflict as well as the political will to change course.

Trade and conflict

The international trading environment, and specifically the trade policy of the rich countries, is a significant determining factor of economic well-being in poorer countries. The latter currently have little influence over global commodity prices; they suffer from major terms of trade disadvantages and have in reality had little say in the global trade liberalization agenda of the past decade.

There is considerable evidence of a link between economics and conflict. One study of 40 sub-Saharan African countries between 1983 and 1999 showed a strong correlation between economic growth and the incidence of civil conflict: a negative growth shock of five percentage points increased the likelihood of major civil conflicts by over one half (Miguel et al, 2003). Another analysis points out that 'economic studies of civil war have successfully identified an empirically robust relationship between poverty, slow growth and an increased likelihood of civil war and prevalence' (Sambanis, 2003).

History and bitter experience have demonstrated that low-income countries are particularly prone to conflict. Poverty undermines human security and creates the conditions for conflict to turn violent. The United Nations Conference on Trade and Development's (UNCTAD) analysis is that low-income countries are particularly conflict prone, with the proportion of low-income countries experiencing civil conflict in the period 1990–2001 more than twice that of middle-income countries. It points out, however, that low income levels alone are not a sufficient condition for the onset of civil conflict; rather, what appears to be important is the interaction of low income levels with other adverse conditions such as economic shocks, stagnation or recession. Most Least Developed Countries (LDCs) in which civil conflict broke out in the 1990s experienced either negative or sluggish growth rates in the 1980s, suggesting that the events of the 1990s were a reaction to the economic experience of the 1980s (UNCTAD, 2004, p164).

The link between economics and conflict is explicitly recognized, to one extent or another, by most governments and international institutions. For example, the UK's Department for International Development (DFID) notes that 'continuous economic decline plays a major part in state collapse and conflict', and that sections of the populations become 'disillusioned, marginalized and frustrated' as a result of the economic decline, which in turn brought about by massive debt and unfavourable terms of trade. DFID notes that 'economic shock is a … direct cause of conflict' and that 'the sudden shift in the terms of trade in Nigeria in 1992/3 halved Nigeria's income, introduced hyperinflation and led to violence and the overthrow of the government'. DFID also notes that 'countries whose economies are dependent on natural resources such as oil and minerals, face a high risk of conflict' – the so-called 'resource curse' (DFID, 2001).

Various trade policies promoted by the OECD states have severe impacts on people in poor countries. By depriving vulnerable countries of government revenues and by impacting severely on specific groups of people, the basic argument here is that these policies aggravate the risk of conflict and/or undermine post-conflict reconstruction efforts. This chapter now considers four important issues in this regard:

1   the tariff and non-tariff barriers, escalating tariffs for processed goods and stringent technical/scientific standards that restrict the access of developing country products to rich developed world markets and inhibit developing country efforts to diversify their economies;
2   the use by northern states of domestic and export subsidies that regularly result in the dumping of subsidized produce, often below the costs of production, undermining industries and food security in developing countries;
3   the continuing dependence of many developing countries on the export of a small number of commodities, which have suffered falling, volatile prices over the past five decades;
4   the aggressive promotion of an increasingly globalized trading system, often for the benefit of northern states, in which developing countries are being required to implement trade liberalization commitments that reduce their policy 'space' to promote policies suited to their national or local circumstances.

Market access restrictions

OECD country trade policy constructs a number of daunting barriers to developing country exporters. Access to developed country markets is often limited by quotas, the exclusion of specific products, tariff barriers and tariff peaks (often for goods that developing countries produce more efficiently than Europe, such as dairy products, vegetables, nuts and fruit), higher duties for processed goods and 'rules of origin' clauses which prevent manufactured goods that require components from outside the region from entering developed country markets.

Tariff escalation is a particularly pernicious measure in which developed countries apply low tariffs to imports of raw commodities but rapidly rising rates to intermediate or final products. For instance, in Japan tariffs on processed food products are seven times higher than on first-stage products, while in Canada they are 12 times higher. In effect, tariff escalation prevents developing countries from adding value to their exports, inhibits industrialization and locks them into dependence on exporting price-volatile, low value-added commodities (UNDP, 2005, p127). There can be little doubt that such barriers have been a major brake on development in some of the world's poor countries.

Existing schemes trumpeted by OECD countries as improving market access for developing countries tend to be the subject of considerable exaggeration. The EU's Everything But Arms (EBA) initiative, which took effect in March 2001, grants duty-free access into the EU to imports of almost all products from the LDCs. However, domestic and corporate lobbies successfully diluted the initiative by keeping import duties on sugar and rice until 2009 and on bananas until 2006 – among the most important exports of developing countries. While the EBA is a welcome step, it is a much smaller one than generally assumed.

A study commissioned by Oxfam soon after the EBA was agreed, for example, showed that the 'static' gains (i.e. at current levels of exports) of the EBA to poor countries would be just $7 million. It was likely to result in more 'dynamic' gains (i.e. as countries began to take advantage of more open markets) but the extent of these was hard to predict. The analysis showed that the gains to the LDCs were likely to be so low because only $95 million worth of exports were actually affected (Stevens and Kennan, 2001).

A subsequent World Bank report suggested that LDC exports affected by the EBA amounted to $73.6 million in 2000 (equivalent to around 0.5 per cent of total LDC exports to the EU), $63 million of which were exports in the areas of delayed liberalization – sugar, rice and bananas. It noted that the changes introduced by the EBA initiative are 'relatively minor for currently exported products, primarily because over 99 per cent of EU imports from the LDCs are in products which the EU had already liberalized' (Brenton, 2003). The EU is not, of course, offering duty-free market access to the non-LDC developing countries.

The US African Growth and Opportunity Act (AGOA), passed in 2000, gives preferential access to US markets for several products, such as textiles, and has helped to increase export growth in some countries in Africa. But there are major limitations. The scheme suffers from limited product coverage, uncertain duration and complex eligibility requirements (UNDP, 2005, p128). A recent World Bank study concludes that only a small number of countries receive substantial benefits from AGOA and that LDCs that do not receive preferences for clothing exports have yet to see any impact on their overall exports (since most LDC exports to the US were already duty free). Preferences for clothing products have led to significant transfers to a small group of beneficiaries, but for most countries the overall impact of AGOA preferences is likely to amount to no more than one tenth of 1 per cent of GDP. Seven beneficiaries account for almost all the transfers resulting from AGOA, while the remaining 31 beneficiaries gain little (Brenton and Ikezuki, 2004). US imports under AGOA were valued at just over $14 billion in 2003, a 55 per cent increase over 2002. Yet these imports are highly concentrated among major oil suppliers and South Africa: the latter plus Nigeria, Angola and Gabon accounted for 83 per cent of US imports in 2003.[1]

Market access alone is no panacea

While market access restrictions are serious for many developing countries, notably non-LDCs, simply ending those restrictions and opening markets is *by itself* no panacea. Even if markets in the North are more open to them, developing countries will still face major constraints in taking advantage – such as supply-side constraints and competing with heavily subsidized northern farms. An UNCTAD agricultural trade experts meeting has described the various internal and external barriers facing developing countries as such:

> *These countries continued to face domestic capacity limitation in the areas of production, infrastructure and research and development of technologies to improve productivity... Agricultural producers, especially small-scale farmers, had also to cope with the need for investment and limited access to finances to meet incremental working capital needs either because of the non-existence of financial facilities or because of a general credit crunch... Lack of capacity and expertise in the international marketing and transport of their products... A highly oligopolistic market structure in some major commodity markets controlled by large TNCs. Certain product sectors of the world agricultural market, for instance, are highly concentrated and dominated by TNCs, which contribute up to 80 percent of the market share in international agricultural trade... Such a trading environment would place small-scale farmers in developing countries at a permanent competitive disadvantage unless complementary actions were taken to strengthen their position.* (UNCTAD, 1999, p5)

However, blunt strategies to increase exports on the part of developing countries do not automatically help the poor or directly benefit wider society. As noted above, a concentration on exports, for example, needs to be well managed and a range of domestic policies need to be in place to ensure that vulnerable groups benefit from overall economic growth; vulnerable groups can become even more adversely affected by a focus on exports, which can lead to instability. In Ghana, for example, expanding cocoa production for export took up increasing amounts of land, pushing women farmers onto marginal lands with steep slopes and poor soil (Curtis, 2001, p66). A World Bank study notes that 'any favourable effects of improved market access on growth could, in principle, be offset by a direct effect on conflict risk. Indeed, we have found that exports can have a direct, adverse impact on the risk of conflict, namely through the rents on primary commodities' (World Bank, 2003, p139).

It is clear that other policy changes need to occur alongside greater market access. High quality capacity-building support to developing countries, to enable them to benefit from market access opportunities, can be vital. Donors have recognized the importance of this area in recent years and an extensive set of aid measures has emerged under the Trade-related Technical Assistance and Capacity Building programme which provides over $2 billion to help developing countries relieve supply-side constraints and build institutional capacity. However, the programme is severely marred by a multiplicity of technical assistance initiatives, weak coordination and, in many cases, limited ownership on the part of recipient governments, with assistance often narrowly geared to implementing WTO agreements of little benefit to developing countries (UNDP, 2005, p144).

The problem of domestic and export subsidies

Rich countries spend billions of dollars each year in payments to their farmers that subsidize the production and export of agricultural goods. These subsidies depress world prices for key developing world products like sugar and cotton, deny developing world farmers valuable export markets and constitute an unfair playing field that undermines growth in the developing world. Both domestic production subsidies (which undermine the ability of producers in poor countries to compete) and export subsidies (which promote export dumping) can have devastating impacts. UNDP estimates that the real costs for developing countries of rich country agricultural protectionism and subsidies may be as high as $72 billion a year – equivalent to all official aid flows in 2003 (UNDP, 2005, p130).

Agricultural subsidies that result in export dumping cause farmers in developing countries to suffer low prices, lost market share and unfair competition. In 2003, dumping by US-based food and agribusiness companies meant that wheat was exported at an average price of 28 per cent below the cost of production, soybeans at 10 per cent, corn at 10 per cent, cotton at 47 per cent and rice at 26 per cent. Since the WTO was established, US-based companies, for example, have engaged in steady, high levels of agricultural dumping in their global sales of the five most exported commodities. The WTO rules formally prohibit dumping but the practice is regular, and the rules make it complicated and expensive for poor countries to establish grounds for anti-dumping actions (IATP, 2005, pp127–129).

The EU is the dominant user of export subsidies, accounting for 90 per cent of all subsidies from 1994 to 1997. Brussels sets the European sugar price at three times international prices and subsidizes exports of its sugar onto world markets. Oxfam notes that this blocks developing country exporters from European markets, undercuts developing countries in valuable third markets, such as the Middle East, by subsidizing exports to prices below international costs of production, and depresses world prices by dumping subsidized and surplus production, thereby damaging foreign exchange earnings for low-cost exporters (Oxfam, 2002). The EU spent around $41 billion in 2003 on agricultural subsidies, much of which involves export subsidies (Oxfam, 2002). One study estimates that EU subsidies and market restrictions on sugar imports cost Mozambique $38 million and Malawi $32 million in 2004.[2] Subsidy levels are also partly hidden: the US, for example, provides 200 times more export support than it declares, equivalent to $6.6 billion (€5.2 billion) a year (Oxfam, 2005, p3).

The EU and the US claim to have cut their domestic subsidies over the years but in reality there has been little substantial reduction, simply a relabelling of existing support. Since the Uruguay Round of trade negotiations started in 1986, overall agricultural support in developed countries has remained at around $250 billion annually (Oxfam, 2005). The July 2004 framework agreement that guided the recent WTO negotiations until their collapse actually expanded the ability of developed countries to support their own farmers. Developed countries have managed to change the criteria that would allow them to provide support to their farmers under the 'blue box' system,[3] instigated mainly at the behest of the US, which wants to shield its 'countercyclical' payments to farmers (i.e. subsidies paid to producers when commodity prices fall below specific levels).

Oxfam estimated that such box-shifting would allow the US to increase its trade-distorting support by $7.9 billion a year from current levels, and the EU by $28.8 billion a year (Oxfam, 2005). Meanwhile, there are no current restrictions on the amount of resources that countries can devote to payments to their farmers through another domestic support mechanism, the 'green box',[4] so the US and the EU have significantly increased the use of this category of support.

The EU's desire to maintain the status quo can be attributed to fears that changes to the green box could jeopardize the recent reforms of the Common Agriculture Policy, through which the EU has shifted a significant part of its support of agriculture to the green box. For the US, payments under the green box already represent a large proportion of its support to agriculture, so changes in the criteria would lead to important modifications in its system of support.

A US proposal in early October 2005 was widely trumpeted by US officials as involving substantial cuts in domestic support. Yet, closer analysis shows that the proposal would result in negligible cuts to the subsidies paid to farmers while it also called for developing countries to cut agricultural tariffs by more than developed countries. Argentina's ambassador to the WTO suggested that the proposal would mean that US subsidies could actually increase (TWN, 2005).

The WTO's Doha declaration of 2001 agreed to a 'reduction of, with a view to phasing out, all forms of export subsidies'. Until the WTO negotiations collapsed in July 2006, OECD countries had finally agreed to phase out export subsidies by 2013. The US had proposed eliminating them in five years, as had the G20 group of countries. Yet the EU had put forward several conditions for eliminating export subsidies: all countries to agree to 'parallel elimination' not only of export subsidies but also of 'all forms' of export subsidies such as export credits, and progress in this area to be linked to developing countries' movement on liberalization in industrial products and services (South Centre, 2005b).

Commodity dependence and price volatility

Perhaps the most serious trade issue facing many developing countries is the volatility and decline in the prices of the primary commodities on which their economies rely. Ninety-five of the world's 141 developing countries are more than 50 per cent reliant on commodity exports (Benn, 2005). This dependence makes many developing countries highly vulnerable to fluctuations in the price of key commodities – with the impact only increasing for those dependent on fewer and fewer commodities. Poor countries have little influence over the international price of their exports and are less able to manage the impacts of volatile prices.

Between 1997 and 2001 the combined price index for all commodities fell by 53 per cent in real terms. This means that African exporters had to double export volumes to maintain incomes at constant levels (UNDP, 2005, p118). While there has been a recovery in the price of some commodities since then, the current high prices – if history is any teacher – are unlikely to last. The UN estimates that for every \$1 in aid received by sub-Saharan Africa since the early 1970s, \$0.50 has been lost as a result of deteriorating terms of trade (UNCTAD, 2001).

A 2000 World Bank report noted that commodity price crashes can induce the growth collapses that increase the risk of violent conflict. The report also notes that for countries that are heavily dependent on commodity exports, the world price of these commodities significantly affects the duration of the conflict: when prices are high the conflict is less likely to end than when prices are low (World Bank, 2003, pp126, 132, 144).

Of course there is no *automatic* connection between falling commodity prices and the outbreak of violent conflict. However, the steep peaks and slumps in commodity prices that have become a feature of the modern economy can administer severe shocks to a country's political and economic stability. Ethiopia and Burundi rely on coffee for between 60 per cent and 80 per cent of their export earnings: the two-thirds fall in the price of coffee between 1980 and 2000 devastated rural livelihoods, slashed government revenues already strained by debt repayments and radically undermined health and education programmes – all of which can be drivers for conflict. It has been convincingly argued that the sinking price of coffee in the early 1990s in part precipitated the Rwandan genocide of 1994 by halving export revenues, eroding livelihoods and exacerbating ethnic tensions (Halle et al, 2004, p13).

Although the World Bank recognizes the link between dependence on primary commodity exports and conflict, it has played a leading role in encouraging the over production and export of primary commodities as part of advice programmes to increase growth. However, such over production will only depress prices through excess supply, leaving many countries reliant on unfavourable terms of trade (Hanlon, 2003). Thus, this is a fundamental policy area that needs to be addressed by OECD governments if they are serious about addressing the economic causes of conflict and aiding post-conflict reconstruction.

On the issue of managing commodity price shocks, Gilbert identifies five sets of possible policy responses:

1   price agreements based on either producer cartels or pacts between consumers and producers;
2   stabilization of producer/consumer prices by variable export tariffs or taxes, marketing boards and domestic stockpiles;
3   compensatory financing of individual producers by domestic governments or international institutions;
4   producer government revenue stabilization funds;
5   the use of risk instruments such as forward contracts to stabilize producer revenue. (Gilbert, 1993, p8)

Auty and Le Billon have noted that the first three measures have a long track record, with mixed success, while the latter two have received more attention recently, and their analysis considers the experience of these mechanisms further. What can be said here is that there are no simple solutions to the crisis in global commodity markets, but that a number of policy areas present themselves (see Chapter 6).

First, diversification away from commodity dependence – a cornerstone of development thinking for decades – must remain a vital priority for many developing countries, and for international aid strategies. But developed country trade policies are also critical, since restrictions on market access through tariff escalation and phytosanitary standards, for example, act as a major brake on diversification.

Second, commodity price agreements mainly collapsed in the 1980s, not least due to pressure and opposition from developed countries, but also as a result of disputes over the form such agreements might take. Yet it can be strongly argued that such schemes need urgent reconsideration today, and should not be opposed as unworkable by OECD governments.

Third, existing compensation arrangements need to be greatly improved. The IMF established a Compensatory Finance Facility (CFF) in 1963 with the aim of providing short-term loans to countries experiencing declines in income from commodities and who were unable to borrow on commercial terms. But, as the UNDP has recently argued, it currently provides finance on terms that are unaffordable to most low-income countries in Africa (UNDP, 2005, p142). The EU's Flex scheme, introduced in 2000 to replace Stabex,[5] initially provided budgetary support to African, Caribbean and Pacific (ACP) countries registering a 10 per cent loss of export earnings and a 10 per cent worsening of the programmed public deficit. Yet these criteria have proved too stringent. As a result only US$12 million a year on average was disbursed in 2000–2003 to just six of the 51 countries that applied (Auty and Le Billon, p35; UNDP, 2005, p142). Currently, there are too few schemes to adequately deal with commodity price volatility, urgent though this is, while existing schemes have proven largely ineffective.

Fourth, it should be more widely recognized that OECD country trade policies can amplify commodity price volatility. For example, if OECD governments increase their subsidies to domestic producers when the world price of an agricultural commodity is low, then the effect will be to amplify price shocks. The recent increase in US cotton subsidies to farmers had the effect of further reducing the incomes of cotton farmers in the Central African Republic (World Bank, 2003, p133).

Trade liberalization and policy space

Recent years have witnessed a fierce debate about the role of trade liberalization in development. It is important to distinguish between two separate issues: the debate about whether trade liberalization *in the South* is good for development and poverty eradication in the South; and the debate about opening up OECD country markets to southern country exporters (i.e. liberalization *in the North*). The latter issue has received much greater international media attention and is often conflated with the conception of 'fair trade'. Greater access to northern markets is a vital issue for developing countries and this analysis takes it as read that import restrictions have major adverse impacts on many poor countries, as discussed above. Yet the issue of liberalization in the South is also, and perhaps more, important for many developing countries, linked as it is to the critical question of developing greater domestic industrial and agricultural capacity and the longer-term ability to compete in global markets.

Northern governments – and many southern governments – now advocate trade liberalization as the best strategy for growth and development in the South; many, if not most, northern and southern civil society groups are opposed to this as a standard model and advocate greater policy flexibility for developing countries, sometimes involving de facto protectionist strategies. The meeting ground between these two contending views is often in the area of 'special and differential treatment' (SDT), which essentially provides longer time periods for developing countries, and especially the LDCs, to implement multilateral liberalization commitments. Here, the argument is often made that SDT provisions for longer time periods are sufficient. Many NGOs, on the other hand, often contend than long time periods and other SDT provisions do not provide developing countries with sufficient policy flexibility and often question whether the liberalization model is right in the first place.

The evidence that trade liberalization per se is good for development is actually very weak. One analysis by UNCTAD, for example, shows that in a sample of 36 countries classified according to their degree of trade 'restrictiveness' and 'openness' at the end of the 1990s, poverty rose both in those countries that adopted the most open trade regimes and in those that continued with the most closed regimes. 'But in between these extremes there was a tendency for poverty to decline in those countries that had liberalized their trade regimes to a lesser extent, and for poverty to increase in those countries that had liberalized their trade regimes to a greater extent.' The conclusion was that 'from this evidence there is no basis for concluding that trade liberalization, in the short run, reduces poverty or leads to a more virtuous trade-poverty relationship' (UNCTAD, 2004, p188). Another analysis by UNCTAD of growth rates in developing countries between 1997 and 2001 shows that of 108 countries studied, only 10 out of 35 classified as the 'most open' have high GDP growth and only 7 out of 36 countries classified as 'restrictive' have low GDP growth. There are 37 countries that have either high GDP growth with a 'restrictive' trade regime or low GDP growth with an 'open' trade regime (UNCTAD, 2004, p86).

There is evidence of the adverse impacts of trade liberalization on certain groups of poor people. In particular, cheap agricultural imports – especially but not exclusively of subsidized produce from the North – have at times had a severe impact on farming communities. Imports of cheap subsidized US rice into Haiti, for example, have driven thousands of poor farmers out of business, and forced many people off their land, with many in effect becoming internally displaced (Curtis, 2001, pp153–157). In Zambia, World Bank/IMF-induced policies to reduce tariffs on textiles resulted in cheap imports putting 30,000 people out of work (World Development Movement, 2004). NGOs have reported similar impacts of cheap imports in Sri Lanka, Guyana, Trinidad & Tobago, the Philippines, Mexico, The Gambia and Brazil, among others (Curtis, 2001, pp41–42).

Of course, cheap imports can also benefit certain groups of people and often it is the capacity to manage the shocks that flow from liberalization that will determine whether liberalization has good or bad effects. Poor countries tend to have fewer mechanisms, such as adequate welfare programmes, to cushion the effects on people of such adverse impacts.

The UN's Food and Agricultural Organization (FAO) notes that 'since the 1980s, with trade reforms and unilateral trade liberalization in many developing countries, there have been more frequent import surges by country and by product' (FAO, 2003a). Indeed, the FAO has identified 1217 cases of import surges on just eight commodities in 28 developing countries for the period 1984–2000. An import surge means either that the volume of imported goods rises sharply or that import prices reduce sharply so that they undermine or threaten to undermine domestic production. A surge is defined as a 20 per cent deviation from a five-year average of imports. Since this analysis is highly selective by product and also considers only a small proportion of all developing countries, the real extent of import surges must be much greater (FAO, 2003b). There are few mechanisms that developing countries have in practice to keep such imports out: the process is expensive, onerous or politically difficult. As the FAO has pointed out, currently 'developing countries lack resources to protect producers from artificially low import prices. The potential for raising duties is limited and will decline with lower bound rates' (FAO, 2003b).

The outstanding cases of successful poverty eradication in the post-war world – that is, those in East Asia such as Taiwan and South Korea – all rejected policies to completely open their economies at key stages in their development. These countries often protected their domestic industries, for limited periods and with clear performance requirements, often tended to give preference to domestic companies on the grounds of promoting long-term industrial development, and actively intervened in the economy through policies of regulation and financing investment. These policies were part of a mix that included those of liberalization now advocated by the WTO, but were far from restricted to them. In a report for the United Nations Research Institute for Social Development (UNRISD), Kwame Jomo, Professor of Economics at the University of Malaya, Kuala Lumpur, notes:

> *There is now considerable evidence that high growth in East Asia was due to successful and appropriate developmental public policy interventions rather than economic liberalization. Clearly then, South Korea and Taiwan have not only achieved far more in terms of growth, industrialization and structural change than Thailand, Indonesia and Malaysia with significantly lower inequality as well. The better economic performances of the first two were due to more effective government interventions, especially selective industrial policy, while lower inequality was partly due to significant asset (especially land) redistribution before the high growth period, full employment and social development to ensure support for developmental public policies.* (Jomo, 2003, p31)

A key point about successful development in East Asia was that these countries were not subjected to 'big bang' or shock liberalization. Rather, their industrialization had long preceded that of the 1980s and had advanced on the basis of a wide range of trade and industrial policies designed to encourage the emergence of higher value-added activities and the production of high-tech and capital intensive products. In particular, foreign investment was strategically managed to ensure it supported domestic efforts to continue strengthening and upgrading domestic productive capacities (Kozul-Wright and Rayment, 2004, pp15–16).

Advocates of trade liberalization often argue that it can make available new technologies, undermine elite privilege, and thus contribute to greater political liberalization and overall economic growth. This can be true, but so can the opposite – that imported technology can crowd out investment, while corruption can be induced by new links with foreign corporations. In short, whether trade liberalization benefits people often depends on other factors than trade liberalization, such as governance, income distribution and policies of equity promoted by the government. The same applies much more generally to increasing exports – the wealth generated can either be funnelled to domestic elites or benefit society more widely, again depending on domestic circumstances. Whether trade (not just trade liberalization) benefits the poor again also depends on other domestic factors.

There is a particular fear that the EU's push in Economic Partnership Agreements (EPAs) with regional groups of ACP states will expose poor countries even more to the dangers inherent with promoting full liberalization. EPAs are based on the concept of reciprocal liberalization, where both the EU and the ACP regions will open their markets to exporters from the other. Developing countries may be even more exposed to the dumping of EU agricultural surplus goods, such as dairy, cereals and beef, under a reciprocal liberalization agreement (Fraser and Kachingwe, 2003).

The evidence suggests that reciprocal liberalization does not benefit both actors equally – those that primarily benefit will be those able to take advantage of market opportunities. For example, an FAO study of the impact of the WTO's Agreement on Agriculture found that 'while trade liberalization [in developing countries] led to a quick increase in food imports, exports did not rise similarly or proportionately. This has implications for the pace of liberalization for countries where supply constraints and other market entry difficulties do not allow them to take advantage of market opportunities as quickly as other suppliers are able to export to them.'[6] There are currently major concerns that reciprocal liberalization being pushed by the EU in the area of industrial goods (i.e. non-agricultural market access) could have major adverse impacts on domestic industry in developing countries, even causing 'de-industrialization' in many of them (EPA Watch, 2004).

The importance of greater trade policy flexibility

The WTO's agenda of 'progressive liberalization' seeks to promote a one-size-fits-all model of economic strategy in developing countries, reducing their flexibility to pursue possible policies more suited to local circumstances. UNDP has stated that 'the rapidly increasing multilateral agreements – the new rules – are highly binding on national governments and constrain domestic policy choices, including those critical for human development. They drive a convergence of policies in a world of enormous diversity in conditions – economic, social and ecological' (UNDP, 1999, p35). There are various WTO agreements that constrain the ability of developing countries to promote adequate policy flexibility:

- Developing countries are not allowed to raise their agricultural import tariffs beyond a certain level to protect themselves from cheaper imports. Some types of agricultural subsidies previously used by developing countries – for example, for land improvement – are now banned under WTO rules, although the LDCs are (unlike other developing countries) exempt from being required to reduce their overall level of domestic support (subsidies and tariffs) to agriculture.
- The WTO's Trade-related Investment Measures agreement covers conditions on investment related to trade in goods and bans many laws, policies and administrative regulations that favour domestic over foreign capital inputs. These include: local content policies, where governments require a corporation to use or purchase domestic products; trade balancing measures, where governments impose restrictions on the import of capital goods by corporations to reflect the level of exports; and foreign exchange balancing requirements, where a corporation's permitted imports are tied to the value of the export so that there is a net foreign exchange earning (Curtis, 2001, p52).

- The WTO's Agreement on Subsidies and Countervailing Measures (ASCM) prevents governments from providing subsidies to encourage the use of domestic over imported goods ('import substitution subsidies'). According to a study for UNCTAD, 'the ASCM bans exactly the type of subsidies primarily used by developing countries (while allowing the subsidies for research, regional development or for the adoption of environmental standards which are typically used by developed countries)' (Nefeld, 2001).

Certainly, these kinds of policies have not always been successfully used by developing countries in the past, and many could be criticized as being ineffective development strategies over the long term. Nonetheless, many such policies have been successfully used – and for this reason it must be a source of concern that they are no longer options.

OECD governments have been decidedly hypocritical when it comes to policy flexibility. On the one hand, they have consistently stated that developing countries must themselves decide and follow their own development path. On the other hand, they have a strong presumption in favour of promoting economic models and international rules that entail onerous restrictions on the same countries.

Policy flexibility and the extent of SDT provisions are critical for fragile states at risk of conflict or emerging from conflict. These countries' economies are often even more vulnerable to the kinds of adjustment costs that liberalization can entail. They must be able to benefit fully from the exemptions from liberalization commitments envisaged in current SDT arrangements. But the argument from this analysis is that especially the poorest and most fragile states should have greater flexibility than in current arrangements to promote policies suited to their own national circumstances, and that their policy options should not be limited to liberalization.

In June 2005, the G33 group of developing countries called for 'more meaningful special and differential treatment' in the WTO negotiations, including a framework on 'special products' and a special safeguards mechanism (SSM). They stated that products that meet the criteria of food security, livelihood security and rural development should be designated as special products, which should be exempt from tariff reduction commitments. The SSM would 'provide more operationally effective remedy for developing countries against import surges and price depressions', should be available to all agricultural products, and would be invoked if the volume of imports of the product concerned exceeds the average volume of imports of the preceding three years, or if the price of the imports falls below the monthly average over the previous three years – in which case a duty or quantitative restrictions could be applied for a maximum of a year (South Centre, 2005a, pp309–311).

Even though protection has become heretical in the WTO orthodoxy, its potential importance as a policy instrument is often still recognized. UNCTAD, for example, noted in a report from 2000 with regard to agriculture in the poorest countries that 'small farmers involved have no way of withstanding large-scale international competition. They need protection if large-scale unemployment and the spread of poverty in these countries are to be limited. They should be allowed flexibility [in the WTO agreements] regarding import restraint and domestic subsidy in order to protect and support household subsistence farming and small-scale farming' (UNCTAD, 2000, p24).

That protectionist policies have been badly used by some developing countries in the past is beyond dispute. However, the reason why protection is off the radar screen of OECD countries has in this author's view little to do with the past effectiveness (or not) of such policies and much more to do with serving the interests of the private companies in OECD countries that stand to benefit most from open markets globally.

Addressing conflict-sensitive trade policy

Some donors and international institutions are beginning to recognize the importance of trade policy for conflict prevention. But this is happening only slowly. Donors are increasingly thinking about conflict prevention but are rarely thinking of trade policy in that context. And trade analysts rarely factor in conflict to their thinking. Within the WTO, for example, there has been little attempt to systematically address the issue of conflict and trade. There are few mentions of conflict in the various WTO rules and, as a further indicator, a search on the WTO website reveals almost no sources of information or analysis on the subject of conflict and trade or on fragile states.

The EU has produced numerous documents detailing its commitment to conflict prevention and the Council has stated that 'all relevant institutions of the Union will mainstream conflict prevention within their areas of competence' (EU, 2001). A Conflict Prevention Unit has been established in the External Relations Directorate of the European Commission (EC), responsible for mainstreaming conflict prevention priorities within Community policy. Within the Council, a Policy Planning and Early Warning Unit has been introduced to provide capacity for analysis and initiatives to support conflict prevention. Common Foreign and Security Policy working groups and committees, such as the Africa Working Group and Political and Security Committee, are increasingly reflecting on strategies to prevent and manage conflicts and feeding these approaches into decision-making (Bayne, 2003).

Since 2001 the EU's conflict prevention unit has developed the EC Checklist for Root Causes of Conflict, which aims to increase awareness and prompt early action in conflict-prone fragile states. The checklist requires staff to determine the extent of a particular state's income dependency, 'capacity to react to natural disasters or international conditions (i.e. massive swings in commodity prices)' and ability to attract investment.[7] The checklist is reviewed when country and regional strategy papers are drafted and, in theory at least, helps draw attention to the conflict prevention activities that aid should target (EU, 2002).

The Commission noted in 2002 that 'trade policy can be identified as a priority area for future work. The Commission is well-placed to ensure a proper examination of the relationship between trade integration, political stability and economic progress and make proposals for targeted use of trade policy instruments...' (EU, 2002).

In April 2005 the European Council adopted a common position on conflict prevention and resolution in Africa. It notes that EU policy will address conflict prevention 'by seeking to address the more structural root causes while targeting the direct causes – trigger factors – of violent conflict', and aid reconstruction 'by supporting the economic, political and social rebuilding of post-conflict states and societies'. The position mentions trade policy, noting that:

The EU shall seek:

- *to support the mainstreaming of conflict prevention perspectives within the framework of Community development and trade policy and its associated country and regional strategies;*
- *to introduce, as appropriate, conflict indicators and peace and conflict impact assessment tools in development and trade cooperation so as to reduce the risk of aid and trade fuelling conflict, and to maximize the positive impact on peace-building...;*
- *to improve development and trade cooperation with regional, sub-regional and local actors to ensure consistency between initiatives and to support African activities.'*

The position also commits the EU to 'work to ensure that regional trade integration measures, within a policy context comprising safety nets for vulnerable groups, support conflict prevention and resolution' (EU, 2005).

While the EU has made some progress at the declaratory and practical level of addressing conflict prevention through development policies, many major policy gaps remain. The EU – and indeed rich countries generally – could be doing far more to help countries trade their way out of poverty. It could, for example, do much more to help reduce their dependence on primary commodity exports, to prevent them being adversely affected by inappropriate liberalization and to help ensure that its trade policies support conflict prevention and reconstruction. Some of these have been noted above, particularly policies on market access, trade flexibility and commodity prices, among others. These are clearly major political or 'high policy' changes that may involve difficult negotiations. Then there are other more 'technical', institutional reforms:[8]

- Make conflict prevention a stated objective of the Common Foreign and Security Policy.
- Strengthen the capacity of the Conflict Prevention Unit to analyse the links between trade policy and conflict, particularly in the case of the Economic Partnership Agreements, and ensure these are more adequately fed into the decision-making system.

- Develop more effective peace and conflict impact assessments.
- Strengthen annual reviews of conflict prevention policies.
- Ensure that the EU advocates conflict-sensitive development policies in multilateral forums.

The World Bank has launched conflict-sensitivity assessments that focus on resource distribution patterns and emphasize inclusiveness of opportunities; its Conflict Analysis Framework aims to 'enhance conflict sensitivity and conflict prevention potential of World Bank assistance' (Picciotto et al, 2005, p31). The Bank has a conflict analysis framework and is discussing how to make poverty reduction strategy papers (PRSPs) conflict sensitive. It has also developed a framework for engaging in countries emerging from conflict – the so-called Low Income Countries Under Stress initiative. To become conflict sensitive, the Bank would have to systematically assess the risks of violent conflict likely to be created by, or have an impact on, an operation. Similarly, perhaps IMF programme design and surveillance could incorporate an evaluation of the risks of conflict when discussing trade-offs between policy choices (Lefrancois, 2004). In reality, it would seem that these assessment processes, which are relatively new, need to become much more deeply embedded and mainstreamed within policy formation.

Policy towards fragile states

US economist Dani Rodrik has written that 'societies that benefit the most from integration with the world economy are those that have the complementary institutions at home that manage and contain the conflicts that economic interdependence triggers'. These include strong institutions in the areas of governance, the judiciary, civil and political liberties, social insurance and education.[9] This view is important for this study since many developing countries do not, of course, have such strong institutions, including most that are at risk of, or emerging from, conflict. This applies especially to fragile states.

In recent years many donors have begun to reform their aid programmes to focus more explicitly on the particular circumstances of fragile states, a process has been partly driven by the attacks of 11 September 2001 and the US 'war on terror' (Christian Aid, 2004). But while various donors have recently produced official strategies towards fragile states, none has explicitly focused on how trade policy specifically can play a role.

The *Fragile States Strategy* of the United States Agency for International Development (USAID) produced in early 2005, notes that 'there is perhaps no more urgent matter facing USAID than fragile states' and that a 'different and more strategic approach' to fragile states is needed. This should include: analysis and monitoring of the internal dynamics of fragile states; priorities reflecting the realities of fragile states; programmes focused on those priorities and the sources of fragility; and an Agency business model that allows for timely, rapid and effective response. The overall impetus for the new US focus on fragile states is mentioned in the conclusion: 'Fragile states have long posed a problem for the United States and are now recognized as a source of our nation's most pressing security threats. Driven by a dramatically changed landscape, responding more effectively to fragile states has moved to the centre of the foreign aid agenda.'

The analysis does not specifically mention trade policy anywhere in its 11 pages. USAID does produce a 'fragility framework' that considers security, political, economic and social policies needing to be in place to address better governance in fragile states – but the analysis there, to this author, looks like it could refer to any developing country rather than the specificities of fragile states. The economic section simply refers to the importance of 'economic and financial institutions and infrastructure that support economic growth (including jobs), adapt to economic change and manage natural resources' and of 'economic institutions, financial services and income-generating opportunities that are widely accessible and reasonably transparent, particularly related to access to and governance of natural resources'.

Later, the analysis mentions 'illustrative' economic policies for vulnerable states – such as 'foster institutional and policy development that promotes economic growth and effective management of natural resources' and 'improve revenue generation/tax systems and expenditure'. It also lists 'illustrative' policies for states in crisis: 'focus on reviving the economy, with particular attention to basic infrastructure, job creation, income generation, early market reform, natural resource management, independent central banks and tax codes'; 'distribute seeds, fertilizers and tools and provide related training, and rehabilitate farm-to-market roads'; and 'advance transparency of resources, particularly in countries rich in natural resources and where profits from these resources are used to fuel conflict'. The latter point is the only mention of a trade-related policy, and is restricted to concerns of 'transparency' (USAID, 2005).

DFID's policy document, *Why We Need to Work More Effectively in Fragile States*, released in January 2005, recognizes that 'fragile states are the hardest countries in the world to help develop' but makes only passing reference to trade, stating that: 'For the international community to provide effective support to fragile states, it needs to combine aid with diplomacy, security guarantees, human rights monitoring, trade policy and technical assistance (such as in tracking down criminal activity)' (DFID, 2005).

In its summary of an international forum on aid effectiveness in fragile states in London in January 2005, the OECD's Development Assistance Committee (DAC) notes that:

> *There is increasing recognition by donors of the need to apply policy approaches that are tailored to the needs of fragile states… Meeting the special needs of fragile states often requires the use of a range of instruments in addition to aid including diplomacy, security and financial measures such as debt relief. A coherent, whole of government approach is therefore required of international actors, which involves those agencies responsible for security, political and financial affairs, as well as those responsible for development aid and humanitarian assistance.*

The DAC's stress on coherence is important, but noticeable is the absence in this report of any mention of trade policy (DAC Chair, 2005).

The EU's *European Security Strategy*, produced in December 2003, calls on the EU to be 'more active in pursuing our strategic objectives' and notes that 'this applies to the full spectrum of instruments for crisis management and conflict prevention at our disposal, including political, diplomatic, military and civilian, trade and development activities. Active policies are needed to counter the new dynamic threats' (EU, 2003). The strategy highlights state failure as one of the five threats facing Europe, but the EU has devoted less attention to addressing this than the other identified threats, such as terrorism and proliferation of weapons of mass destruction.

Although the EU has great potential to address the problems of fragile states, given the wide range of policy instruments available to it, and given the large number of declaratory statements recognizing the importance of conflict prevention, noted in a previous section, at present the EU does not apply these instruments effectively (Saferworld and International Alert, 2005). EU action remains often fragmented and uncoordinated, lacking an overall strategy and direction. Two prominent NGOs working in this area, for example, note that 'the institutional disconnect between the Commission and the Council means that the complementary conflict prevention and development programming is not integrated into the strategic and operational planning of crisis management operations' (Saferworld and International Alert, 2005).

As well as the range of policies identified above, there are further ways in which EU policies could specifically address fragile states. The Council could agree on a common position for fragile states, which would help to ensure a coherent, strategic approach. More development assistance could be targeted to fragile states, which could include trade capacity-building support and otherwise be cohered with other trade policies. The EU's institutional understanding of how trade policy can help fragile states needs to be significantly enhanced, and this analysis must be fed into the decision-making system. The EU also needs to focus on fashioning more proactive development cooperation strategies for fragile states that take more account of the specificities of fragile states and that ensure coherence between the EU's different policy instruments.

Conclusion and recommendations

OECD countries are taking some steps to prevent future conflict. Yet if governments and institutions recognize some of the economic causes of conflict, their policies often betray little of this understanding. The political will to address some critical policy areas is, frankly, lacking. And the importance of trade policy to conflict-prevention and post-conflict reconstruction has yet to be fully taken on board and is a missing piece in the jigsaw.

It is hard to disagree with a report for International Alert arguing that 'international responses to insecurity and violent conflict reflect a prevailing assumption that the problem essentially consists of episodic and contained events, rather than coherent manifestations of entrenched structural global causes and dynamics' (Alexander and Smith, 2004, p9). It is precisely these entrenched causes, often directly related to OECD country policies, that need to become much more seriously addressed if conflict-sensitive trade policy is to become a reality rather than an aspiration on the part of some sections of the development community.

In summary, OECD states need to:

- take increased steps to abolish market access barriers to poor country exports and abolish export subsidies in the developed world;
- recognize more clearly through better research the links between trade policy and conflict and increase efforts to design conflict-sensitive trade policies;
- increase support for developing country efforts to diversify their economies – specifically, identify and remove the trade-distorting subsidies and protectionist import standards that inhibit economic diversification in the developing world;
- improve trade policy flexibility so that poor countries can take greater advantage of trading opportunities that are currently available under the WTO's SDT provisions.

As regards fragile states in particular:

- While the immediate need is often (good quality) aid and reconstruction, trade policy is also critical even for immediate development needs in the case of countries dependent on commodities, and certainly in the medium term. Research needs to be conducted to assess the importance of trade policy in fragile states and to ensure this is incorporated into the design of overall development cooperation packages. DFID notes, for example, that 'before we decide whether to deploy significant resources, we need to improve early warning of instability and understand more about the political economy of the states concerned' (DFID, 2005). This applies to trade policy as well as to aid.
- OECD countries need to improve and cohere approaches to failed states and engage in better research to design appropriate trade policies and ensure this is incorporated into the design of overall development cooperation packages. As recommended in a paper commissioned by the DAC on aid policy in difficult environments, conflict-sensitivity criteria should be mainstreamed in macroeconomic advice, fiscal policy and public expenditure reforms, PRSPs and public expenditure reviews. It also recommends to 'privilege diplomacy, private investment, trade and security assistance over aid in donor engagement in fragile states but provide sufficient aid to make the other instruments effective' (Picciotto at al, 2005, p10).
- Donors could provide more capacity-building support specifically to fragile states to enable them to jump-start their trading activities. A ring-fenced financial fund could be established for this purpose. More aid

could also help support fragile-state attempts to manage future economic shocks. DFID, again, notes that 'economic shocks have the potential to turn fragility into a crisis and poverty into destitution. The capacity to manage shocks, whether natural disasters or economic, is crucial for fragile states. Fragile states are seldom able to do this without help from the international community' (DFID, 2005).

Notes

1   See the Africa Growth and Opportunity Act at www.agoa.gov/.
2   Cited in O. Brown, 2005, pp6–7.
3   These are domestic support programmes that are linked to production-limiting programmes; for example, if the level of payments is based on fixed areas and yields, or per head of livestock.
4   These are support payments to farmers that are deemed non-trade distorting and thus exempt from reduction commitments.
5   Stabex was a stabilization system under which ACP States were eligible for compensation if their export revenues from trade with the EU dropped compared to a six-year average. Such a drop would trigger an automatic compensation payment to the affected government for use in aiding economic diversification and to benefit producers in the affected sector.
6   Cited in Konandreas, 2000.
7   See the EC checklist for root causes of conflict at www.europa.eu.int/comm/external_relations/cpcm/cp/list.htm
8   See, for example, Bayne, 2003.
9   Cited in Trocaire, 2003.

References

Alexander L. and Smith, D. (2004) *Evidence and Analysis: Tackling the Structural Causes of Conflict in Africa and Strengthening Preventive Responses*, London, International Alert

Bayne, S. (2003) 'Conflict prevention and the EU: From rhetoric to reality', in BOND, *Europe in the World: Essays on EU Foreign, Security and Development Policies*, London, BOND

Benn, H. (2005) 'Trade and security in an interconnected world', in Dodds, F. and Pippard, T. (eds) *Human and Environmental Security: An Agenda for Change*, London, Earthscan

Brenton, P. (2003) 'Integrating the Least Developed Countries into the world trading system: The current impact of EU preferences under Everything but Arms', *Policy Research Working Paper*, Washington DC, World Bank

Brenton, P. and Ikezuki, T. (2004) 'The initial and potential impact of preferential access to the US market under the African Growth and Opportunity Act', *World Bank Policy Research Working Paper 3262*, Washington DC, World Bank

Brown, O. (2005) *EU Trade Policy and Conflict*, Geneva, IISD

Christian Aid (2004) *The Politics of Poverty: Aid in the New Cold War*, London, Christian Aid

Curtis, M. (2001) *Trade for Life: Making Trade Work for Poor People*, London, Christian Aid

DAC Chair (2005) 'Chair's summary: Senior level forum on development effectiveness in fragile states', London, 13–14 January 2005, Paris, OECD DAC

DFID (Department for International Development) (2001) *The Causes of Conflict in Sub-Saharan Africa: Framework Document*, London, DFID

DFID (2005) *Why We Need to Work More Effectively in Fragile States*, London, DFID

EPA Watch (2004) 'Trade traps: Why EU–ACP economic partnership agreements pose a threat to Africa's development', www.epawatch.net/general/text.php?itemID=263&menuID=28 accessed in 2005

EU (European Union) (2001) *EU Programme for the Prevention of Violent Conflicts*, Brussels, European Union

EU (2002) 'One year on: The Commission's conflict prevention policy', www.europa.eu.int/comm/external_relations/cpcm/cp/rep.htm accessed in 2005

EU (2003) *A Secure Europe in a Better World: European Security Strategy*, Brussels, European Union

EU (2005) 'Council Common Position 2005/304/CFSP of 12 April 2005, concerning conflict prevention, management and resolution in Africa and repealing Common Position 2004/85/CFSP', *Official Journal of the European Union*, Aberdeen

FAO (Food and Agriculture Organization of the United Nations) (2003a) 'FAO support to the WTO negotiations: The need for special safeguards for developing countries', www.fao.org//docrep/005/y4852e/y4852e05.htm accessed in 2005

FAO (2003b) 'FAO trade policy briefs on issues relating to the WTO negotiations on agriculture: No.9, A special safeguard mechanism for developing countries', ftp://fao.org/docrep/fao/008/j5425e/j5425e01.pdf accessed in 2005

Fraser, A. and Kachingwe, N. (2003) 'Cotonou and the WTO: Can Europe's trade agenda deliver a just partnership with developing countries?', in BOND, *Europe in the World: Essays on EU Foreign, Security and Development Policies*, London, BOND

Gilbert, C. (1993) 'Domestic price stabilization schemes for developing countries', in Classens, S. and Duncan, R. (eds), *Managing Commodity Price Risk in Developing Countries*, Baltimore, Johns Hopkins University Press, pp30–67

Halle, M., Switzer, J. and Winkler, S. (2004) *Trade, Aid and Security: Elements of a Positive Paradigm*, Geneva, IISD, IUCN, CEESP

Hanlon, J. (2003) 'World Bank admits its policies caused war', www.brettonwoods project.org/art.shtml?x=4543 accessed in 2005

IATP (Institute for Agriculture and Trade Policy) (2005) 'A decade of dumping on world agricultural markets', *South Bulletin*, 30 March 2005, pp127–129

Jomo, K. (2003) *Globalisation, Liberalisation and Equitable Development: Lessons from East Asia*, Geneva, UNRISD

Konandreas, P. (2000) 'Overview of implementation experiences and possible negotiating objectives', paper presented at seminar on WTO negotiations on agriculture, Geneva, South Centre/IATP/ActinAid/Focus on the Global South

Kozul-Wright, R. and Rayment, P. (2004) 'Globalisation reloaded: An UNCTAD perspective', *UNCTAD Discussion Paper No. 167*, Geneva, United Nations

Lefrancois, F. (2004) 'World Bank, IMF: Helping peace or creating conditions for war?', www.brettonwoodsproject.org/art.shtml?x=43345 accessed in 2005

Miguel, E., Satyanath, S. and Sergenti, E. (2003) 'Economic shocks and civil conflict: An instrumental variables approach', *Journal of Political Economy*, vol 112, no 4, pp725–753

Nefeld, I. N. (2001) 'Anti-dumping and countervailing procedures – use or abuse?', *Policy Issues in International Trade and Commodities,* study series No.9, New York/Geneva, UNCTAD

Oxfam (2002) 'Europe's double standards: How the EU should reform its trade policies with the developing world', *Oxfam Briefing Paper No. 22,* London, Oxfam

Oxfam (2005) *A Round for Free: How Rich Countries Are Getting a Free Ride on Agricultural Subsidies at the WTO,* London, Oxfam

Picciotto, R., Alao, C., Ikpe, E., Kimani, M. and Slade, R. (2005) 'Striking a new balance: Donor policy coherence and development in difficult environments', DAC background paper, Paris, OECD

Saferworld and International Alert (2005) *Developing an EU Strategy to Address Failed States: Priorities for the UK Presidency of the EU in 2005,* London, Saferworld and International Alert

Sambanis, N. (2003) 'A review of recent advances and future directions in the quantitative literature on civil war', *Defence and Peace Economics,* vol 13, no 3, pp215–243

South Centre (2005a) 'G-33 Ministerial Communiqué: Food and livelihood security vital', in *South Bulletin,* vol 106, 30 June 2005, pp309–311

South Centre (2005b) *State of Play in Agriculture Negotiations: Country Groupings' Positions July 2005,* Geneva, South Centre

Stevens, C. and Kennan, J. (2001) *The Impact of the EU's Everything but Arms Proposal: A Report to Oxfam,* Sussex, IDS

TWN (Third World Network Information Service) (2005) 'US agricultural proposal criticized as inadequate and ignoring SDT for developing countries', www.twnside.org.sg/title2/twninfo268.htm accessed in 2005

Trocaire (2003) 'Conflict sensitivity and peace building in development', Trocaire discussion paper, Ireland

UNCTAD (1999) *Report of the Expert Meeting on Examining Trade in the Agricultural Sector, April 1999,* TD/B/COM.1/23, Geneva, United Nations

UNCTAD (2000) *Subsidies, Countervailing Measures and Developing Countries,* UNCTAD/DITC/COM/23, Geneva, UNCTAD

UNCTAD (2001) *Economic Development in Africa: Performance, Prospects and Policy issues,* New York/Geneva, United Nations

UNCTAD (2004) *The Least Developed Countries Report, 2004,* New York/Geneva, United Nations

UNDP (1999) *Human Development Report 1999,* New York/Geneva, United Nations

UNDP (2005) *Human Development Report 2005,* New York/Geneva, United Nations

USAID (US Agency for International Development) (2005) *Fragile States Strategy,* Washington DC, USAID

World Bank (2003) *Breaking the Conflict Trap: Civil War and Development Policy, Vol 1,* Washington DC, World Bank

World Development Movement (2004) 'Zambia: Condemned to debt', www.wdm.org.uk/campaigns/colludo/zambia/index.htm accessed in 2005

Chapter 2

Developing Conflict-sensitive Aid: The Relationship between Aid and Conflict

Ian Smillie

This boy is Ignorance. This girl is Want. Beware them both, and all of their degree, but most of all beware this boy, for on his brow I see that written which is Doom, unless the writing be erased.

Charles Dickens, A Christmas Carol, 1843

This chapter is about constructing aid policies that are 'conflict sensitive'. Many donors today support a wide range of projects related to 'peace-building' – efforts aimed at resolving conflict, at promoting post-war reconciliation and the strengthening of institutions that contribute to social peace. More specifically, such efforts may deal with the demobilization and reintegration of combatants, support for truth and reconciliation commissions, the creation of civil society partnerships and conflict-sensitive media and communications strategies. This chapter is not about that sort of peace-building, although it touches upon it. The chapter is about the wider role of official development assistance and where it fits in relation to conflict and conflict prevention.

Lessons of history: See no evil

Rwanda

Critics of development assistance have long said that aid can make things worse, that it can ignore signs of trouble, and that in supporting bad governments it can help set the stage for conflict. There is no country in recent years more studied than Rwanda, because the violence that erupted there in 1994 was so devastating, and because the outside world did so little to stop it. Many studies have pored over the warnings that were available in the months before the genocide began in April 1994, and many have condemned the unwillingness or the inability of the international community to take the warnings seriously. The UN peacekeeping force, installed in 1993 to deal with the country's low-grade civil war, had only 2500 troops and 80 serviceable vehicles recycled from a UN operation in Cambodia when the real violence erupted. At that point, the UN Security Council could have done one of two things: it could have done more; or it could have done less. It did less, and the rest is history.

But the prologue to the story is longer and more complex than many histories have shown. Where foreign aid is concerned, it was not so much a matter of ignoring or misreading the signs, but of actively building the capacities of a government with murder on its mind. One of the most damning studies has been written by a Swiss-born former NGO worker, Peter Uvin. Uvin lays bare the contradictions between the genocide and the attitude of donors who had until the last moment regarded Rwanda as a model of development in Africa. Rwanda had certainly showed promising performance in almost all development indicators – economic growth, government services and food security. Up to the last minute, Uvin says, 'thousands of technical assistants and foreign experts were building roads, extending credit, training farmers, protecting the environment, reorganizing ministries, advising finance officials and distributing food aid, at a cost of hundreds of millions of dollars a year – the lion's share of all government expenditures. For most of these people, up to the end, Rwanda was a well-developing country – facing serious development problems, but dealing with them much more effectively than were other countries' (Uvin, 1998, p2).

The development enterprise in Rwanda was, Uvin says, by and large a noble one. Rwanda was of little political interest to any of the major donors, and aid came with few of the strings and caveats of the Cold War and immediate post-Cold War period. But the truth about Rwanda, understood largely in retrospect, was more complex than what outsiders saw and understood. The majority of Rwanda's people lived in absolute poverty, with few prospects for improvement. Aid programmes had made little difference. An uneducated, ill-informed public was treated in an authoritarian and oppressive manner by an arrogant government with a solid track record of corruption and human rights abuse. Regional and ethnic inequality was palpable, exacerbated by a history of state-sponsored racism. And violence had erupted in the past. Uvin says that these factors – exclusion, inequality, pauperization, racism, structural violence and oppression – all interacted with processes of development assistance to lay the groundwork for the genocide. Foreign aid contributed through action – in supporting and building the capacity of the government – and through inaction – in ignoring unmistakeable warning signs and in failing to mitigate the worst aspects of poverty, exclusion and violence.

Uvin ends his book with a question: 'Could and should aid have acted differently?' As to whether donors should, or could have done anything differently, these questions relate in part to concepts of what foreign aid is all about, and to questions of conditionality and state sovereignty. These will be addressed later in more detail; however, 1994 was not exactly the dark ages of human rights awareness and donor conditionality. By the 1990s human rights as a component of good governance was well understood. Patchy as the donor application of human rights criteria may have been over the years, this was not *terra incognita*. And by 1994, donors had almost two decades of aid conditionality under their collective belt. Most of this, however, related to good economic, rather than good political or social governance, manifesting itself largely in structural adjustment programmes and what became known as the 'Washington Consensus'. This consensus was based on less rather than more government, trade liberalization and building the groundwork for enhanced foreign investment.

Rwanda was familiar with this kind of conditionality. A $90 million structural adjustment programme had been concluded with the World Bank in 1991, with additional loans negotiated in 1992 and 1993. A 40 per cent devaluation of the Rwandan franc led to higher rates of inflation. This, along with increased user fees in the health, education and water supply sectors only exacerbated the poverty in which much of the population lived. Rwanda's debt rose from 32 per cent of GNP in 1990, to 62 per cent in 1993. On top of a civil war and bad political governance, it is perhaps not surprising that the economic chemotherapy failed to work.

Many lessons have been drawn from Rwanda, but lessons drawn are not the same thing as lessons learned or lessons applied. The following pages will examine current conditions in two other countries that are the recipients of considerable foreign assistance, and where certain parallels with the Rwanda of 1994 can be discerned.

Nigeria

Nigeria, of course, is not exactly Rwanda. It is a vast country with a population the size of Germany and Italy combined. At more than 130 million people, Nigerians represent nearly a quarter of all those living in sub-Saharan Africa. Seventy-five per cent of the land is arable, and Nigeria has abundant resources of coal, tin, gypsum, columbite, gemstones, marble, uranium and other resources. Nigeria is the sixth largest oil producer in OPEC, and at the 2005 production rate of 2.6 million barrels day, current reserves are predicted to last for 40 years or more (CIA World Fact Book, 2006).

And yet Nigeria is a mess, from almost every point of view. More than 70 per cent of the population lives on less than a dollar a day, one out of every five Nigerian children dies before the age of five and at least four million people are living with, and dying from, HIV/AIDS. Half of the country's adults are illiterate, and only half of the children attend primary school. Despite a 1999 return to civilian rule after decades of military mismanagement and corruption, the government has been unable to rectify some of the worst aspects of economic and political mismanagement. Inflation is high, growth is weak, and most of the wealth is in the hands of a small and incredibly rapacious elite.

While freedom of expression and media independence are better than in the past, opposition leaders and journalists take their lives in their hands if they are overly critical of government. Human Rights Watch has documented a wide range of attacks and killings – often by police – of journalists, human rights activists and opposition politicians (Human Rights Watch, 2003). In a 2003 report, the US State Department noted that 'The government's human rights record remained poor ... the national police, military and security forces committed extra-judicial killings and used excessive force to apprehend criminal suspects and to quell several incidents of ethno-religious violence' (US Department of State, 2002).

Between 1967 and 1970, Nigeria's devastating civil war took the lives of something between one and three million people – in the hostilities, and from other war-related causes. Another three million people were displaced, many of them for years. One of the triggers for the war was communal violence – committed largely by Muslim northerners against Christian Ibos from the south. These riots took the lives of 6000–8000 people (de St. Jorre, 1972, p86). Today, inter-communal violence in Nigeria has become commonplace, with riots in Kaduna, Kano and Plateau State taking the lives of more than 50,000 people between 2001 and 2004 alone. Since 2000, 12 northern Nigerian states have introduced Sharia law, exacerbating tensions between Muslims and Christians, and are using the new laws as the basis for committing a wide range of human rights abuses.

Thousands of people have also been killed in the Niger River delta area in recent years as a result of inter- and intra-communal violence, violence between criminal gangs, and violence committed by security forces sent in to quell disputes.

While many reports on Nigeria say that things are better today than when under military rule, it is hard to imagine that the cumulative violence, human rights abuse, corruption and mismanagement – along with the country's crippling poverty – are not taking a major toll. The words Uvin uses to describe Rwanda in 1994 could as easily be used to describe Nigeria today: exclusion, inequality, pauperization, racism, structural violence and oppression.

In 2005, the National Intelligence Council in Washington produced a scenario that is widely discussed in Nigeria, but rarely in writing – the potential for outright collapse. 'While currently Nigeria's leaders are locked in a bad marriage that all dislike but dare not leave, there are possibilities that could disrupt the precarious equilibrium in Abuja.' The report says this could perhaps be triggered by a military coup. Whatever the cause, 'If Nigeria were to become a failed state, it could drag down a large part of the West African region. Even state failure in small countries such as Liberia has the effect of destabilizing entire neighbourhoods' (National Intelligence Council, 2005).

Bangladesh

Bangladesh gained its independence from Pakistan in a bloody war. The country began its life in 1971 as a kind of 'failed state' before it was actually a state, and predictions for its 70 million people – living in a country the size of Maine – were dire.

Defying logic and prediction, Bangladesh – which had a 10-million ton annual food deficit in the 1970s – has today become largely self-sufficient in rice and wheat, even though the population has doubled. Bangladesh has reduced child mortality, eradicated polio and has enjoyed annual GDP growth rates averaging 5 per cent over the past decade. Despite a stormy political history, the country has been governed by a parliamentary democracy for the past 15 years. Emerging from a conservative Muslim tradition, women have taken an increasingly important role in society, and both prime ministers since 1991 have been women. These are remarkable achievements that few among even the most optimistic would have dared to predict 30 years ago.

But there is another side to Bangladesh. It is the most densely populated country in the world. Half the population lives in abject poverty, and despite its remarkable agricultural track record, the prospects for the 240 million people who are likely to live in Bangladesh by 2020 are not hopeful. Donors optimistically say that with good public policies, strengthened institutions and sustained levels of growth, some of the MDGs could actually be met in Bangladesh by 2015.

But Bangladesh does not have good public policies, strong institutions or the levels of growth that will be needed. The parliamentary democracy that has succeeded 20 years of coups, counter-coups and military government is fragile. In opposition, each party makes it as difficult for the other to govern as possible. The general strike or *hartal*, initiated by Gandhi as a demonstration of peaceful resistance to British rule, has become the order of the day, disrupting and paralysing government on a regular basis. Between 1990 and 2002 there were 827 *hartals*, estimated to have cost the economy 3–4 per cent of GDP (UNDP, 2005a).

All donors recognize that poor governance threatens everything in Bangladesh – growth, security, human rights and democracy. In August 2005, more than 300 small bombs were set off within minutes of each other in Dhaka, causing panic in the streets and even greater panic in the corridors of power. Leaflets found at bombing sites called for the imposition of Islamic law. More bombs followed. The erosion of what few democratic processes remain is rampant; communal violence is largely ignored as a concession to increasingly militant fundamentalist parties; and Bangladesh, along with Nigeria and Haiti, now finds itself at the very bottom of Transparency International's corruption index. Like Nigeria, Bangladesh bears all the hallmarks of Peter Uvin's Rwanda: exclusion, inequality, pauperization, racism, structural violence and oppression.

And like Nigeria, Bangladesh has experienced serious violence. The consequences were calamitous – not just for Bangladesh, but for its neighbour, India. Independence came to Bangladesh after a brutal Pakistani army crackdown following a national election that might have given national power to a regional Bengali political party. Throughout 1971 a campaign of suppression led to a huge number of deaths and displacement. In December of that year,

India stepped in, declaring war on Pakistan and forcing a surrender before the new year. The issue here is not the cause of the cataclysm, but the result in human terms. UNDP placed the number of refugees fleeing the country at 10 million – certainly the greatest refugee crisis since World War II. The number of internally displaced was perhaps as high, and as many as a million people died. The cost of collapse today – in human terms, political terms and in regional terms – would arguably be as high or higher.

Foreign Policy places Bangladesh 17th on a list of 60 countries described in a 'failed state index'. Many of the countries on the list are far from 'failed', but using indicators that include demographic pressures, human rights, uneven development, economic decline and delegitimization of the state, Bangladesh finds itself with the same ranking as Burundi, and only slightly ahead of Zimbabwe and North Korea (*Foreign Policy*, 2005).

Both Nigeria and Bangladesh are recipients of large amounts of foreign assistance – $1.4 billion in the case of Bangladesh in 2003, and $318 million in the case of Nigeria. Apart from objective need, donors view both Nigeria and Bangladesh from a political perspective. As USAID puts it, 'Bangladesh is one of the world's few moderate, democratic Islamic nations. If its fragile democratic institutions or growing market economy do not advance, the consequences for its neighbors and for U.S. interests could be quite serious' (USAID, 2004a). Quite. In its 2005 Congressional budget justification for Nigeria, USAID says, 'As the most populous sub-Saharan African nation and as an established leader in regional initiatives, including the New Partnership for Africa's Development (NEPAD), Nigeria's prosperity and stability are essential to growth and stability in West Africa, and more generally to the continent as a whole. Nigeria also supplies about 10 percent of U. S. crude oil requirements, is our second-largest trading partner in Africa, and is the recipient of significant U.S. foreign investment' (USAID, 2004b).

Rather than Uvin's question about Rwanda – 'Could and should aid have acted differently?' – the question about Nigeria and Bangladesh, and a dozen other fragile states relates to the present: 'Are aid agencies doing the right thing, right now?' Or are they ignoring unmistakeable warning signs and failing to mitigate the worst aspects of poverty, exclusion and violence? The warning signs, in fact, are not being ignored – in the sense that new emphasis is now being placed by many donors on 'good governance', which includes good policies and administration, democracy, human rights and conflict prevention. USAID will spend $7 million of its planned $50 million 2006 budget in Bangladesh on the promotion of governance and democracy. And in Nigeria, where it is the largest donor, it will spend $8 million out of $46 million on governance and democracy.

But to the question 'are they doing the right thing', the answer is at least a partial 'no' in the sense of overall quantity of aid and the urgency with which the problems – both those related to governance and those related to poverty reduction – are being addressed. Where governance is concerned, three or four or five million dollars is not insignificant but, even when tripled to account for all other donors, is hardly enough to make a dent in countries where governance is as bad as it is in Nigeria and Bangladesh, where politics have been seriously criminalized, and where the consequences of collapse are so dire.

A more critical question about spending on governance is, 'Are aid agencies doing things right?' This question will be addressed in the pages that follow.

Governance

Human rights and economic governance

'Governance' and more especially ideas about '*good* governance' have come late to the development agenda, appearing in tentative form in the mid-1980s, but remaining constrained by the Cold War until its unexpected demise in 1989. Today the term covers a multitude of meanings, but it is essentially about building effective institutions and rules imbued with predictability, accountability, transparency and the rule of law. It is about relations between institutions and processes, governmental and otherwise.

The discourse on good governance and its manifestation in aid programming began with human rights, moved into concerns about economic management and structural adjustment, and began to concern itself with democracy and the rule of law in the 1980s. The issue of good governance is important to conflict-sensitive aid programming, not just because well-governed states are thought to be less inclined to conflict than others, but because pushing too hard on buttons marked 'governance' without understanding all the possible consequences can lead to unforeseen results, and sometimes to conflict.

In its earliest incarnation, and still unnamed as such, concern about governance was manifested in human rights conditionalities. The 1975 Helsinki Accords were an early influence on communist signatories in the field of human rights. The Carter administration stressed human rights in US aid allocations – if somewhat selectively – and other countries began to introduce human rights into their development programming at about the same time.

A variation on the governance theme, although not labelled as such at the time, was growing concern about economic management in developing countries. The oil crisis of the 1970s, global recession, famine and drought, and commodity and debt crises led one country after another into difficult IMF stabilization agreements. Structural adjustment became the watchword of the decade under the general rubric of governance – or more pointedly, *economic* governance. During the 1970s, the IMF engaged in about 10 stabilization programmes a year. In 1980 the number rose to 28 and by 1985 there had been 129 more. Typically, adjustment programmes had three components: expenditure reduction; expenditure switching (exchange rate devaluation, reductions on subsidies, import controls and taxes); and institutional and policy reforms (trade liberalization, privatization, fiscal reform, and less state involvement in the economy). This approach became known as the 'Washington Consensus'.

By the late 1980s, the side effects of structural adjustment were proving worse in many cases than the disease. In 1987, UNICEF produced an influential review of the experience thus far and concluded that 'overall, prevailing adjustment programmes tend to increase aggregate poverty, or in other words the number of people – and of children – living below the poverty line' (Cornia et al, 1987, p66). For most donors, however, the governance issue remained fixed for several more years on the economic agenda. It is only in more recent times that imposed economic formulae were seen to be failing, and in some cases making matters worse. The 'IMF riot', commonplace across the developing world, from Malaysia to Uganda to Bolivia, was hardly what might be called a conflict-sensitive aid outcome. As Joseph Stiglitz, former vice president of the World Bank puts it, 'The very notion that one could separate economics from politics, or a broader understanding of society, illustrated a narrowness of perspective. If policies imposed by lenders induce riots ... then economic conditions worsen, as capital flees and businesses worry about investing more of their money. Such policies are not a recipe either for successful development or for economic stability' (Stiglitz, 2002, p47).

Democracy

Many studies over the past 15 years have made a direct link between the spread of democracy and reductions in armed conflict, thus supporting and encouraging donor involvement in these areas (Weart, 1998; Diamond, 2002; Windsor, 2003). The UN has invested a decade, not just in the idea, but in holding elections and promoting democratic institutions from Cambodia to Sierra Leone, from East Timor to Burundi. NEPAD, widely endorsed by African and donor governments, has as its first principle, 'good governance as a basic requirement for peace, security and sustainable political and socio-economic development'. NEPAD does not hedge on the word *governance* as some donors do; for NEPAD, governance and democracy go hand in hand: 'democracy *and* good, political economic and corporate governance'.[1]

During the 1960s, the 1970s, and well into the 1980s, the Cold War dampened any serious discussion of democratic development in a wide range of superpower client states – Zaire, Liberia, Somalia, Ethiopia, Afghanistan, Mozambique, Angola. Other truants, such as Indonesia, Pakistan and China, were also excused from the discussion for strategic or commercial reasons. But a burst of democratic change in Latin America during the 1980s sparked change elsewhere, and the last year of the 1980s was a seminal moment for democratic development. In 1989, a wave of independence surged across a dozen Soviet vassal states, and the Cold War stumbled to an unexpected end. Suddenly, the gloves were off and 'democracy' could be discussed in polite company. In its 1989 DAC report, the OECD said, 'Now that the word "democracy" has become an acceptable word to use in development circles, we are also hearing more often concerns about "corruption"... We are even beginning to hear that one-party systems do not work' (OECD, 1989, p16). It went further, saying that 'There is a vital connection, now more widely appreciated, between open, democratic and accountable political systems, individual rights and the effective and equitable operation of economic systems' (OECD, 1989, pii).

Elsewhere in the governance debate, some are beginning to cast doubt on the idea that there might be a correlation between democracy and growth. 'As a whole,' writes David Gillies, 'the empirical evidence directly linking democracy and economic growth is ambiguous at best. There is no iron-clad law defining the relationship between democracy and economic growth' (Gillies, 2005). It might be noted, of course, that there is, in fact, no ironclad law defining the relationship between *anything* and economic growth.

But legitimacy is an important part of effective governance, and while historically it has taken many forms, Francis Fukuyama observes that 'in today's world the only serious form of legitimacy is democracy' (Fukuyama, 2004, p28). Accountability is important, but it is unlikely to be adequate or effective if allegiance is owed more to donors and international financial institutions than to the citizenry. And while the relationship between development and democracy may be contested, the argument could be stated another way. There is no correlation – and certainly no ironclad law – linking authoritarian governance and economic growth, as countless dictators have demonstrated in recent years. Amartya Sen has demonstrated how a free press and accountable politicians can help to avert famine. Certainly, he says, democracies are more likely than dictatorships to enjoy long-term political stability (Sen, 2000). And in a democracy, a bad government can at least be defeated at the polls.

Justice

Justice is seen by the victims of conflict as an important part of coming to closure. At the conclusion of many of today's wars, however, justice is reduced to a 'Truth and Reconciliation Commission', a process that serves a cathartic purpose, perhaps, but one from which justice is largely absent. Listen to the words of a Sierra Leonean in a camp for people who had their limbs hacked off by rebel soldiers:

> *We were told to forgive, but forgiveness doesn't hold any water without restitution, and we are not getting any. We continue to suffer, we can't afford education for our children, and our families scatter because we can't look after them... The ones who did this to us are getting support – training, kits, money, and jobs. They actually got compensation for what they did. The security everyone talks about is at risk, not just for us but also for our children, the next generation. I am supposed to forgive, but what about my children – deprived of education and a life? For us, if there is to be security, this matter has to be settled.* (Donini et al, 2005, p43)

Multiply that personal tragedy by a million or two stories from developing countries, and consider how long it took to bring Charles Taylor, Liberia's former warlord president and the progenitor of untold horrors across West Africa, to justice. Forced to step down in 2003 in a deal to end a dozen years of bloodshed in Liberia, Taylor was given asylum in Nigeria, despite an indictment for murder and war crimes by a UN-backed international war crimes court in Sierra Leone. Taylor languished with impunity in a Calabar villa until March 2006, when Liberia's newly elected government finally asked Nigeria to hand him over. The Security Council could have made the request any time during the intervening 30 months, but did not. And it did nothing when The Netherlands refused for months to allow the trial venue to be moved – for safety reasons – from Freetown to The Hague. It could be said that all's well that ends well: an African tyrant will now face justice, something of a precedent. But it happened *despite*, and not because of the efforts of the world's largest donor governments and the UN Security Council. Had tiny Liberia not made its request to Nigeria, Taylor would still be free in Calabar, the beneficiary of an all-too-frequent conflict-insensitive arrangement with long-term negative implications for peace.

Civil society

The term 'civil society' entered the democratic governance discourse in the early 1990s, but the ideas about the importance of civil society as an alternative to the state, or as a buffer, go back to the writings of De Tocqueville, Hegel and Gramsci. Certainly NGOs and other civil society organizations – trade unions, educational institutions and professional associations – have long been programming actively in developing countries, usually with significant support from their home governments. But it was not until the publication of Robert Putnam's 1993 study of governance in Italy that ideas about civil society's role in the promotion of democracy began to gel. *Making Democracy Work: Civic Traditions in Modern Italy* found – through a detailed analysis of 500 years of documented Italian history – that it was civic institutions and what Putnam called 'social capital' that made the difference between the north of the country, where democracy and good governance in the north of the country were established, and the south, where they were not.

Soon, there were university courses and a small publishing industry devoted to the subject. Definitions and descriptions proliferated. But as with other big new ideas, the civil society bloom was short-lived. Although it still enjoys a kind of half-life, civil society is no longer touted as the answer to all problems, and in many developing countries the idea of building the capacities of civil society is no longer so much about buffering against the state as creating alternative service providers where the state had been downsized and emasculated courtesy of the Washington Consensus. Instead of supporting civil society organizations as development institutions in their own right, many donors tend to instrumentalize them as contractors, persuading them into government and donor-led priorities. Too few civil society organizations today, especially in developing countries, have the financial wherewithal to undertake independent study and to engage in the advocacy and policy dialogue that Putnam saw as so essential to democratic development.

Programming for good governance

Today, a billion, or perhaps even two billion people, live in poverty-stricken informal economies, making lives for themselves that are almost completely outside the formal structure of the state. This is not to say, however, that they do not understand concepts of good governance. Unlike the many donor governments that actively supported the criminalization of governance in Zaire, Liberia, Angola and a dozen other places over three or four decades, most citizens of these countries could always tell the difference between a political right and a political wrong. Whenever they are given the opportunity, hundreds of thousands of illiterate and desperately poor people go to the polls in hopes of electing a better government. Even the poorest villager in Africa knows what corruption is, what a judge is supposed to do and why there are police.[2]

The problem is not so much knowing what good governance is, but how to promote, achieve and sustain it. As Kofi Annan has put it, 'Obstacles to democracy have little to do with culture or religion, and much more to do with the desire of those in power to maintain their position at any cost. This is neither a new phenomenon nor one confined to any particular part of the world' (UNDP, 2002, p14).

Sue Unsworth, formerly Chief Governance Advisor at DFID, suggests – under the heading 'rethinking governance' – that donors must 'increase their understanding of political and institutional context ... [they must] increase their awareness of the impact of external interventions on local initiatives and capacity for action' (Unsworth, 2005, p12). She suggests a number of other ideas familiar to donors in other settings: the need for donor coordination and harmonization; predictable funding; giving real meaning to the idea of local ownership; finding out what is working and why; and limiting expectations.

Merilee Grindle writes about the long, expanding and overwhelming nature of the good governance agenda. She says that 'there is little guidance about what's essential and what's not, what should come first and what should follow, what is feasible and what is not. If more attention is given to sorting out these kinds of issues, the end point of the good governance imperative might be recast as "good enough governance", that is, a condition of minimally acceptable government performance and civil society engagement that does not significantly hinder economic and political development and that permits poverty reduction initiatives to go forward' (Grindle, 2002, p1). More to the point, she suggests that donors should keep their eye on the ball, making as clear a connection as possible between 'good enough governance' and poverty reduction. In the short and medium term, some improvements in governance may be less important than others in helping to reduce poverty. Most importantly, she suggests, good governance – especially good enough governance – requires research and critical analysis (Grindle, 2002, p27). And presumably, it requires a willingness among donors to apply the lessons that are being learned in this highly complex field.

Greed, grievance and the resource curse

Economic agendas

Economic agendas are not a new factor in war. In fact many wars have been fought almost exclusively for economic purposes – to gain access to land, oil, the sea. As a Soviet writer once put it, wars are fought for 'freedom, or iron, or coal, or the devil knows what' (Van Crevald, 1991, p187).

Civil wars in Africa over the past three decades have been seen largely in terms of power and grievance – ethnic grievance, political grievance, territorial grievance, religious grievance. Apart from an unbridled quest for power, however, the wars of the 1990s in countries like Angola, Sierra Leone and Liberia were baffling to journalists, diplomats and academics alike, unfamiliar with Africa and grappling with a change in the way wars were being fought. No longer something that took place mainly between nations and between formal armies fighting pitched battles, conflict was now something that occurred mainly within countries, often between inchoate groups with unclear ambitions and ideologies.

In fact, while many of these groups may have been (and may still be) inchoate, with unclear ideologies, their ambitions never have been vague. Foday Sankoh's Revolutionary United Front (RUF), Charles Taylor's National Patriotic Liberation Front in Liberia, and Jonas Savimbi's União Nacional para a Independência Total de Angola (UNITA) in Angola demonstrated clearly that their concerns about injustice and bad government were far less important to them than gaining power. All were prepared to use whatever means they could to further their aims, including child soldiers, all-out attacks on civilian populations and the most barbaric tactics imaginable. They, and later counterparts in the DRC, were pioneers in developing a new technique to pay for their wars. In the declining presence of great-power patrons in the post-Cold War world, they discovered that they could occupy land, harvest saleable natural resources, and trade them for weapons. Savimbi became a master at selling Angolan diamonds, at one time exporting hundreds of millions of dollars worth in a year. Charles Taylor financed his war by cutting down some of Liberia's best hardwood forests. And Foday Sankoh, with assistance from Taylor, went on a looting rampage in Sierra Leone's alluvial diamond fields.

A 1999 conference on 'economic agendas in civil wars' led to an edited volume the following year entitled *Greed and Grievance: Economic Agendas in Civil Wars*. The chapters shed light on the contours of 'economic agendas', but the details were still vague. Paul Collier at the World Bank, for example, wrote: 'A country that is heavily dependent upon primary commodity exports, with a quarter of its national income coming from them, has a risk four times greater than one without commodity exports' (Collier, 2000, p97).

It is true that poor countries with significant resources – of oil, for example – have suffered from conflict. Copper was a major factor in the Bougainville secessionist movement, and drugs have played a role in several conflicts. Collier explored some of these issues, but missed at first a key point that Sankoh, Taylor and Savimbi did not. Had the resource in their case been oil, they would not likely have had anywhere near the success they did, because none of them had the technology or the investment required to exploit oil. The Bougainville Revolutionary Army may have been fighting to gain control over copper, but it was never able to mine and sell copper in order to buy guns. As Laurent Kabila did in the DRC, it might have been able to sell 'futures' to unscrupulous entrepreneurs, but this requires business savvy, connections and time. The key distinction in Angola, Liberia and Sierra Leone, and later in the DRC, was the *lootability* of timber, coltan and diamonds, and an ability to sell the goods into a ready market that had little regard for legality.

Some lessons from the diamond trade

The implications of this for the international community became clearer as the ugliness of the wars grew, and as reports from NGOs began to pinpoint the issue more clearly. Global Witness focused on Angola and Partnership Africa Canada investigated Sierra Leone, publishing articles and starting a campaign that by the middle of 2000 had spooked the diamond industry into engagement. The Kimberley Process, as it became known, produced a global certification scheme for rough diamonds in almost record time – 40 months from the date of the first meeting in May 2000. This was significant not only because of the amazingly short time it took to reach an agreement of this type, but because it brought together NGO campaigners, industry and the governments of some 60 different countries.

Some countries were excluded: Liberia because of UN Security Council sanctions, which were imposed in 2000, and the Republic of Congo (Brazzaville), which was expelled in 2004 because it could not explain where the diamonds it was exporting had originated. The impact of the Kimberley Process was clear and it was important. The fact of the negotiations alone helped choke off the money supply to UNITA, the RUF and Charles Taylor, and all were soon in military difficulty. And once the agreement had been made, legitimate diamond exports from conflict countries grew quickly. The DRC exported more diamonds in 2004 than in any other year in its history. Sierra Leone's official exports grew from almost nothing in 1999 to more than $126 million in 2004. The Kimberley Process remains a work in progress, but it has been remarkably effective in helping to reduce or stop conflict in four countries, has significantly boosted the official exports earnings of three, and has helped to clean up an industry that on its margins had become seriously criminalized.

Surprisingly, aid agencies played a remarkably small role in the Kimberley Process. DFID and the Canadian International Development Agency (CIDA) co-financed some of the work done by NGOs, but governments at the Kimberley Process negotiating table were always represented by their foreign ministries or their mining ministries. Bilateral aid agencies, the World Bank and UNDP almost never appeared at Kimberley Process meetings. This perhaps made sense, given the limited mandate that the Kimberley Process set for itself, but the issue of conflict diamonds goes deeper than achieving better control over imports and exports.

There are more than a million alluvial artisanal diamond diggers in Africa. Most are in the informal sector, and most earn less than a dollar a day. It is a casino economy in which people hope to get rich quickly, but where most end up living in absolute poverty, working in conditions where health and safety are everyday hazards. The alluvial diamond fields of Africa were easy pickings for rebel armies, and they remain a destabilizing influence on local, national and regional economies across Africa. But because alluvial diamonds are close to the surface and are spread over hundreds of square kilometres, governments have never been able to regulate their exploitation very well or for very long. The expulsion in 2004 and 2005 of some 200,000 Congolese diamond diggers from Angola is an example of the human scale (and the human tragedy) associated with alluvial diamonds. Worse, as a solution to illegality it is unlikely to be effective for long.

The bigger picture

Lootable resources aside, World Bank research has demonstrated that there is a high correlation between conflict and three conditions: low average incomes (i.e. poverty), low rates of growth and a high dependency on the export of primary products (World Bank, 2003). When average incomes double, the risk of civil war declines by half. The reasons are not hard to fathom. Poverty and low growth breed resentment and may well be associated with bad governance. The exploitation of natural resources – especially if done in developmentally or environmentally unsound ways – can exacerbate the situation, deepening resentment and widening the gap between rich and poor. In Nigeria, for example, people in the delta regions see little return on the oil being pumped from their region. It is a short step from unrequited civil disobedience to damaged pipelines, government retaliation and outright conflict.

In addition to improving the international governance of natural resources and shutting rebel organizations out of the market – which is what the Kimberley Process aims to do – the World Bank suggests a number of other things that can be done:

- *Focus aid on poor countries.* While this seems obvious, donors need constant reminding. The risk of conflict is higher in the poorest countries than in others. (Focusing on the poorest makes sense for other reasons as well, not least because that is what taxpayers think their governmental aid agencies actually do.)
- *Promote good governance*, especially in countries with weak policies and institutions, and where democratic processes are weak. Use aid to reinforce good governance and democratic processes. (As noted above, this is a lot easier said than done. See Chapter 3)
- *Reduce the exposure of poor countries to price shocks.* Many of Africa's current economic problems were triggered by the oil crisis of the 1970s. Price volatility in oil and other commodities remains a problem and is especially problematic in countries where policies and institutions are fragile.

- *Attract more reputable resource extraction companies.* Like all of the recommendations above, this too is much easier said than done. It is especially difficult for countries emerging from conflict to attract solid investors, but countries with weak governments and bad track records on probity and transparency will find themselves choosing among untried junior mining companies and unattractive bottom feeders. Donors need to think about how they can assist in attracting a better class of investor to countries where governance and democratic processes are improving (World Bank, 2003, pp175–184) (See Chapter 5).
- *Increase the transparency of natural resource revenues* (and tighten scrutiny on illicit payments). It is essential that resource revenues be well used; it is equally important that citizens of and donors to developing countries *see* that resource revenues are being well used. This calls for much greater degrees of transparency in resource management. The NGO-led 'Publish What You Pay' (PWYP) campaign and the Extractive Industries Transparency Initiative (EITI) promoted by the British government encourage greater transparency (see Chapter 6).

To this list might be added some imprecations from a 2005 study commissioned by UN Global Compact: *Enabling the Economics of Peace; Public Policy for Conflict-sensitive Business* (UN Global Compact, 2005). This study, initiated by the German government, speaks about the importance of strengthening and harmonizing inter-state efforts to govern cross-border economic transactions in order to prevent conflict, corruption and criminality. And it says that donor and host governments need to develop policies and practices to support private sector efforts to reduce the negative impact of business operations in societies susceptible to conflict.

The smaller picture

Artisanal and small-scale mining (ASM) goes well beyond the million or so alluvial diamond diggers in Africa, described above. Between 13 and 20 million people in more than 50 developing countries are involved in small-scale mining, and another 80–100 million depend in some way on this sector for their livelihoods. ASM touches gold, silver, tin, coal, coloured gemstones, coltan, amber and a dozen other minerals. Artisanal and small-scale miners live in a high-risk, low-pay environment, fraught with health and safety perils. ASM is a vector for malaria, HIV/AIDS and other diseases and is a sink of female exploitation and child labour. Artisanal miners are easy prey for bandits, rebel armies and money launderers, and are often at the centre of low-grade conflicts that carry on for years.

A Communities and Small-scale Mining initiative has been funded by DFID since 2001, with a small secretariat based at the World Bank.[3] But there is a major problem where donors are concerned. While there is no lack of interest in ASM by the governments of countries where it exists, they and others working in the area have had great difficulty in attracting donor interest.

Although ASM can be directly related to seven if not all eight MDGs, the word 'mining' seems to be a significant turnoff for the donor community.[4]

Humanitarian assistance[5]

Emergency humanitarian assistance is usually, by its very nature, 'conflict sensitive', but much of it is driven by non-humanitarian concerns: geo politics, growing apprehensions about security, domestic considerations of donor countries, sometimes even commercial concerns. Far too often there are no provisions for the longer-term development assistance required to prevent a recurrence of hostilities. And donor 'priority setting' – a nice term for earmarking and cherry-picking – fosters unseemly competitive scrambles among executing agencies and leads directly to ineffective multilateral response and a weakening of humanitarian principles.

Predictable funding is a key element in all successful planning and implementation, not least in the humanitarian sector. Short donor time frames lead to unpredictability and therefore poor planning. The management of humanitarian assistance is exacerbated by a compartmentalization in donor agencies of funds and departments, reducing the possibility of funding for recovery and reconstruction, and for linking relief and development.

The most prominent characteristic of global humanitarianism as it is practiced today is its voluntary nature. Donor governments, like individuals, provide assistance – if they feel like it. There are no obligations beyond the moral, no consequences (for the givers) of doing less than enough, or of doing nothing. This is true of all foreign aid, but the negative consequences are more dramatic where life-saving is concerned. There is often more calculation than compassion, calculation that is too often narrow, inward and myopic. For the victims of calamity, there are no assurances of any kind, and many are condemned to live – if they are lucky – through what the world has come to call, euphemistically, 'forgotten emergencies'.

At the centre of the humanitarian enterprise lies the UN, created to save and protect the world from the scourge of war. Despite the UN and its agencies, however, despite the Red Cross, which can sometimes act as an alternative or a complement, and despite the many forums for coordination and shared learning, each donor undertakes its own, often painstakingly slow analysis of a given emergency, each applies its own policies and strategies, and its own organizational and political imperatives. Each 'earmarks' its funding to emergency appeals – to UNICEF, for example, not UNHCR; UNHCR, not the World Food Programme; the Red Cross, not the UN. It goes on: Liberian refugees, not Guinean; Darfur, not Somalia; food not cash; women rather than men; children rather than adults. The multiplicity of actors, the overlapping and underlapping mandates, weak collaboration at the field level, and the competition for funds by front-line agencies all undercut the coordinating mandate and potential of the UN.

This earmarking, which is tantamount to a bilateralization of the UN, has to a large extent crippled the humanitarian role of the UN and it has robbed front-line delivery agencies of their principles, their independence and much of their efficiency. The results could be seen in the 18,000 Angolan refugees in the summer of 2003, living on half rations in the miserable refugee camps of Namibia. They could be seen at Ituri in the Congo, where people were buffeted back and forth between rebel armies for years with little or no humanitarian assistance. They could be seen in Haiti, where exit strategies were more important than lasting results and where 'Operation Uphold Democracy' faded with the headlines in the mid-1990s, setting the stage only for another international intervention a few years later.

With each major emergency there is a promise to learn from the confusion that inevitably occurs. 'Next time will be different' is a constant donor and practitioner refrain. Afghanistan was to be an example of that, but the scramble was no different from what had happened a dozen times before. The European Commission's Humanitarian Aid Office (ECHO) says it will focus in the future on 'forgotten emergencies' (i.e. presumably it will stop forgetting). A 2003 donor meeting debates humanitarian definitions and principles but cannot 'agree' or 'endorse' them, settling finally on the word 'elaborate'. It '*elaborates* a plan for good humanitarian donorship'. This 'plan', recognizing the problems of the late, short-term and unpredictable funding to front-line UN agencies, 'strives to ensure predictability' and says it will 'explore the possibility of reducing, or enhancing the flexibility of, earmarking, and of introducing longer-term funding arrangements' (Good Humanitarian Donorship, 2003).

The results the following year, 2004, were disappointing. Overall, UN emergency appeals received 64 per cent of what they requested. But some, as usual, did considerably better or worse than others. Angola received 96 per cent of what was requested. The Darfur appeal was 76 per cent subscribed, although in 2005, halfway through the year, it had received less than 30 per cent of the request. In 2004 there continued to be losers as well. Liberia received 59 per cent of the UN request, Côte d'Ivoire got 32 per cent, and – demonstrating clearly that emergency assistance is anything but independent, neutral and proportional to need – Zimbabwe received only 11 per cent of what was requested (OCHA, 2005).

Then a tsunami occurs, and almost everything anyone has ever said about coordination, proportionality and 'remembering' goes out the window as governments, agencies, politicians and rock stars clamber for the microphones. This 'worst disaster of all time' trumps everything else, including the Congo, where six times more people have died over the past five years as a result of that country's on-going emergency.

There are several things that would contribute to a more conflict-sensitive emergency aid system, one that would focus more on those in need and downplay the 'ad hocism', egocentricity and the haphazard, take-it or leave-it approach that characterizes today's humanitarian planning and activities.

The creation of a conceptual humanitarian centre

The experience of Sierra Leone, East Timor, Afghanistan and elsewhere shows that humanitarian principles of proportionality, independence and neutrality almost always take a back seat to the political and commercial concerns of donors. Efforts are too often focused narrowly on particular issues and on the short term, or they are distracted by clamorous events elsewhere. There is no lack of humanitarian definitions, policies, concepts and frameworks. The problem is the lack of an anchor, and of accountability for them among donors and implementing agencies.

There has to be a conceptual centre – not so much a physical entity as a catalytic function – where definitions and norms for humanitarian action are set and maintained. The UN is best suited for this role – as a 'standard bearer', as a 'visionary leader', as a place where a global humanitarian framework can be created and where assessments of response can be considered against future action. The UN should serve as the catalyst enabling the outcomes of global humanitarian assistance to become more than the sum of its parts.

Linking relief and development

There must be much better synergies between the humanitarian mandate and operations within donor agencies and those of their development counterparts. Investments in the transition from relief to development, and in post-emergency reconstruction efforts are very much an ad hoc affair. Each humanitarian agency winds down according to its own institutional imperatives, making whatever arrangements for follow-on activities it deems best, which in many cases means none at all. The longer-term factors that contributed to the crisis in the first place are often ignored completely.

If huge investments in humanitarian assistance are to bear fruit, it is essential that longer-term development issues be approached in a comprehensive manner *during* the emergency phase. Donors must develop common strategies to address relief and development issues concurrently, and to plan for the longer term. Different mandates within individual donor governments should not be allowed to interfere with transition planning and funding.

A strengthened multilateral core

At the centre of humanitarian action lie the multilateral ideal and its manifestation in the UN: the software and the hardware of combined efforts to achieve common objectives. And yet UN agencies are usually in competition for donor funding with each other, with NGOs, with commercial and political interests, and sometimes even the military. The major humanitarian challenge today, for the UN and for member governments, is to create a strengthened multilateral core that has the capacity, resources and mandate from its members to meet humanitarian needs in a more impartial and effective manner. Such a core would have to insulate the humanitarian mandate of the UN from the current and individual political concerns of its member states. It would require the services of a strong, managerial but non-operational UN humanitarian agency that could assess needs, set priorities and allocate funds. Some aspects of this exist in the UN Office for the Coordination of Humanitarian Assistance (OCHA) and in the newly created UN Peacebuilding Commission, but they need a strong mandate to do more than 'coordinate'; they must lead, and they must have the *authority* to lead. The humanitarian focal point must have access to significant amounts of humanitarian funding that is predictable, timely and non-earmarked. A substantial portion of this funding must be derived from assessed rather than voluntary contributions, like assessed contributions for UN peacekeeping operations

To propose that even some of the contributions made by governments to humanitarian activities should be 'assessed' rather than 'voluntary' may seem unrealistic, even hare-brained, under current political circumstances. But reliance upon hundreds, if not thousands of inadequate, earmarked voluntary contributions from a score of donors throughout any given fiscal year makes as much sense as trying to run a fire brigade in a big city on nothing but voluntary contributions. The result is not a 'system'; it is a self-serving, hit-or-miss charitable free-for-all.

A giant step in the right direction emerged from a UN General Assembly resolution in December 2005. It mandated the creation of a Central Emergency Response Fund (CERF), which will give the UN some of the core funding it needs in order to ensure predictability. The fund, set at $450 million in voluntary contributions, will allow for greater speed in humanitarian response; it will provide a much-needed degree of flexibility; and it will help to reduce the problem of earmarking. Much will depend on whether the fund is able to generate the voluntary contributions required, and whether it be managed in a way that encourages governments to renew pledges as the fund is drawn down. But the CERF is a major step forward.

Greater realism about NGOs

Much is made of the unseemly NGO scramble that seems to attend so many humanitarian emergencies. But NGOs are an extremely important part of the humanitarian response, and appearances can be misleading. An estimated 10–15 per cent of all humanitarian assistance is generated in the form of private donations to NGOs, churches and the Red Cross family – as much as $1.5 billion annually. On top of that, NGOs receive about one third of all bilateral contributions to the humanitarian effort in the form of grants and contracts. And they programme as much as half of what goes through the UN system. NGOs, therefore, programme as much as 60 per cent of all humanitarian assistance, or roughly $6 billion per year. And although it is true that there are hundreds of NGOs, it is safe to say that 75 per cent of their humanitarian spending is handled by fewer than 15 large transnational organizations.

The size, professionalism and importance of these major NGOs are not recognized, however, in the way monies are allocated, dispensed and reported.

Most donors moved to multi-year programme funding for the development work of these organizations two decades ago. But where emergencies are concerned, even the largest and most professional NGOs are kept on short donor leashes and are provided with woefully inadequate support.

Capacity building for local civil society in conflict prevention and emergency assistance needs to be taken much more seriously. It should become an automatic feature of donor funding in any emergency that extends beyond three months.

In protracted emergencies, donors and the UN must find ways to make longer-term allocations, even if they are notional and conditional. This would help implementing agencies to plan better, to find and retain good staff, to develop greater synergies between relief and development, and to become more professional in other ways.

Better accountability

UN agencies and NGOs have been much criticized for their failings where emergency assistance is concerned. Some of the criticism is deserved, but many of the failings of front-line agencies could be diminished if there were a more open and forthright approach to evaluation, learning and accountability.

In its standard application, evaluation contains a large element of control – and threat. Because of low donor tolerance for failure and because effective humanitarian action involves a high element of risk and innovation, accountability processes as currently applied can actually drive real lessons underground, especially the important lessons that might be derived from failure. The upshot is an approach to evaluation that is limited in scope, imagination, and the potential for learning. Useful lessons can be learned from the evaluation of difficult and risk-prone enterprises, even failed efforts, if punishment is not a likely outcome. This is not to suggest that wilful or repeated mistakes should be ignored but that mistakes are much less likely to be repeated if they are identified and addressed.

There should be a more holistic approach to evaluation that puts *learning* at centre stage. If this is done well, the accountability requirements of donors will also be satisfied, but as a by-product rather than as the only product. Evaluations should transcend one organization, one emergency and one donor. And the focus should be broadened from the delivery end of the chain to encompass the entire system, from design and supply to end result.

More cash

From a global vantage point, the humanitarian effort is underfunded by at least half, if not significantly more. The only individual emergencies that may have received adequate funding in recent years are East Timor and the Asian tsunami.

The question is not really whether more money is needed for humanitarian work, but where it will come from and how to prevent it from reducing development spending. Given how little most OECD member countries devote to overseas development aid (ODA) as a whole, however, an increase in global aid spending, with at least a portion being devoted to the humanitarian effort, does not seem too much to ask.

Conditionality and ownership

It is generally conceded that ownership is a key to good development. The objects of the development enterprise must also be the subjects; they must feel that they are the 'owners' of policies and projects from change. This, of course, is not at all the way it works.

Despite the advent of sector-wide approaches, PRSPs and the Comprehensive Development Framework over the past 15 years, conditionality – often of the most ruthless and detailed variety – has been the order of the day. Donors design their own programmes and strategies often, if not usually, without reference to the objective needs and priorities of the recipient country. Plans are drawn up and programmes are executed by advisors, consulting firms, external suppliers and foreign NGOs, often with only rudimentary local consultation. Timetables, volumes and reporting requirements bear little resemblance to local needs and systems, and most vary from one donor to the next.

The most dramatic forms of conditionality have related to what is euphemistically known as 'policy dialogue' on economic reform. Joseph Stiglitz says that 'Those who valued democratic processes saw how "conditionality" – the conditions that international lenders imposed in return for their assistance – undermined national sovereignty' (Stiglitz, 2002, p7). The net effect of the policies set by the Washington Consensus 'has all too often been to benefit the few at the expense of the many, the well-off at the expense of the poor. In many cases, commercial interests and values have superseded concern for the environment, democracy, human rights, and social justice' (Stiglitz, 2002, p20).

Conditionality is probably one of the hardest things to handle well in a business that wants more than anything else to be a 'partnership', but where great amounts of cash have vanished without a trace, and without effect. UNDP has moved to 'national execution', and many donors now pointedly refer to their development effort as international 'cooperation' rather than as 'aid'. Some are no doubt sincere in wanting joint ownership of projects and programmes. Money, however, means that partnerships and ownerships are inevitably lopsided, and when push comes to shove, the donor view will always prevail.

At the end of the day, the issue in the conditionality debate is not so much whether there should be conditions. Peter Uvin's example of Rwanda at the outset of this chapter suggests that donors have more than a little responsibility for how their money will be spent. The issue is about how the conditions should be negotiated, and more importantly about how deep, how rigid and how formulaic they should be. Years ago the IMF insisted that the Jamaican government remove subsidies on petrol. The government, knowing what the impact would be in several sectors, pleaded – to no avail – for reconsideration, more time, a phased approach. The result: taxi drivers overturned and burned cars in tourist areas, and Jamaica's number one foreign exchange earner went into the toilet for three years.

Security: Whose protection?

Security from violence, according to a 2005 OECD publication, 'is fundamental to people's livelihoods and to sustainable economic, social and political development. Where violence breaks out, within or between countries, development is arrested. Security matters to the poor and other vulnerable groups, especially women and children, and has emerged as a vital concern for development, reducing poverty and achieving the Millennium Development Goals' (OECD, 2005, p3).

Effective and accountable security systems can reduce the potential for conflict, and 'security sector reform', now added to the many items on today's development agenda, is undoubtedly an important element in constructing a conflict-sensitive aid programme. Since the September 11 2001 terrorist attacks on New York and Washington, however, discussions about security have led to concerns about the diversion of long-term development aid and short-term relief assistance – not so much to the security of people in developing countries, but to the new anti-terrorist agenda of wealthy countries.

Until recently, security remained a background issue as far as the general aid establishment was concerned. The paradigm began to change with the 1999 North Atlantic Treaty Organization (NATO) intervention in Kosovo, which added the question of state sovereignty to more general issues of security. Not long afterwards, the government of Canada funded an international commission to examine the intervention–sovereignty conundrum. The commission's December 2001 report, *The Responsibility to Protect*, defined sovereignty not on the basis of the prerogatives of the state, but on the state's responsibility to protect its citizens.

It broke the responsibility to protect into three elements:

1   *The responsibility to prevent.* To address the root causes and the direct causes of internal crises that place people at risk.
2   *The responsibility to react.* To respond to conditions of compelling human need with appropriate measures, including sanctions, international prosecution and, in extreme cases, military intervention.
3   *The responsibility to rebuild.* To provide assistance in a post-conflict situation for recovery, reconstruction and reconciliation (International Commission on Intervention and State Sovereignty, 2001, pxi).

These are nice, uplifting ideas, but the slow, patchy response to the Darfur crisis demonstrates that there is still a long way to go in embracing human security and the responsibility to protect in any meaningful way. How the R2P concept – endorsed by the UN General Assembly in September 2005 – will evolve is not yet clear, but the ground continues to shift under the issue of security.

One way of insulating the ODA budget from security sector incursions is the creation of special funds to deal with security sector reform and related issues. Britain created two such funds in 2001 – a Global Conflict Prevention Pool and an Africa Conflict Prevention Pool. The former is managed by the Foreign Office and the latter by DFID, but each has input from the other as well as the Ministry of Defence and Treasury. Funds have been used, for example, to support African peacekeeping missions in Sudan, Burundi, Côte d'Ivoire and Liberia. In Sierra Leone it has funded the creation of a national security policy, to restructure and train the armed forces, to provide a military advisory team and to carry out other reforms in the security sector. These are things that might or might not have been done in the past, but they would certainly not have involved DFID. Bringing a development aspect to security reform in a country where security problems have been the number one constraint to development over the past decade is important, and may help to make the interventions more sustainable. The cost, however, will only be charged to Britain's ODA budget where it conforms to ODA definitions. A similar 'Stability Fund' has been created in The Netherlands, and Canada has recently created a Global Peace and Security Fund.

MDGs and other false-bottom boats

It happened in Monterrey, and without thinking twice …

Mabel Wayne, King of Jazz, *1930*

Aid critics say that aid does not work, and judging from the broad numbers of people living in absolute poverty, it is not difficult to see why they might reach that conclusion. The criticism is usually unfair, however, and overly generalized when it is not. The most vociferous critics seldom differentiate between aid that vaccinates a boy or educates a girl, and aid that subsidizes helicopter and locomotive sales, or pays for the installation of high-end, rich-country technology in settings where it is guaranteed to fail.

When the aid critics become too shrill, World Bank economists set to work to show that if countries do a), b) and c), aid really does have a positive impact.[6] Usually, however, economists think in terms of overall growth rates, rather than what happens to poor people, ignoring Herman Daly's important dictum: 'When something grows, it gets bigger. When something develops, it gets different.'[7]

Donors, NGOs, academics and critics pore relentlessly through the ruins of past aid programmes, searching for ever more sophisticated ways of dealing with problems. New fads roll relentlessly over the aid business like waves on a beach, wiping out the sandcastles of yesterday's big new idea: population control, integrated rural development, the basic human needs approach, growth-with-equity, the sectoral approach, structural adjustment, appropriate technology, women in development, gender and development, environmental sustainability, political sustainability, social sustainability, micro-finance, civil society, capacity building, good governance, security sector reform and a dozen others that will no doubt in due course be consigned to the development dumpster.

In considering how to construct conflict-sensitive aid policies, it seems almost naive to return to the basic ODA goal of poverty reduction. But virtually all of the lessons about conflict suggest that poverty and exclusion are the most fertile breeding grounds for social violence and larger-scale conflict. Historically, ODA has focused its main efforts on economic growth, not in itself a bad thing but, alone, insufficient. As John Kenneth Galbraith said many years ago, the trickle-down theory is like feeding oats to a horse. If you feed it enough, some will find its way through to the road for the sparrows.

Some things, in fact, *are* growing. Development assistance, for example, is growing. In 2004 it reached an all-time high of $79 billion, a reversal of the fifteen-year downward trend. And in addition to the five countries that currently spend more than 0.7 per cent of national income on ODA (Denmark, Finland, Luxembourg, Norway and Sweden), six more have promised to do so by 2015. Most of the recent increase, however, has been used for debt relief and emergency assistance. Neither of these is a bad thing, but they do not create much in the way of new money for development, especially in the poorest countries where most debt repayment has stopped anyway. As a percentage of the overall gross national income (GNI) of rich countries, ODA – at a quarter of one per cent – remains significantly below 1990 levels, and significantly short of 0.7 per cent.

Donor countries give, but they also take away. Key exports from developing countries – clothing, agricultural products, textiles – remain subject to high tariffs in rich countries. And agricultural subsidies in rich countries not only give them an unfair trading advantage, they also seriously undercut the productivity of farmers in developing countries. It is estimated that free trade in farm products alone would be worth $20 billion to developing countries. The Doha Round of WTO trade negotiations that began in 2001 saw rich countries promising to reduce agricultural subsidies. Instead, they have done the opposite. Rich countries provide $1 billion a year in agricultural assistance to poor countries, but they spend $1 billion *a day* subsidizing over production at home (UNDP, 2005b, p10). The dismal effort to keep the Doha Round alive at the WTO Conference in Hong Kong in December 2005 managed little more than a half-hearted promise by rich countries to stop subsidizing their agricultural exports by 2013. Other subsidies and high tariffs against imports from developing countries remain untouched.

Other things are growing, and not in a good way. The number of people in Africa living on a dollar a day (or less) increased from 227 million in 1990, to 313 million in 2004. And lest we get lost in dollar-a-day numbers, it is worth noting that an estimated 2.5 billion people, more than half of those living in developing countries, survive on less than two dollars a day (UNDP, 2005b, p24).

We take heart, however, from positive changes in Asia, where absolute poverty ($1 a day) has declined from 936 million in 1990, to 703 million in 2004, a remarkable achievement resulting mainly from sustained growth in China and India. But Branko Milanovic, a lead economist with the World Bank, puts a different spin on the numbers. In what he calls a 'downwardly mobile world', Milanovic shows that globally, the gap between rich countries and poor countries is growing. For example in 1960 there were 41 rich countries, 19 of them non-Western. By 2000 there were 31 rich countries, only nine of them non-Western. And almost all of the non-Western middle-income countries had dropped to the ranks of the poor. In India and China, widely quoted average growth rates conceal huge levels of inequality between urban and rural populations (Milanovic, 2005).

Targets and pledges have been useful in the ODA business, not so much as goals that governments have any intention of reaching, but as *ex post facto* demonstrations that donor promises have an awfully hollow ring to them. The famous aid target of 0.7 per cent of GNI for donor countries has proven impossible for a dozen rich countries over the 35 years it has been out there, even through rich countries have, during that time, enjoyed some of the most accelerated growth periods in a century.

In 1978, senior government delegates meeting at a celebrated WHO-sponsored world health summit in Alma-Ata pledged 'health for all by the year 2000'. It was not an idle or ill-considered target; the goal, relating almost exclusively to primary health care, was more achievable in that 22-year time frame than the current health-related targets of the 15-year MDGs. Needless to say, the 'health for all' slogan went out the window not long after donor representatives returned home. The development business, in fact, is littered with the empty promises of donor governments. Meeting at a United Nations Educational, Scientific and Cultural Organization (UNESCO) conference in Jomtien in 1990, governments solemnly pledged to provide 'education for all' at some unspecified future date. At the time there were 100 million children with no access to primary education. Today the number has risen to 115 million.

And now we have the MDGs, the most comprehensive set of development targets ever set down on paper. Time-bound and measurable, they have unprecedented political support and are – or at least were, in 2000 – believed to be achievable. But progress during the first five years was not good. 'If current trends persist,' says UN Secretary General Kofi Annan, 'there is a risk that many of the poorest countries will not be able to meet many of them.' Given the dismal findings in a 2005 UN progress report and in UNDP's 2005 *Human Development Report*, this is something of an understatement (United Nations, 2005). The Secretary General goes on to say, 'Let us be clear about the costs of missing this opportunity: millions of lives that could have been saved will be lost; many freedoms that could have been secured will be denied; and we shall inhabit a more dangerous and unstable world.'

Foreign ministers of developed countries issued a 'statement of resolve' under the banner of the Paris Declaration on Aid Effectiveness in March 2005, endorsing once again the MDGs. The 2005 G8 Summit was an occasion for more promises. 'We have agreed,' the leaders said in their communiqué, 'to double aid for Africa by 2010. Aid for all developing countries will increase, according to the OECD, by around $50 billion per year by 2010, of which at least $25 billion extra per year [will be] for Africa' (G8 Gleneagles, 2005). *According to the OECD?* With the leaders of several of the wealthiest donor countries shying away from clear financial commitments of any kind, it is not hard to see why they would rely on the OECD for a statistic rather than the calculators all of them undoubtedly took with them to the meeting.

In fact it was all the leaders of the assembled United Nations could do at their World Summit in September 2005 to avoid having the US throw the MDGs right out of the window. Hama Amadou, the Prime Minister of Niger, told the BBC afterwards, 'A few years ago, developed countries made some promises; but since then, very few concrete actions were implemented.' Bob Geldof said, less diplomatically, that the tepid result of the meeting was 'bloody outrageous' (BBC, 2005). There must have been a hollow ring to the applause that followed General Assembly President Jan Eliasson's adoption of the final General Assembly document, which, he said, 're-affirms our commitment to achieving the Millennium Goals by the year 2015'.

Conclusions

This chapter has examined several aspects of the development assistance enterprise and how it might become more sensitive to the prevention of conflict. This is an important issue, because conflict takes lives and destroys investments in long-term development. It is important because the levels of conflict over the past decade rose dramatically. Between 1994 and 2003, an estimated 13 million people died in large-scale conflicts, 12 million of them in Africa, western Asia and southern Asia. In 2003 there were an estimated 37 million refugees and internally displaced people, but this number includes only those covered by the United Nations High Commissioner for Refugees (UNHCR), whose mandate with regard to the displaced is limited.

This deadly time may be a temporary shaking-out; a settling of old scores in the post-Cold War world. The situation may even be improving.[8] But there is no guarantee that it will end any time soon, or that it will confine itself, as it once did, to the increasingly artificial borders of what used to be called the 'Third World'. The effects of poverty, state collapse and conflict have leeched dramatically into the wider world in the form of pollution, illegal refugees, terrorism and disease.

Many books have been written about development assistance over the past 40 years. One of the most instructive is the 1969 *Pearson Commission Report*, because it outlined most of the challenges that still confront the post-millennium world. Had donors and recipients done half of what the report recommended – on aid levels, on debt relief,[9] on trade liberalization, on tied aid, in health, education and infrastructure – the development challenges of today would be a lot less severe.

The most important books on development assistance are those that caution policy makers and practitioners against hubris, stressing the need for adaptive learning. There are not many of these. In the late 1960s, William and Elizabeth Paddock, American academics who had worked for 10 years in Central America, set off on a journey to find and document aid projects that worked. They didn't find very many, but they wrote about what they learned in *We Don't Know How: An Independent Audit of What They Call Success in Foreign Assistance*, published in 1973. This was not an attack on foreign aid, it was a critique of the way aid was being applied, and of the way experience was being institutionalized. The Paddocks said they learned two things in the course of their research. 'First, development professionals do not know how to carry out an effective economic development program, either a big one or a small one. No one knows how – not the US government, not the Rockefeller Foundation, not the international banks and agencies, not the missionaries. I don't know how. You don't know how. No one knows how.' Second, and more to the point, 'We don't *know* that we don't know how.' Overconfidence, cultural and geographic distance, arrogance and impatience all contribute to the problem (Paddock, 1973, p300).

Ten years later, Robert Chambers published *Rural Development: Putting the Last First*. Chambers noted the same constraints to *knowing* as the Paddocks, but much of his book is about *how* to learn – how to listen and how to apply knowledge. It is about making choices, and not trying to do everything. 'It is not the practice of (successful) generals,' he writes, 'to attack on all fronts, because they cannot say that one is more important than the other.' The second failure of analysis, according to Chambers, 'is the ritual call for integration and coordination, and even maximum integration and maximum coordination. These words,' he says, 'slip glibly off the tongues of practiced non-thinkers.'

In *Rural Development* and other books, Chambers writes about working directly with poor people. Dennis Rondinelli wrote in 1993 about the accumulation and application of knowledge to higher levels of development administration. In *Development Projects as Policy Experiments*, he says that the development experience of half a century has led to three fundamental discoveries: first, conventional theories of development based mainly on the acceleration of growth have not achieved their purpose; second, sustainable benefits for poor people have been disappointing; and third, as development strategies become more complex, their success becomes less certain. The upshot is a major dilemma for development administration: 'Planners and managers, working in bureaucracies that seek to control rather than to facilitate development, must cope with increasing uncertainty and complexity; but their methods and procedures inhibit the kinds of analysis and planning that are most appropriate for dealing with the development of problems effectively' (Rondinelli, 1993, p3).

Rondinelli's thesis is that aid managers cannot acknowledge that they 'don't know how'. Overwhelmed by a technocratic mindset, an extremely low tolerance for failure and a rush to the Next Big Thing, they front-load all of the available brainpower into the planning for a project, creating rigid structures that are almost incapable of adaptation as the project gets underway. Rondinelli says that if we knew how to undertake effective poverty reduction, we would certainly have had a lot more success by now. This is not a reason for despair, however. All projects, he says, are experiments. If they are seen that way, they can contribute to an adaptive, learning approach to development, as opposed to the rigidities that are so common. Writing about the world of business, Henry Mintzberg makes the same point in *The Rise and Fall of Strategic Planning*: 'We have no evidence that any of the strategic planning systems – no matter how elaborate, or how famous – succeeded in capturing (let alone improving on) the messy informal processes by which strategies really do get developed' (Mintzberg, 1994, p296). Successful strategies cannot be handed over on a silver platter; they are most likely to be emergent, and they must be adaptive. And where conflict-sensitive aid is concerned, they may have to be entrepreneurial, taking advantage of good opportunities that arise on short notice.

All this is by way of reiterating some of the points made throughout this chapter about conflict-sensitive aid. These are mostly generic points about development assistance, rather than issues immediately related to conflict prevention:

- One size does not fit all.
- Over-high expectations and rigid battle plans will result in disappointment.
- Slavish loyalty to precast logical frameworks and results-based planning almost guarantees failure.
- But failure – honest failure – can be as important as success if it teaches lessons. The problem in a failure-intolerant business, where lack of success is usually met with punishment and the cancellation of funding, is that failure is driven underground. Evaluation becomes ritualistic, flaws are hidden, success is exaggerated. And so there is an inherent failure to learn from failure.
- Understanding local cultures, histories and pathologies – which takes time and the combined ability of listening and remembering – is essential to any kind of success.
- The long tradition of overloading the ODA agenda with short-term political and commercial considerations, and now with an impulsive security agenda, has only deflected it from its stated long-term primary objective. The much-advertised poverty reduction goal has been treated for the past 40 years only as a possible, even casual, by-product of initiatives aimed largely at fostering growth, rather than as the goal itself.

Poverty could perhaps be ignored with greater impunity during the Cold War, when the great powers could be counted upon by badly governed, poverty-ridden states for assistance with money, advice, weapons and even troops to put down rebellion. Donors could be counted on to turn a selective, if not a blind, eye to repression and human rights abuse. Poverty could be more easily ignored when the only real form of international communication for the poor was the transistor radio, when there were no cell phones, no television, no internet, no apparent allies for those living in isolated pockets of discontent. But the idea of a better life can no longer be hidden so easily from the poor. Poverty, even where it is on the decline, is the most dangerous social problem of our time, and it is also the greatest threat to peace and the longer-run well-being of all.

This is not a new lesson; Pearson said it in 1969, Kofi Annan's High-Level Panel on Threats, Challenges and Change said it in 2004. But the message is becoming much more urgent. And four decades of ineffectual development assistance suggest that there is still not nearly enough serious willpower or money to deal with it.

Notes

1 For more on NEPAD, see www.nepad.org/2005/files/inbrief.php.
2 For a discussion about local perceptions, see Donini et al (2005).
3 Information on the CASM initiative can be found at www.casmsite.org/about. html.
4 Assuming that donors *could* be persuaded to take a greater interest in the subject, USAID has produced a useful document called 'Minerals and conflict: A toolkit for intervention', USAID, Office of Conflict Management and Mitigation, Washington, 2004.
5 This section has been adapted from Chapter 10 of Smillie and Minear (2004).
6 See, for example, Collier and Dollar (1998).
7 Daly has used this line to good effect several times. See, for example, Daly and Townsend (1993), p267.
8 The 2005 *Human Security Report* says that this is changing, that the number of armed conflicts around the world has declined by more than 40 per cent since the early 1990s and the number of refugees dropped by 45 per cent between 1992 and 2003. It also reports that there are 300,000 child soldiers serving around the world today, and then says 'not one of these claims is based on reliable data' (Human Security Centre, 2005, pp1–2).
9 A landmark agreement to forgive more than $40 billion in debt for the world's poorest countries, mostly in Africa, was reached by the IMF in September 2005. This was the result of 10 years of negotiation, during which time the governments of some heavily indebted poor countries (HIPC) ceased to exist in all but name. Benin's finance minister, Cosme Sehlin, welcomed the agreement, but said, 'The devil is clearly in the implementation details.'

References

BBC (2005) 'UN reforms receive mixed response', news.bbc.co.uk/1/hi/world/americas/ 4255106.stm accessed 17 September 2006

CIA World Fact Book (2006) 'Nigeria', www.cia.gov/cia/publications/factbook/geos/ ni.html accessed 17 September 2006

Collier, P. (2000) 'Doing well out of war', in Berdal, M. and Malone, D. (eds) *Greed and Grievance: Economic Agendas in Civil Wars*, Boulder, CO, Lynne Rienner

Collier, P. and Dollar, D. (1998) *Aid Allocation and Poverty Reduction*, Washington DC, World Bank

Cornia, G. A., Jolly, R. and Stewart, F. (1987) *Adjustment with a Human Face: Protecting the Vulnerable and Promoting Growth*, Oxford, Oxford University Press

Daly, H. and Townsend, K. (1993) *Valuing the Earth: Economics, Ecology and Ethics*, Cambridge, MA, MIT Press

de St. Jorre, J. (1972) *The Nigerian Civil War*, London, Hodder and Stoughton

Diamond, L. (2002) *Winning the New Cold War on Terrorism: The Democratic-Governance Imperative*, Policy Paper No. 1, Washington DC, Institute for Global Democracy

Donini, A., Minear, L., Smillie, I., van Baarda, T. and Welch, A. (2005) *Mapping the Security Environment: Understanding the Perceptions of Local Communities, Peace Support Operations and Assistance Agencies*, Feinstein International Famine Center, Medford, MA, Tufts University

Foreign Policy (2005) *Failed State Index*, Foreign Policy and the Fund for Peace, July/August

Fukuyama, F. (2004) *State-Building; Governance and World Order in the 21st Century*, Ithaca, Cornell University Press

G8 Gleneagles (2005) 'Chair's summary, Gleneagles summit, 8 July', www.g8.gov.uk/servlet/Front?pagename=OpenMarket/Xcelerate/ShowPage&c=Page&cid=1119518698846 accessed in 2005

Gillies, D. (2005) 'Democracy and economic development', *IRPP Policy Matters*, vol 6, no 2

Good Humanitarian Donorship (2003) 'Implementation plan for good humanitarian donorship, elaborated in Stockholm', www.odi.org.uk/hpg/papers/Implementation%20Plan.pdf accessed in 2005

Grindle, M. (2002) *Good Enough Governance: Poverty Reduction and Reform in Developing Countries*, Cambridge MA, Kennedy School of Government, Harvard University

Human Rights Watch (2003) *Nigeria: Renewed Crackdown on Freedom of Expression*, Washington DC, Human Rights Watch

Human Security Centre (2005) *Human Security Report*, Vancouver, University of British Columbia

International Commission on Intervention and State Sovereignty (2001) *The Responsibility to Protect*, Ottawa, IDRC

Milanovic, B. (2005) *Worlds Apart: Measuring International and Global Inequality*, Princeton, Princeton University Press

Mintzberg, H. (1994) *The Rise and Fall of Strategic Planning*, New York, The Free Press

National Intelligence Council (2005) *Mapping Sub-Saharan Africa's Future*, Washington DC, National Intelligence Council

OECD (Organisation for Economic Co-operation and Development) (1989) *Development Cooperation in the 1990s*, DAC Report, Paris, OECD

OECD (2005) *Security System Reform and Governance*, Paris, OECD Publishing

Paddock, W. and E. (1973) *We Don't Know How: An Independent Audit of What They Call Success in Foreign Assistance*, Ames Iowa, Iowa State University Press

Rondinelli, D. (1993) *Development Projects as Policy Experiments*, London, Routledge

Sen, A. (2000) *Development as Freedom*, New York, Anchor Books

Smillie, I. and Minear, L. (2004) *The Charity of Nations: Humanitarian Action in a Calculating World*, Bloomfield, Kumarian Press

Stiglitz, J. (2002) *Globalization and its Discontents*, New York, Norton

UN Global Compact (2005) *Enabling the Economics of Peace: Public Policy for Conflict-sensitive Business*, New York, United Nations

UNDP (United Nations Development Programme) (2002) *Human Development Report 2002*, New York, United Nations

UNDP (2005a) *Beyond Hartals*, Dhaka, United Nations

UNDP (2005b) *Human Development Report 2005*, New York, United Nations

UN (2005) *The Millennium Development Goals Report 2005*, New York, United Nations

United Nations Office for the Coordination of Humanitarian Assistance (OCHA) (2005), ochaonline.un.org/cap/index.htm accessed in 2005

Unsworth, S. (2005) *Focusing Aid on Good Governance*, Global Economic Governance Programme, University College, Oxford

US Department of State (2002) *Country Reports on Human Rights Practices – Nigeria*, 31 March 2002

USAID (2004a) *2005 Congressional Budget Justification for Bangladesh*, Washington DC, USAID

USAID (2004b) *2005 Congressional Budget Justification for Nigeria*, Washington DC, USAID

Uvin, P. (1998) *Aiding Violence: The Development Enterprise in Rwanda*, Bloomfield, CT, Kumarian Press

Van Crevald, M. (1991) *The Transformation of War*, New York, The Free Press

Weart, S. (1998) *Never at War: Why Democracies Will Not Fight One Another*, New Haven, Yale University Press

Windsor, J. (2003) 'Promoting democracy can combat terrorism', *Washington Quarterly*, Washington DC, Summer

World Bank (2003) *Breaking the Conflict Trap: Civil War and Development Policy*, Washington DC, World Bank

Chapter 3

Promoting 'Good' Governance through Trade and Aid: Instruments of Coercion or Vehicles of Communication?

Oli Brown

'Good governance' and security

Since the early 1990s, the importance of governance to peace and security has climbed steadily up the international agenda. As K. Y. Amoako, Executive Secretary of the Economic Commission for Africa, argues, 'The creation of capable states is one of the most fundamental challenges... A capable state is one in which peace and security are guaranteed and sustained. Without peace, there can be no long-term development. And without good governance, there is seldom peace' (Economic Commission for Africa, 2005, piii).

But despite more than a decade of efforts at governance reform, progress has been limited and difficult to sustain. A big part of the problem is that there is little agreement on what 'good governance' actually is – and even less consensus on how the international community should go about spreading it.

The link between governance and insecurity is clear: autocratic and unaccountable regimes, corruption, environmental degradation, poor provision of basic services, weak legislation and lax enforcement have contributed to a downward spiral to violence in fragile developing states across the world. The civil wars in the DRC and Nepal, instability in Zimbabwe, rebellion in the Solomon Islands, violence in Nigeria and paralysing demonstrations in Bolivia represent only a few recent examples. Countries with ineffective or corrupt institutions are less able to ensure economic growth, to address their environmental challenges or to maintain peace and stability. And governments that abuse their citizens' human rights make poor neighbours.

Trade and aid are two of the main ways in which the developed world interacts with the developing world. The direction and priorities of trade and aid policies, largely decided by the rich countries of the North, have profound impacts on the societies, economics and stability of the poorer countries in the South. Unsurprisingly, good governance has become an explicit objective of both aid and trade policies (Hout, 2002). As such they can be a powerful way to communicate reforms to other countries. But they can also be used as instruments of coercion in ways that can ultimately prove counter-productive.

There is a great deal of debate about what puts the 'good' in good governance. Is it the bargaining process between citizen and state over tax? A vocal and aware civil society? A meritocratic civil service? An independent judiciary that upholds the rule of law? A written constitution? Free and fair elections?

In fact, many of these are both a cause and consequence of good governance. For example, a vocal and influential civil society is facilitated by the absence of political repression, but it also reinforces good governance by holding its government to account. Similarly, a meritocratic civil service implies low levels of corruption but it also helps to ensure that a government can deliver on its promises. This 'chicken or egg' debate is both important and poorly understood but is not the primary focus of this chapter.

Instead, this chapter asks whether and how trade and aid policies can be used to encourage, even to coerce, governance reforms (whatever those reforms may be) in developing countries that are unwilling to embark on reforms themselves. The chapter examines the four ways that aid and trade policies are typically used to promote governance change overseas: through the 'carrot' of conditionality, the 'stick' of sanctions, capacity building and, lastly, through closer trade integration. It then outlines some of the successes, dilemmas and pitfalls involved in trying to encourage good governance in other countries.

Almost inevitably, this chapter deals with the 'tools' or 'levers' at the disposal of the more developed, richer countries to encourage the reform they think is appropriate in poorer, less developed countries. The purpose of the chapter is not to endorse a paternalistic, top-down approach in which developed countries force change on others. Rather it recognizes that rich country trade and aid policies can be highly influential for governance and security in developing countries – both positively and negatively.

What makes governance 'good'?

Restless definitions

The question of whether trade and aid policies can bring about 'good' governance is complicated by the fact that very few people actually agree on what constitutes 'good' governance. The concept is vague, contested and covers a wide spectrum of possible regimes. As Joachim Ahrens notes, 'there are still no clear or settled ideas about how effective governance should be suitably defined, let alone how key governance issues can be appropriately incorporated into externally financed programmes of policy reform' (Ahrens, 2001, p54). Sue Unsworth, former chief governance advisor for DFID, notes, 'The main actors have different, often vague definitions of what they mean by good governance, though the implicit model ... is the reproduction of Weberian norms and democratic political systems as found in OECD countries' (Unsworth, 2005, p2).

For some, like the IMF and the World Bank, good governance is mainly about fiscal performance and, in particular, levels of government income, spending and debt. Accompanied by a strong neoliberal ideology, this idea began with and survived the structural adjustment programmes of the 1980s and 1990s. It also reflects the World Bank's founding charter, which forbids the Bank from taking political considerations into account when designing aid programmes (Santiso, 2003). The unspoken assumption is that if economic vital signs such as a government's balance of payments, corruption and inflation are brought under control then economic reforms will somehow automatically spill over into wider political and social reform.

By contrast, USAID sees democracy at the core of good governance. Governance, it argues, is 'the ability of government to develop an efficient, effective and accountable public management process that is open to citizen participation and that strengthens rather than weakens a democratic system of government' (USAID, 2005). On the other hand, analysts like Carlos Santiso argue that while democracy tends to refer to the legitimacy of a state, good governance is about a state's core effectiveness and its capacity to deliver basic services to its citizens (Santiso, 2001, p2). The Economic Commission for Africa conflates ideas of legitimacy and effectiveness, arguing that, 'a core element of good governance is a capable democratic state – a state embedded in the public will, relying on legitimacy through the democratic process, with strong institutions promoting the public interest' (Economic Commission for Africa, 2005, p26).

DFID has taken a deliberately wider view of good governance, which turns on whether a government demonstrates commitment in three core areas: first, a clear focus on poverty reduction in government programmes; second, a demonstrable respect for human rights and compliance with other international obligations; and third, basic financial management that reduces the risk of funds being misused through weak administration or corruption (DFID, 2005, piii).

But even if there were agreement on what good governance is, it would still be very hard to quantify. Like legitimacy, accountability and transparency, 'good governance' has the habit of shrugging off objective, numerical indicators. While there have been attempts to capture the qualitative aspects of good governance – such as the aggregate indicators developed by the World Bank Institute (Hout, 2002, p516) – none are particularly compelling, nor do they capture the nuances at play in different countries.

First, the quality of a country's governance is too complex a subject to capture in one or even a few indicators. Second, the reliability of measurements compared across a number of different countries is low. Third, it is hard to disaggregate the impact of external influence from existing processes of internal reform. This has tended to result in an overemphasis on economic performance, which is only part of the picture, but one of the easiest to quantify (Hout, 2002, p515). It also results in limited insights into what actually catalyses governance change, and to a lack of systematic evaluation of governance interventions (Unsworth, 2005, p5).

In the context of this book we understand good governance primarily as the package of domestic institutions and policies helping to ensure that natural resource and aid revenues are used effectively and equitably. It implies accountability, transparency, sound environmental management, respect for the rule of law and low levels of corruption.

Moving goalposts

Despite disagreeing about the nature of the objective, over the past three decades, Northern policy makers have arrived at 'The Answer' to improved governance – over and over again. The UK's Institute of Development Studies (IDS) notes, 'In quick succession, donors have advocated state-led development, then marketization and the retrenchment of government from core functions, followed by democratization, decentralization, the establishment of autonomous agencies, the creation of public–private partnerships, and civil society participation in the delivery of core services' (IDS, 2005, p1).

Each time, the governance goalposts shift. Each time, developing countries are pressed and cajoled into making dramatic domestic policy changes in line with the latest development wisdom, regardless of their administrative capacity for change, or the public appetite for it. According to the IDS, 'All this has been imposed on poor countries, with weak institutions, many of them still in the process of basic state building, and in the context of a rapidly changing global environment' (IDS, 2005, p1). And, although they are pulled in many different directions by the policies of developed countries, responsibility for poor governance is typically laid firmly at the feet of developing country governments.

In effect, developing countries have become the subject of repeated state-building experiments carried out by unaccountable (and often ill-informed) developed country donors. The good governance agenda has turned into 'a constant restless search for the next 'fix'; a rapid succession of new remedies, often poorly understood by harassed programme managers, and dictated more by fashions or changing preoccupations in developed countries than by a good understanding of processes of change in developing countries' (Unsworth, 2005, p4).

Since 2000 the focus of international attention has been on the MDGs, a wide-ranging and urgent set of goals established by the world's leaders for achievement by 2015. It is difficult to argue with the importance of the goals, including as they do universal primary education and a two-thirds reduction in child mortality. However, in order to achieve the MDGs (very much a donor-driven agenda), poor countries are expected to put in place institutions and policies that are far more sophisticated than were present in OECD countries at a similar stage in their development – all within the space of 15 years.

Although good governance is not a stated objective of the MDGs, ideas of good governance are implicitly embedded within the MDG framework. Good governance is a precondition for the success of the goals. For example, it would be difficult to reduce poverty significantly in the presence of continuing corruption. However, there are real concerns that in the drive for the MDGs donors may be establishing parallel systems of governance to provide basic services, particularly for health and education, which may distract attention and ultimately detract from good governance in the developing world (Therkildsen, 2005, p28).

'Good enough' governance

In 2002, predicting this debate, Harvard academic Merilee Grindle questioned the daunting and often unrealistic length of the good governance 'project'. The wide-ranging good governance agenda can touch on pretty much every aspect of the public sector: 'From institutions that set the rules of the game for economic and political interaction, to decision-making structures that determine priorities among public problems and allocate resources to respond to them, to organizations that manage administrative systems and deliver goods and services to citizens, to human resources that staff government bureaucracies, to the interface of officials and citizens in political and bureaucratic arenas' (Grindle, 2002).

Grindle argues that not all governance deficits need to be, or can be, tackled at the same time. She suggests that donors should instead focus more pragmatically on 'good enough' governance: the elements of governance that are absolutely essential to political and economic development (Grindle, 2005, p1). This concept of 'good enough' governance requires that interventions be questioned, prioritized and made relevant to individual countries. Grindle suggested that interventions should be assessed in light of each country's specific context, and should be selected carefully in terms of their contributions to particular ends such as poverty reduction and democracy (Grindle, 2005). By making progress in fundamental areas, the argument goes, a country can build the capacity to implement more ambitious reforms in the future. In effect, Grindle makes a pragmatic distinction between the essential and the merely desirable.

Trade, aid and 'good governance'

Improved trade and aid policies have the potential to increase transparency and accountability, promote the rule of law, and build domestic governing capacity. Aid and trade deals can be, and often are, created in ways that encourage and reward 'good' behaviour, in addition to sharing new skills, structures and policies. They can also be used to deter 'poor' behaviour. In short, if one country wants to influence another, two of the most obvious ways it can express approval or disapproval, short of military action, are through its aid and trade policies.

Of course the use of trade and aid policies to influence the domestic policy of another country is not a new phenomenon. Historically, trade and aid policies have often been used to communicate particular ideas of 'good' governance, with voices that have run the spectrum from gentle persuasion to outright coercion; US sanctions on Cuba throughout the regime of Fidel Castro being just one example.

Broadly speaking, the levers available to promote good governance are either 'carrots' – inducements for positive behaviour such as preferential trade access and aid packages, or 'sticks' – reactive punishments for poor performance such as trade sanctions or the suspension of aid. In addition, capacity building and technical assistance aim to transfer skills, policies, institutions and experiences from the developed to the developing world. Finally, some countries, particularly the European states and the US, are enthusiastically promoting regional integration – typically spearheaded by regional trade agreements – as a mechanism to improve governance, promote interdependence between countries, develop economic incentives for peace and construct non-military ways to resolve disputes. The following section will expand on each of these areas in turn.

Carrots and conditionality

Conditionality is not new to aid, but it is evolving. For many years donors have made aid packages and loans conditional on the implementation of fiscal reforms. These reforms were typically aimed at setting criteria for national budgeting and government spending. More recently the trend has been to move beyond operational conditionality to governance (or 'second generation') conditionality, where the aid is used to extract much wider and deeper change. The reforms have varied hugely, but market liberalization, government transparency, democratic institutions and reduced (or increased) social spending have all been subjects of donor conditionality.

The use of conditionality expanded greatly during the 1990s. Between 1989 and 1999 the proportion of IMF programmes with attached structural conditions rose from 60 per cent to 100 per cent (IMF, 2001, p11). And governance conditions represent the bulk of conditions imposed by the International Financial Institutions (IFIs) – between 50 per cent and 70 per cent of the IMF's conditionality by the late 1990s (Santiso, 2001, p12).

Governance conditionality is also becoming a common feature of trade arrangements. For example, the EU's Economic Partnership Agreements (EPAs), being negotiated with blocs of African, Caribbean and Pacific states, are conditional on certain negotiated governance reforms. The 2000 Cotonou Agreement, a precursor of the EPAs, lists three 'essential elements' of the partnership: respect for human rights, democracy and the rule of law. If contravened, these conditions can lead to the suspension of cooperation – including the cancellation of preferential access.

Such trade deals can include carefully targeted conditions designed to promote good governance and peace-building. An innovative example is the US trade protocol with Israel and Egypt of December 2004, which was specifically designed to accelerate rapprochement between the two countries. The deal created five special zones where Egyptian goods have free access to US markets, as long as 35 per cent of the goods are the product of Israeli–Egyptian cooperation (Saleh, 2004).

Meanwhile, a more generous version of the Generalized System of Preferences (GSP) scheme (which offers preferential trade terms) is offered as an incentive to countries that tackle the drug trade more effectively. There is currently debate over whether and how to introduce a similar scheme to reward countries that are enthusiastic participants in the 'war on terror'. In 2002, Pakistan, for example, was given an increased textile quota allowance by the EU in tacit recognition of its cooperation with the US-led invasion of Afghanistan.[1] At its June 2002 Seville meeting, the European Council agreed to incorporate a terrorism clause in all EU agreements, including free trade agreements, as an inducement against state support of terrorism (EU, 2002, p4).

Of course the extent to which countries are influenced by conditionality tends to relate, in direct proportion, to the size of the aid or trade package in question, and the degree to which the country is dependent on aid from, or trade with, the negotiating country. Conditionality tends to proliferate (and be most influential) when countries are economically or politically weakened. The 1980s debt crisis significantly changed the balance of power between developed and developing countries – at least for a time. It reduced the latter to, in Ajit Singh's words, 'supplicants before the IMF... In return for balance of payments support, countries were asked to privatize, to deregulate and essentially follow neo-liberal economic policies'. The same was true after the Asian economic crisis of 1997–98, where Indonesia was subject to particularly broad conditionality in order to receive IMF bridging loans. However, individual countries often have relatively little leverage over resource-rich countries, particularly when commodity prices are high (as the relative value of aid packages falls) and strategic or commercial interests rather than wider 'good governance' objectives cloud the priorities of bilateral donors.

In practice, conditionality has a mixed record. Aid and trade conditionality can certainly provide a powerful incentive for good governance and some direction as to what might be done. However, conditionality has often been inconsistently and ineffectively applied. Developing countries have agreed to conditions even where they have not been convinced of the case for change. Unsurprisingly, conditions have often been ignored in such circumstances. Paul Collier, former director of research at the World Bank, notes, 'the IFIs have radically overestimated their own power in attempting to induce reform in very poor policy environments' (Collier, 1999).

For their part, donors have often continued financial assistance even when conditions are not met. One problem is that conditionality, for whatever purpose, does not fit neatly into aid ministries or IFIs, where the incentive structure puts a premium on how much and how fast aid can be disbursed. Conversely, donors have also stopped or reduced aid for domestic political reasons, unrelated to whether or not specific conditions were met. Understandably many developing countries have become deeply cynical of conditionality and the way it is applied.

Recognizing that heavily prescriptive conditionality has not proved particularly effective, in early 2005 DFID set out a new approach to conditionality that tries to be both more flexible and more predictable. Reflecting their view of 'good' governance, the policy states that all new DFID aid partnerships will be based on three objectives: first, reducing poverty and achieving the MDGs; second, respecting human rights and other international obligations; and third, strengthening financial management and accountability.

These deliberately vague objectives also establish the circumstances under which the UK will consider reducing or interrupting aid: if a country moves *significantly* away from agreed poverty reduction objectives, is in *significant* violation of human rights or other international obligations, or if there is a *significant* breakdown in financial management and accountability. DFID argues that this approach will support policy leadership in developing countries without imposing DFID's own views on those countries. The crucial word here is, of course, '*significant*' – which is subjective and open to interpretation. While it may be easier for countries to predict whether a particular policy will trigger a cut in aid, it seems unlikely to result in real change to the nature or extent of conditionality placed on developing countries.

Persuading unconvinced or unwilling countries to take up reforms is obviously difficult. Conversely, if a government perceives the need for a particular reform already, it should not need prompting by donors. As Tom Porteous, writing as a conflict management adviser at the UK Foreign Office, argues, 'In the absence of a genuine commitment on the part of a capable leadership to adopt sensible policies, and the institutional capacity to implement them transparently, development assistance will not be effective. But where neither the commitment nor capacity is there, it is very hard for the foreign donors to conjure it up out of nothing' (Porteous, 2005, p292).

Conditionality or selectivity?

World Bank economists David Dollar and Craig Burnside published research in 1998 suggesting that aid is most effective at reducing poverty and promoting growth in countries with sound economic management and robust government institutions (World Bank, 1998). Their influential and controversial report recommended a systematic and selective targeting of aid to poor countries with, to the World Bank's eyes, sound policies and effective institutions. The idea of aid selectivity is to create a system where aid is selectively given to countries on the basis of their existing performance, not their plans or promises.

The most prominent example of aid selectivity is the US Millennium Challenge Account (MCA) launched by President Bush at the Monterrey summit on financing for development in 2002 (Woods, 2005). In 2005 the MCA was promised \$2.5 billion – a large amount, but one dwarfed many times by the money spent pursuing other US security priorities in Iraq and Afghanistan (Woods, 2005). The MCA uses 16 criteria to assess the policy performance of countries, which must demonstrate their commitment to just and democratic governance, economic freedom and investing in their own people.

Underneath this 'tough love' rhetoric are some glaring problems. The MCA has struggled to find enough candidates that meet its strict criteria. In fact it took more than two years for the MCA to disburse a single grant. The problem is that aid selectivity is difficult to implement in practice as, almost by definition, it is the worst-performing countries that have the weakest policies and institutions. Consequently, if you only reward those countries that are performing well, poor performers become increasingly isolated (Santiso, 2001, p11). In other words, aid selectivity actively ignores the very countries that are likely to be most in need of governance reforms.

Sticks and sanctions

Sanctions are the middle ground between words and war. Economic sanctions are normally chosen when diplomacy has proven ineffective, but when a state or states are unwilling or unable to use military force. Sanctions can be unilateral (of the kind imposed on Cuba by the US), regional (such as EU sanctions on Serbia) or multilateral (UN sanctions mandated through the Chapter VII powers of the Security Council – such as those imposed on Iraq during the 1990s).

Aid sanctions or the threat of aid sanctions are a common response to perceptions of poor governance. As aid funds are inherently discretionary, they can be swiftly and unilaterally suspended – typically without serious political or economic consequences for the sanctioning nation. In a cynical world they are also useful for domestic reasons to show that politicians in a donor country are 'doing something'.

Depending on how much a country trades, and with whom, trade sanctions can carry more economic weight than aid sanctions. Obviously, to be most effective trade sanctions need to be agreed upon by a wide range of countries. However, in the face of competitive pressures between countries for markets and resources, trade sanctions are politically harder to construct and sustain than aid sanctions. For example, by the mid-1990s Nigeria's record on human rights, democracy, corruption and organized crime was among the worst in Africa. NGOs and the media were demanding that pressure be put on the military regime of General Sani Abacha. There were practical as well as moral grounds for action: military rule appeared to be driving the country and the region towards economic and political meltdown. But usable western leverage was limited. Europe and the US had valuable commercial interests in Nigeria, mainly in oil, and were relying on the Nigerian military to maintain regional stability in West Africa, particularly in Liberia and Sierra Leone (Porteous, 2005, p285). The result was inertia and inactivity, until the military head of state died and internal change could begin.

That said, effectively implemented multilateral economic sanctions send a tremendously powerful signal of disapproval. Wide-ranging economic sanctions, such as those imposed on Libya, Burma and apartheid South Africa, can cut government revenues, increase unemployment and erode the standard of living. It is widely believed, for example, that trade and financial sanctions (alongside the threat of military action) imposed by the US, Russia, the UK, France and Germany played an important role in forcing Serbian President Slobodan Milosevic to accept the 1995 Dayton Peace Accords, which finally ended the war in the former Yugoslavia (Boyce, 2002b, p20). The dilemma, of course, is that broadly applied aid or trade sanctions usually cannot be applied against a particular government without adversely affecting ordinary people.

But sanctions, like conditionality, have a relatively weak track record where real change is concerned (Le Billon, 2005, p4). They tend to have a sharp impact in the short term, but their influence tails off as countries learn how to adapt and divert their trade through non-sanctioning countries (Torbat, 2005). In fact, decades of US sanctions on Cuba and Iran have helped to entrench the very regimes that sanctions were supposed to displace, in part by providing them with a convenient enemy against which to focus public discontent. Likewise, the EU has been unsuccessful in forcing any significant changes on the Mugabe regime in Zimbabwe – despite a wide variety of inducements and punishments (Porteous, 2005, p291). In part this is because disagreement among members of the EU, principally France and the UK, over how to tackle Zimbabwe have hampered the development of a coordinated EU policy (Porteous, 2005, p293).

Since the UN-managed 'oil for food' programme in Iraq collapsed amidst allegations of corruption and ineffectiveness, the international community's appetite for sanctions has melted away. In addition, WTO rules tend to constrain the ability of countries to impose unilateral trade sanctions (Cleveland, 2002, p136). Instead there has been a shift toward targeted trade sanctions, such as embargoes on arms shipments. These may be buttressed by targeted non-trade sanctions such as travel bans or financial freezes. In theory, by applying selective sanctions to the subset of aid or trade that is of greatest benefit to political leaders, pressure can be applied in a way that has a more limited impact on the general population. As described in Chapter 4, targeted sanctions on conflict resources can disrupt the sale of natural resources used to finance conflicts and, as was the case with the multilateral UN sanctions on timber and diamonds from Liberia, can directly help to end conflict by undermining the protagonists' economic incentives for continued conflict.

Capacity building and technical assistance

Effective reform requires the capacity to implement it. As such, technical assistance has become a central pillar of the good governance agenda. Behind this is an assumption that many problems with poor governance in the developing world stem from a lack of skills, experience, structures and institutions rather than, say, political will. In recent years about a quarter of all development aid, or more than $15 billion each year, has gone into technical assistance, most of which is ostensibly aimed at building governance capacity (OECD, 2006, p7).

Until recently, capacity development was seen mainly as a technical process, involving the simple transfer of skills or institutional models from North to South. The implicit conclusion is that once the 'right' institutions are in place, good governance would automatically follow. Traditionally, northern policy makers have found it difficult to conceive of legitimate public authority except in terms of models, policies and institutions that have worked in their own countries. As a report by the IDS notes, 'The focus has been on the formal institutions rather than the informal relationships that shape the way they work. The approach is ahistorical – there has been virtually no attempt to understand the processes whereby current institutional models were negotiated or the social, economic and political circumstances in which they were conceived' (IDS, 2005, p2).

It is perhaps unsurprising then that overall, capacity building has a rather poor record of success. A 2003 study of technical assistance identified three problems: first, that programmes tend to be driven by donors rather than provided in response to a recipient's priorities; second, that ownership by aid-recipients has been weak and eroded by donor controls and the use of parallel management structures outside normal government procedures; and third, the costs are high while the quality of technical assistance varies (Williams et al, 2003, piii). Too often, building accountable, robust governments has been seen as a technocratic exercise rather than the complex political bargaining process it is, involving protracted negotiations between the state and diverse interest groups (IDS, 2005, p4).

The international community has typically pushed for wide-ranging political, economic and social reforms that may be well beyond the capacity of a government – however worthwhile the reforms. In many cases the funding has far exceeded absorptive capacity, sucking up whatever limited capacity did exist by diverting competent government staff with the lure of higher salaries. For example, by early 2006 there were some 120 laws that were pending approval by the Afghan parliament, drafted by various donors and their consultants. There was little chance of these reforms being adopted in anything but the most token way (François and Sud, 2006, p153).

There is new consensus emerging, articulated most clearly in the 2005 *Paris Declaration on Aid Effectiveness*, which sees capacity building as an endogenous process, driven and led from within a country rather than from outside, with donors playing a supporting role (OECD, 2006, p3). In practice this means that policy makers should understand the environment they are trying to influence much more clearly. The encouraging news is that a few donors are beginning to invest more in careful analysis of the political context in which they are operating.

DFID's 'Drivers of Change' studies are in-depth analyses of the political and social forces at work in recipient countries. The World Bank is funding a similar exercise, called Poverty and Social Impact Analysis, which involves systematic analyses of the impact of policy reforms on the welfare of different stakeholder groups. However, many such studies have been ignored in the past by donors intent on promoting their own prefabricated, one-size-fits-all policy solutions. The extent to which these studies will prove any different remains to be seen.

Trade integration

Less confrontational than sanctions but often more persuasive than aid conditionality, trade integration is increasingly being seen as a more effective, and perhaps more subtle, vehicle for governance reform. The possibility of joining a trading entity like the EU is a very powerful incentive to meet pre-established governance standards – and this has certainly been the impetus behind dramatic reforms in the recent and potential EU accession states in east and south-east Europe.

Meanwhile, regional and bilateral trade agreements are mushrooming around the world. Over the past 15 years regional trade agreements (RTAs) like the North America Free Trade Agreement (NAFTA) have become much more common. Of the 193 RTAs formally notified to the WTO by early 2006, 163 of have come into force since 1990 (WTO, 2006). The growth of regional and bilateral trade agreements is creating a growing and interlocking web of regional commitments, which could have a positive spill-over impact on national governance.

Interestingly, more and more governance criteria are being bundled into trade agreements. As noted above, the 2000 Cotonou Agreement between the EU and countries of the Africa, Caribbean and Pacific (ACP) region is a case in point. The agreement specifically lists three so-called 'essential elements' that should be respected: human rights, democracy and the rule of law. Contravention of any of these 'essential elements' can, as an option of last resort, lead to suspension of cooperation, including the cancellation of preferential trade access.

Similar conditions are being negotiated as a part of the trade agreements that are to succeed the Cotonou Agreement when it expires in 2007. The EPAs are a prime example of the extent to which aid and trade policies are now seen as interconnected. An explicit objective of the EPAs is to improve governance in partner countries. Former EU trade commissioner Pascal Lamy has argued that trade agreements like the EPAs should contain even more extensive conditionality. He suggested that the agreements should allow the EU to ban any imports that do not meet the EU's 'collective preferences'. The term is deliberately vague but would likely allow unilateral trade sanctions in cases of human rights abuse, serious environmental mismanagement or rigged elections (Euractive, 2004). Of course a cynic might point out that this would also give the EU a convenient degree of latitude to use trade sanctions to further its own political or strategic interests under the cover of its 'collective preferences'.

North–South trade integration arrangements like the EPAs are, in effect, a form of trade conditionality where market access is offered (partly) in return for governance reforms. That this is possible at all is indicative of the negotiating and trading power of the rich developed countries. But it is also the case, albeit to a lesser extent, in South–South regional integration processes. One example is the creation in December 2004 of the South Andean Community of Nations, which was modelled explicitly on the EU. Regional groupings such as MERCOSUR (Brazil, Argentina, Paraguay, Venezuela and Uruguay) can become aspirational clubs, and can play a stabilizing role for countries on their borders. They can also provide non-military ways to resolve disputes: agreements such as MERCOSUR have instituted dispute settlement mechanisms to mediate economic conflicts, and have also resolved political tensions.

Developed countries, particularly in the EU, have become enthusiastic proponents of regional integration elsewhere in the world as a 'hands-off' way to improve governance and promote interdependence between countries. EU delegations, for example, are actively encouraged to help 'export' the EU's model of regional integration. This is backed by EU funds that bankroll organizations like the African Union and the Pacific Forum. Often this has the explicit rationale of contributing to the prevention, management and resolution of violent conflict (Council of the European Union, 2004, p3). The same is true of the US, where the Bush senior, the Clinton and George W. Bush administrations have made the spreading of regional economic agreements a foreign policy priority.

Dilemmas and debates

There are compelling arguments in favour of the current focus on good governance in the developing world. It is widely accepted that 'better' governance is an essential precondition for sustainable development, poverty reduction and stability. Donors recognize that aid funds spent in corrupt, unaccountable regimes tend to be much less effective than aid spent in countries with transparent, accountable governments focused on achieving economic growth and poverty reduction.

Moreover, policy makers in the developed world have a legitimate interest in seeing that their resources are spent to the best effect. It is politically unfeasible and practically unwise for most donor governments to give unconditional aid to countries with graphic and well-publicized problems of corruption and human rights abuse. Also, it is not unthinkable that donor governments may have the experience, capacity and resources to help develop well-founded reform of institutions, skills and policies in recipient countries. Consequently it is unsurprising that policy makers often attempt to use the levers of influence at their disposal to encourage what they perceive to be best practice.

Not doing so can have disastrous consequences. In Rwanda in the early 1990s, the international community failed to halt a slide towards the very worst form of governance, state-sponsored genocide, by not applying pressure to a government that was deliberately ramping up ethnic tensions (see Chapter 2). From the late 1980s to the early 1990s, the annual flow of aid rose by half, despite evidence of the regime's complicity in exciting violence by Hutu extremists against the Tutsi minority (Boyce, 2002a, pp1032–1033).

Between April and June 1994 over 800,000 people were massacred in three months of vicious ethnic hatred. Peter Uvin's damning indictment of the international community's inaction during the run-up to the Rwandan genocide is worth quoting at length. Despite plenty of warnings that ethnic tensions were rising and the situation was fast deteriorating, the international community did little to avert the genocide.

> *[P]olitical conditionality was never really implemented in Rwanda: there were few credible threats and even less action to diminish Rwanda's financial lifeline. After all we should not forget that aid to Rwanda greatly increased during that period... In so doing, the aid system sent a message ... and it essentially said that, on the level of practice and not discourse, the aid system did not care unduly about political and social trends in the country, not even if they involved government-sponsored racist attacks against Tutsis. The problem is that we tend to conceptualise our choices as between negative conditionality and the continuation of business as usual. The former is clearly an action fraught with risks and uncertainties, while the latter is perceived to be neutral – amounting to no action at all. That is wrong: the continuation of business as usual is a form of action, it does send signals, and it has an impact on local political and social processes.* (Uvin, 1998, p26)

A British parliamentary report analysing the international community's inaction before the genocide noted how the World Bank and the IMF in Rwanda clung to narrow views of 'economy and efficiency'. The report observed, 'As two of the most powerful international institutions in contact with the Rwandan Government, their concerns if expressed early enough might have proved important interventions. Neither organization recognised the direct link between growing social tension, human rights abuses and the subsequent destruction of the entire economic infrastructure' (House of Commons, 1999).

However, using trade and aid policies to push reform also raises serious problems and dilemmas. Aid itself can undermine governance by making recipient governments more responsive to the requirements of the donors than to their own constituencies. Large revenues from aid and natural resources over time have proved inherently problematic for governance because they undermine accountability and weaken the 'incentives for local collective action, including the incentives for states to engage with taxpayers' (Unsworth, 2005, p11).

Worse still, trade and aid policies can reduce stability and cause resentment if they are misdirected or perceived as overly heavy-handed. In the past, aggressively promoted Western concepts of good governance, market liberalization and democratic reform have proved, at best, highly controversial and often dangerously destabilizing. Certainly, Western taxpayers would revolt if faced with the taxes or the cutbacks in service that have been standard parts of the economic recipe promoted by the IMF and the World Bank. Pressurizing developing countries into dramatic and expensive policy changes can ultimately prove counterproductive in three different ways:

1 It can undermine national sovereignty and policy autonomy. Often con-
   descending and didactic, foreign attempts at national reform have more
   than a hint of missionary zeal about them. Moreover, they can undermine
   public confidence (where it exists) in a government's ability to govern.
2 External governance reform can be fundamentally undemocratic and
   unaccountable. It is ironic that donors force norms of good governance
   on recipient countries, which often include respect for the democratic
   process in ways that can be profoundly undemocratic. Those most affected
   by the policy prescriptions of international policy makers – poor people in
   developing countries – have little recourse against them.
3 Strategic interests can crowd out the interests of long-term development
   and good governance. This was certainly the case during the Cold War.
   The 1990s represented a new opportunity to link aid and trade policies
   with genuine humanitarian and good governance objectives, in contrast
   with the ideologically and geo-strategically motivated aid that sustained so
   many dictatorships during the Cold War. The risk is that this window could
   be closed by the strategic interests of the developed world in the post-9/11
   world of the 'war on terror'. Since late 2001 it seems that a *good ally* is as,
   if not more, important than *good governance*.

Conclusions – the limits of leverage

Good governance is a prerequisite to security. And security is a prerequisite to
sustainable development. As Kofi Annan famously noted in 2005, 'Humanity
will not enjoy security without development, it will not enjoy development
without security, and it will not enjoy either without respect for human rights'
(UN, 2005).

Yet, good governance remains elusive. The core challenge for those
wishing to encourage good governance is to generate constructive influence in
countries that are at risk of instability or conflict. But in the past, many of the
mechanisms used by the international community to promote good governance
have proven neither constructive nor influential. As President Mkapa of
Tanzania said, 'Development cannot be imposed. It can only be facilitated.
It requires ownership, participation and empowerment, not harangues and
dictates' (Benn, 2005, piii).

It is legitimate for policy makers to use the tools at their disposal to try to
promote good governance overseas. However, if aid and trade policies are to
generate real economic growth and build peaceful relationships between and
within countries, decision makers need to understand the full impact of their
trade and aid policies – and the signals those policies send.

There are many examples where conditionality, sanctions, capacity building or trade integration have been ineffective at generating tangible changes in
governance. As a report by the IDS notes, 'Despite a proliferation of projects
to reform the public service, strengthen accountability mechanisms, get
basic services to poor people, improve the regulatory environment and build

democratic institutions, progress (with some exceptions), has been meagre and hard to sustain' (IDS, 2005, p44).

However, it is equally clear that not all conditionality is coercive, not all sanctions are counterproductive and not all technical assistance is ineffective. Often, a mix of measures may be the most effective way to proceed. In Cambodia in the mid- to late 1990s, for example, carefully focused pressure from the international community, applied through a range of aid and trade 'carrots and sticks', helped to move the peace process past several dangerous episodes and consolidate some semblance of peace in the country (Boyce, 2002b, p30).

In 1997 it was estimated that illegal logging was costing Cambodia over $100 million in lost revenues per year and fuelling the continuing conflict with remnants of the Khmer Rouge regime in the remote west of the country. The resumption of IMF financial support was made conditional on the government showing credible attempts to reduce illegal logging and to bring forestry profits back within the government budget. That same year the World Bank made it clear that disbursement of $450 million in aid would be conditional on the Cambodian government dealing with the problem of illegal logging.

The international community, led by the UN, helped to keep progress moving towards national elections in 1998. In February 1999 donors pledged another $470 million in fresh aid to Cambodia. International pressure to crack down on illegal logging led to an announcement by Prime Minister Hun Sen in 2001 that all logging would be suspended (Boyce, 2002b, p32). While progress on the issue of illegal logging has since been slow, with frequent setbacks, it may well have been non-existent but for carefully applied pressure from the international community.

It is clear that aid and trade policies can be powerful tools to promote good governance. However, too often policy makers in developed countries attempt to use trade and aid policies to pursue subjective, changing concepts of good governance. Donors come with different objectives: 'democracy builders see this as an end in its own right, while others pursue better governance as a means to promote growth and poverty reduction, or to counter the security risks posed by collapsed or fragile states' (Unsworth, 2005, p2). All too often they do this without a real understanding of the change they are trying to achieve or the context in which they are trying to achieve it.

Donor aid and trade policies tend to focus on the short to medium term. But governance reform is a long-term process; institutions can't be transferred – they need to be developed. Building trust and accountability in a political process takes time. It is a truism that political change must occur from within a country rather than from outside. Trade and aid policies may be able to help accelerate the pace of reform but they have generally proven ineffective at reversing trends or triggering reforms out of thin air.

Nevertheless, there have been some important successes. In most poor countries large assistance programmes or important trading relationships do at least enable serious dialogue about governance and in some cases this has encouraged reform. Even so, it is difficult to force countries to implement policies they find unconvincing. More often, the most that can be expected is to encourage and nurture incipient reform; 'to push a train that's already moving' (Unsworth, 2005, p6).

Some recommendations

Recommendation 1 *Consider the impact of current aid and trade policies*
For decades poorly constructed trade and aid policies have undermined governance in the developing world: by allowing aid and valuable but opaque revenues from natural resources to be captured by political elites; by locking countries into dependence on volatile and unpredictable revenues from natural resources and aid; and by fuelling the trade in illegal and conflict resources.

Northern policy makers need to concentrate on creating an environment for good governance: by creating conflict-sensitive trade and aid policies, by reducing the economic incentives for war, by building markets for conflict-free goods, by helping countries diversify their economies, by supporting moves for greater transparency – in short by pursuing the policy objectives outlined elsewhere in this book. These are things over which policy makers in the developed world already have control. Only when these fundamentals are resolved will policy makers in the developed world have sufficient credibility to offer their policy prescriptions to others.

Recommendation 2 *Don't travel blind*
All governance interventions are by their very nature highly political. Any external intervention needs a clear understanding of the local political context and the incentives of key actors (as well as the strategic interests of the donor). Independent, rigorous and detailed governance assessments are needed before any intervention. This exercise shouldn't be a preparation to better 'sell' a pre-determined governance agenda, but rather to understand what that governance agenda should be and to understand what impact external interventions might have on local incentives and capacities for action.

Recommendation 3 *Build on existing reforms and align external interventions with domestic priorities*
Rather than offering prefabricated policy solutions, external policy makers need to look at what is working already. Donors need to acknowledge existing power structures and incorporate local policies, working within and from those instead of transferring models, institutions and policies from elsewhere. External actors can offer experience and lessons as well as resources from elsewhere, but the emphasis should be on the word 'offer'. If ownership is to be real, ideas about 'leverage' will need to be reconsidered.

Recommendation 4 *Realize that occasionally aid and trade policies may not be the most effective lever of influence*
Poorly planned, inept attempts at leveraging influence through trade and aid policies have backfired and contributed to deteriorating governance.

Occasionally, in an imperfect world, doing nothing may be the most effective policy.

Recommendation 5 *Acknowledge that one size does not fit all*
In the past, ideologically driven, one-size-fits-all models have proven inappropriate and ineffective. Reforms have to be context-specific. This re-emphasizes the need to understand the local political context, power relationships and incentives. As Sue Unsworth notes '[t]ransitional, unorthodox, bitty arrangements that target local constraints in politically compelling ways may be more effective than trying to transfer ready-made institutions from rich to poor countries' (Unsworth, 2005, p9).

Recommendation 6 *Be patient, consistent and realistic*
There are few 'quick wins' when supporting genuine governance reform. Policy makers in the developed world need to be patient and realistic with what they can achieve in improving governance in other countries, what they cannot accomplish and what they should not tackle. Institutions can rarely be transferred; they must be developed. Building trust and accountability is a political process that takes time. A key to success seems to lie in maintaining a consistent approach and in coordinating policies with other actors – so that the recipient country is not pulled in different directions at the same time. Focusing aid on 'islands of change' within state structures can also help to reward reform-minded elements within a government.

Recommendation 7 *Design trade agreements so that they provide sufficient incentives and clear benchmarks*
Given the right package of incentives and support, coupled with clear objectives and long-term cooperation, trade agreements can be an effective way to promote and support good governance.

Note

1　Following satisfactory cooperation in the fight against terrorism, Pakistan was included in the GSP special arrangement on drugs and a Memorandum of Understanding was signed with the EU increasing the level of textiles and clothing quotas for exports in exchange for increased reciprocal access. The EU was later forced to withdraw this preference following a complaint to the WTO by India on the grounds of unfair treatment. See *Bridges Weekly Trade News Digest*, 'India wins landmark GSP case' vol 7, no 37, 5 November 2003 (www.ictsd.org/weekly/03-11-05/story1.htm)

References

Ahrens, J. (2001) 'Governance conditionality and transformation in post-socialist countries', in Hoen, H. (ed) *Good Governance in Central and Eastern Europe*, Cheltenham, Edward Elgar, cited in Santiso (2003)

Benn, H. (2005) 'Partnerships for poverty reduction: Rethinking conditionality', DFID Policy Paper, London, March 2005

Boyce, J. (2002a) 'Aid conditionality as a tool for peacebuilding', *Development and Change*, vol 33, no 5, pp1025–1048

Boyce, J. (2002b) 'Investing in peace: Aid and conditionality after civil wars', Adelphi Paper 351, London, International Institute for Strategic Studies

Cleveland, S. (2002) 'Human rights sanctions and international trade: A theory of compatibility', *Journal of International Economic Law*, vol 5, no 1, pp133–189

Collier, P. (1999) 'Learning from failure: The international financial institutions as agencies of restraint in Africa', in Schedler, A. et al (eds) *The Self-restraining State: Power and Accountabilities in New Democracies*, Boulder, CO, Lynne Rienner

Council of the European Union (2004) *Council Common Position Concerning Conflict Prevention, Management and Resolution in Africa*, SN 1010/04, January 2004

DFID (2005) 'Partnerships for poverty reduction: Rethinking conditionality', UK Policy Paper, London, DFID, March 2005

Economic Commission for Africa (2005) *Striving for Good Governance in Africa: Synposis of the 2005 African Goverance Report*, Addis Ababa, Economic Commission for Africa

Euractive (2004) '"Collective preferences" is an EU attempt to silence domestic critique: Vandana Shiva', 10 March, www.euractiv.com/Article?tcmuri=tcm:29-113110-16&type=News accessed September 2005

European Union (2001) 'Report of the European Union to the Security Council Committee established pursuant to resolution 1373 concerning counter-terrorism', s/2002/928, European Union

European Union (2002) 'Report of the European Union to the Security Council Committee established pursuant to resolution 1373 (2001) concerning counter-terrorism', s/2002/928

François, M. and I. Sud (2006) 'Promoting stability and development in fragile and failed states', *Development Policy Review*, vol 24, no 2, p141

Grindle, M. (2002) 'Good enough governance: Poverty reduction and reform in developing countries', *Governance: An International Journal of Policy, Administration, and Institutions*, vol 17, pp525–548

Grindle, M. (2005) 'Good enough governance revisited: A report for DFID with reference to the Governance Target Strategy Paper, 2001', Cambridge, Harvard University

House of Commons, International Development Committee (1999) 'Conflict prevention and post-conflict reconstruction. volume I: report and proceedings', cited in Boyce, J. (2002a) 'Aid conditionality as a tool for peacebuilding', *Development and Change*, vol 33, no 5, pp1025–1048

Hout, W. (2002) 'Good governance and aid: Selectivity criteria in development assistance', *Development and Change*, vol 33, no 2, pp511–527

IDS (2005) 'Signposts to more effective states: Responding to governance challenges in developing countries', Brighton, Institute of Development Studies

IMF (2001) 'Structural conditionality in fund-supported programs', PDRD, Washington DC, IMF, cited in Santiso (2001)

Le Billon, P. (2005) 'Aid in the midst of plenty: Oil wealth, misery and advocacy in Angola', *Disasters*, vol 29, no 1, pp1–25

Mansfield, E. (1999) 'Preferential peace: Why preferential trading arrangements inhibit interstate conflict', Philadelphia, University of Pennsylvania

OECD (2006) *The Challenge of Capacity Development: Working Towards Good Governance*, DAC Network on Governance, OECD

Porteous, T. (2005) 'British government policy in sub-Saharan Africa under New Labour', *International Affairs*, vol 81, no 2, p281–297

Saleh, H. (2004) 'Egypt and Israel seal trade deal', BBC, news.bbc.co.uk/1/hi/business/4095011.stm accessed in August 2006

Santiso, C. (2001) 'Good governance and aid effectiveness: The World Bank and conditionality', *The Georgetown Public Policy Review*, vol 7, no 1, Fall 2001

Santiso, C. (2003) 'The paradox of governance: Objective or condition of multilateral development finance?', SAIS Working Paper Series, WP/03/03, Washington DC, John Hopkins University

Therkildsen, O. (2005) 'Major additional funding for the MDGs: A mixed blessing for capacity development', *IDS Bulletin*, vol 36, no 3, pp28–39

Torbat, A. E. (2005) 'Impacts of the US trade and financial sanctions on Iran', *The World Economy*, vol 28, no 3, pp407–434

UN (2005) *In Larger Freedom: Towards Development, Security and Human Rights for All*, New York, United Nations

Unsworth, S. (2005) 'Focusing aid on good governance: Can foreign aid instruments be used to enhance "good governance" in recipient countries?', Working Paper, Global Economic Governance Programme, Oxford

USAID (2005) 'Democracy and government', www.usaid.gov/our_work/democracy_and_governance accessed August 2006

Uvin, P. (1998) *Aiding Violence: The Development Enterprise in Rwanda*, West Hartford, Kumarion Press, cited in Boyce (2002b)

Williams, G., Jones, S., Imber, V. and Cox, A. (2003) 'A vision for the future of technical assistance in the international development system', Oxford Policy Management

Woods, N. (2005) 'The shifting politics of foreign aid', *International Affairs*, vol 81, no 2, pp393–409

World Bank (1998) *Assessing Aid. What Works, What Doesn't, and Why*, New York, Oxford Unversity Press

WTO (2006) 'Regional trade agreements: Facts and figures', www.wto.org/english/tratop_e/region_e/regfac_e.htm accessed 8 June 2006

Chapter 4

Building Markets for Conflict-free Goods

Duncan Brack and *Gavin Hayman*[1]

Introduction

As the introductory chapter made clear, the exploitation of natural resources in poor countries with weak standards of governance is frequently associated with conflict. The presence of some commodities, in particular oil, may make the initiation of conflict more likely; the presence of others, for example gemstones and narcotics, may lengthen the duration of conflicts. Revenues and riches may alter the mindset of combatants, turning war and insurgency from a purely political activity to an economic one; conflicts become less about grievance and more about greed.

In all cases, however, the linkage between natural resources and conflict depends critically on the ability of their exploiters to access external markets. Take away the ability to earn returns from resource extraction and their value to the promoters of conflict falls away, sometimes dramatically. As pointed out in the first section of this chapter, when the Thai and Cambodian governments closed their joint border to log exports in 1995/96, the Khmer Rouge insurgency, which had depended largely on logging revenues, began to disintegrate, leading ultimately to the end of the civil war.

An obvious solution, therefore, is to attempt to exclude natural resources associated with conflict from international markets. The simplest way is to place a trade embargo on the country or countries concerned; the third section of this chapter looks at the record of UN sanctions in this respect, and puts forward proposals for their improvement.

Sanctions may not work when resources extracted in a conflict area are smuggled into neighbouring countries and thereby 'laundered' into legitimate trade; consumers then have no way of knowing whether or not the products they buy are financing conflict. The extension of trade sanctions to the neighbouring countries would clearly be unjust, so a more targeted solution is to establish a licensing system, allowing only those products that can be shown to be conflict-free into international trade. The Kimberley Process on conflict diamonds is just such a system, and has operated with some effect since it was established in 2003.

Other licensing systems exist, or are being set up, to deal with the related problem of natural resources produced illegally, in breach of national laws or international treaty obligations. Illegal trade in wildlife, timber and fish is thought to be worth a minimum of $30 billion a year, 7.5 per cent of the size of the global drugs trade, and perhaps up to 25 per cent of the total legal trade in these products. The fourth section looks at the record of existing licensing systems, and suggests some ways to improve them.

The counterpart of excluding conflict resources and illegal goods from world markets – and a crucial part of the debate, given the importance of international trade to sustainable development – is building markets for legal and conflict-free products. Public procurement policies, and private sector scrutiny over their supply chains, can help to do this, and are examined in the fifth section.

Policies that interfere directly with international trade are subject, at least potentially, to the constraints of WTO rules. The WTO dealt with the Kimberley Process by giving it a waiver from normal trading disciplines, though this procedure, which implied that the Process was subordinate to the WTO, was in itself controversial with at least some Process participants. Despite its growing importance, the topic of excluding illegal products from trade has hardly ever been discussed within the WTO, and its impact remains uncertain. This is discussed further in the final section.

First, before all these policy tools and their implications are discussed, we look in more detail at what conflict resources and illegal goods are and the problems they cause.

Conflict resources and illegal goods

Conflict resources

Natural resource exploitation has played an increasingly prominent role in bankrolling conflict around the world since the end of the Cold War. Previously, many combatants in local insurgencies or low-level nationalistic conflicts were financed by competing superpower blocs. Since such ideological sponsorship is now much harder to come by, and as war remains an expensive business, belligerents have turned to easily accessible and easily convertible wealth from natural resource exploitation.

After Chinese support dried up in the late 1980s, the Khmer Rouge in Cambodia turned to logging and gem-mining to fight the Vietnamese-supported government. Precious minerals such as diamonds, emeralds and lapis lazuli have been used to fund conflicts from Angola to Afghanistan, from Burma to Sierra Leone, whilst tin ore is still being used to fund warring parties in the DRC. Timber sales paid for the human rights abuses committed by Charles Taylor's regime in Liberia, whilst Nepal's insurgent Maoists claim that a significant portion of their income comes from the sale of a rare fungus, highly prized in Asia as an aphrodisiac.

The term 'conflict resources' is one that is easy to grasp, but harder to define. An intuitive definition would be 'natural resources whose extraction or trade funds a war'. However, not all conflict is internationally illegitimate – a state has a sovereign right to defend itself against aggression, provided that it obeys the laws of war embodied by instruments like the Geneva Convention. Similarly, there are certain rebellions and insurgencies, for example against a despotic and genocidal government, that could be considered to be legitimate. The crucial point of international concern is not the existence of conflict in the abstract, but the collateral damage to the ordinary citizenry by freebooters who have made violence and pillage a form of economic activity and who flout the rules of war.

A conflict resource – one on which sanctions should be applied by the international community – is therefore one that is bankrolling a war that is illegitimate, or where the laws of war are broken. The legitimacy of a conflict is, of course, a controversial subject, with the members of the international community very rarely agreeing on this point. The trigger for drawing an international response is likely to be when combatants who are already breaking the laws of war or committing grave violations of human rights abuses are being funded by natural resource extraction. Thus, we can define 'conflict resources' as:

> *Natural resources whose systematic exploitation and trade in a context of conflict contribute to, benefit from or result in the commission of serious violations of human rights, violations of international humanitarian law or violations amounting to crimes under international law.*

The remainder of this section reviews the impact of various conflict resources in the 1990s.

Cambodia

In Cambodia in 1996, corruption watchdog Global Witness was able to expose a deal between the country's co-prime ministers and the Thai prime minister that circumvented an export ban to allow some 1.1 million cubic metres of timber to be exported from Cambodia to Thailand by 18 Thai companies that had based their logging operations in Khmer Rouge areas. The bulk of the revenue derived ($35–90 million) would probably have gone directly to fund the Khmer Rouge war effort. The deal collapsed after it was exposed, and the Cambodian government began to charge Thai loggers a flat rate of $35 per cubic metre for the provision of certificates circumventing the export ban. High-ranking officials were reported to fly by helicopter to Khmer Rouge log collection points inside the Thai border to receive payments and facilitation fees split between Cambodian and Thai prime ministers and other ministers and low-ranking officials at the border.

This is one of the 'bizarre instances of co-operation between forces that are supposed to be locked in combat' that characterizes the political economy of civil wars based around natural resources (Keen, 1998). The ideological content of the struggle had ceased to be important, and instead political and economic disorder was being exploited, simply to enrich participants in the conflict.

Angola

Similar to the Khmer Rouge's reliance on timber when their external assistance dried up, so in Angola, UNITA insurgents, led by the sociopathic Jonas Savimbi, switched in the 1990s from relying on the US and the apartheid South African government for patronage and military assistance to diamond exploitation as their main source of funding. UNITA controlled about 60–70 per cent of the country's easily exploitable diamond fields. Between 1992 and 1998, it earned an estimated \$3.7 billion in diamond sales, supplemented by gold, timber, coffee and wildlife products (Global Witness, 1998). After 1998, however, income declined rapidly to an estimated \$80–150 million a year, due to territorial losses, depletion of some of the diamond deposits, and the impact of UN sanctions on conflict diamonds (Renner, 2002). By the time of Savimbi's death in 2002, UNITA was fighting a losing battle against the Angolan government (which had itself replaced Soviet funding with oil receipts), and entered into peace negotiations soon after.

Despite generating around \$3–5 billion from oil per year (an estimated 87 per cent of government revenue) and maybe another \$1 billion in revenues from diamonds (much going to UNITA), social and economic development in Angola collapsed. At the end of the 1990s, three quarters of the Angolan population was forced to survive in absolute poverty, on less than one dollar a day; 42 per cent of Angolan children aged five or less were underweight, with one child dying of preventable diseases and malnutrition every three minutes (Integrated Regional Affairs Network, 2002). Life expectancy was a mere 45 years, and over 3 million civilians had fled their homes (Integrated Regional Affairs Network, 2001).

Liberia and Sierra Leone

Charles Taylor's insurgency and presidency in Liberia, and his sponsorship of the savage civil war prosecuted by the RUF in neighbouring Sierra Leone, provide perhaps the most stark example of military–political entrepreneurship. Taylor was a freebooter *par excellence* – dedicated to pursuing power and wealth, and prepared to go to any lengths to achieve it.

In the early 1990s, Taylor's rebel group, the National Patriotic Front of Liberia, one of the major forces in the Liberian civil war, earned most of its income (approximately \$75 million a year) from taxing the sale of diamonds and timber (Ellis, 1999). Once he gained power in elections in 1997, he proceeded to use the revenue from the export of diamonds, timber, rubber and other natural resources to support the RUF in its struggle in Sierra Leone, providing arms, supplies and troops, partly in an effort to gain control of the lucrative Sierra Leone diamond fields, less than 160 kilometres from the Liberian border (UN Panel of Experts, 2000). UN sanctions imposed on diamonds from Liberia were introduced in March 2001, forcing Taylor to rely on timber as his primary source of revenue.

Taylor ran a shadow state that completely bypassed normal state institutions, diverting state money to himself rather than the treasury and building up the logging company militias at the expense of the Liberian army. Liberia's revenues from logging were around $100 million in 2000. Only about $7 million of this made it into government coffers. In 2000, this theft of natural resources was regularized through the Strategic Commodities Act, which declared that the president was granted the 'sole power to execute, negotiate and conclude all commercial contracts or agreements with any Foreign or Domestic Investor' (Global Witness, 2001a). Given the inherent instability of Taylor's regime, this 'theft by legislation' also created enormous incentives for the immediate liquidation of natural capital. According to one report, between 1997 and 2001 the production of roundwood in Liberia increased by over 1300 per cent (SAMFU, 2002). UN timber sanctions imposed in July 2003, however, helped reduce this source of funding and, as various rebel groups approached Monrovia, Taylor left for Nigeria in August 2003. After free elections in Liberia in 2005, the new president requested his extradition, and he was sent to The Hague to face trial on 11 war crimes charges.

Democratic Republic of Congo

If Taylor is the ultimate freebooter, then the disintegration of DRC in the late 1990s is the apogee of the problem in which natural resources are bountiful, governance is poor, and war is profitable, with the armies and proxy militias of six different countries (and those of the government itself) engaged in military adventurism, plunder and looting alongside catastrophic levels of civilian casualties – over 3 million and still counting.

The second DRC war started when Laurent Kabila, recently installed as president by a Rwandan and Ugandan-backed insurgency, turned on his erstwhile allies in 1998, with Angolan, Zimbabwean and Namibian help; the Rwandan and Ugandan governments then sponsored rebel groups, which in turn fragmented into numerous factions. Control of natural resources soon became a prime aim of all sides; in 1999, Rwandan and Ugandan troops fought for control of the town of Kisangani and its rich diamond mines, while the mineral coltan, used in electronic devices such as mobile phones and video-game consoles, was exploited, sold and taxed by rebels and Rwandan and Ugandan forces (Global Witness, 2004b). Zimbabwean troops, meanwhile, put down their weapons and went into the tropical timber business. Gold trafficking through Rwanda and Uganda also provided a major source of revenues to rebels in the east of the country (Human Rights Watch, 2005).

By the time the war came to an end with the creation of a transitional government in July–September 2003, DRC was split into many different fiefdoms, each controlled by a different rebel group, many of which were breakaway factions of other rebel groups, created to further the ambitions of their leaders. These divisions continue to this day, albeit in a weaker form as the central government struggles to reassert its sovereignty over the whole of its territory.

Natural resources in other conflicts

The natural resources element in the conflicts mentioned above is well known – it has been recognized at the level of the UN Security Council – even if the international response has been confused and hesitant. Natural resource endowments have also been an important factor in other, less well-known conflicts that have not made it on to the Security Council agenda.

Casamance is the region of Senegal south of The Gambia; it has seen a separatist rebellion since 1982, making it West Africa's longest running civil conflict, if one of its least known (Evans, 2003). By 2003, approximately 1000 people had died as a result of the conflict, and 60,000 (about 5 per cent of the population) had been displaced. Casamance, being more fertile than the rest of Senegal, is rich not only in valuable hardwoods, but also in tree crops such as cashew nuts. Both resources are being harvested illicitly or taxed by the two factions of the Movement of the Democratic Forces of Casamance (MFDC), the North and South Fronts, and the government. All three sides have also been involved in robbery and extortion from the local citizens, while rebel factions have committed extra-judicial executions, and the army has destroyed civilian dwellings and engaged in plundering villages. The army forcibly displaces civilians to their villages, citing security reasons; the North Front uses its monopoly on violence in the areas it controls to impose laws that enrich itself, while the South Front has driven civilians away from the resource-rich areas it controls through terror tactics, violence and the use of mines. The conflict has now reached a state of chronic equilibrium whereby everybody gains – apart from Casamance's civilians.[2]

The Maoist insurgency in Nepal has resulted in 11,000 deaths and over 100,000 people internally displaced since it began in 1996. The rebel Maoist Communist Party of Nepal (CPN) now controls 70 per cent of the country, with the government only in effective control of the area around the capital, Kathmandu. News reports have highlighted the Maoists' taxation of the trade to Tibet of a fungus known as yarshagumba (or yarchagumba), which is used as an aphrodisiac and general tonic in traditional Chinese medicine. One government source claimed that the rebels raised about $700,000 from taxing the yarshagumba harvest in 2003, while the head of the rebels' financial bureau claimed that 75 per cent of the total cost of waging the civil war had been financed by taxation of the trade (Bell, 2004). The irony is that the central government only opened the way for exports in 2001 by opening their border, thereby encouraging consumption in China. This may have helped make the Maoist insurgency economically feasible.

Natural resources can cause or exacerbate conflicts without being conflict resources themselves. In 1988, resentment at the environmental impact of the Panguna copper and gold mine in Bougainville Island, Papua New Guinea (which had generated nearly half of PNG's export earnings in the previous 20 years), combined with a sense that Bougainvilleans were not benefiting sufficiently from the mine's earnings, led to a secessionist conflict that is estimated to have claimed 10,000 lives. The insurgency in Bougainville led to a complete breakdown in exports from the mine within the first year as the local infrastructure was devastated, so the gold exports and revenues themselves played a minimal role in financing the conflict directly.

Booty futures

Enterprising political–military entrepreneurs can draw down on the revenues from future natural resource exploitation that they currently possess, or that they expect to control as a result of the fighting, to bankroll their bid for power. These 'booty futures' have played a part in a number of conflicts (Ross, 2005). We have already seen how Charles Taylor supported the RUF in return for access to Sierra Leone's diamond mines, but perhaps the most striking example is the activities of the French national oil company Elf-Aquitaine, which financed both sides in the 1997 civil war in Republic of Congo (Congo-Brazzaville) between the 'Cobra' militias loyal to Sassou Nguesso and the 'Kokoye' fighters loyal to elected president Pascal Lissouba. The regular army itself split along ethnic lines.

Elf-Aquitaine used its assets and influence to provide Sassou, the final victor, with military assistance from Angola in return for the future rights to exploit Congo's substantial oil reserves (Global Witness, 2004a). At the same time, Elf executives also organized an oil-backed loan (mortgaging future oil production at high rates of interest for up-front money) for Sassou's opponent Lissouba, with which he could purchase arms. The logic of Elf's so-called 'Africa System' (this speculation on war and bet-hedging was also prevalent in Angola and Gabon) was thus partially responsible for a civil war where systematic rape was prevalent, thousands died and hundreds of thousands more were displaced. As Loïk Le Floch Prigent, the former chief executive of Elf, asked: 'How did we get to the point, being the lead oil production company in Congo, of allowing a civil war to develop which transformed the capital city of Congo into a wasteland?' (Global Witness, 2004a).

Illegal goods

Conflict and illegal activity are both, at base, caused or contributed to by failures of governance. Furthermore, as noted above, trade in illegal products shares many of the same characteristics as trade in conflict resources, and sometimes they are the same thing. It is therefore worthwhile to look briefly at the main issues of concern with regard to illegal trade in natural resources.

Over the last three decades the national and international framework for the protection of the natural environment has evolved rapidly. As environmental legislation has expanded, however, so too have opportunities to evade it. Deliberate evasion of environmental laws and regulations by individuals and companies in the pursuit of personal financial benefit, where the impacts are transboundary or global – 'international environmental crime' – is a serious and growing problem.[3] The major categories of natural resources traded illegally are wildlife, timber and fish, looked at in more detail below. It is of course impossible to know for sure their total value, but educated guesses put it at a minimum of $30 billion a year, about 7.5 per cent of some estimates of the size of the global drugs trade, and perhaps up to 25 per cent of the total legal trade in these products. Other natural resources are also sometimes the target of criminal behaviour: the issue of the theft of oil from pipelines in the Niger Delta (called bunkering) has drawn international attention, and some estimates suggest that it may amount to over 5 per cent of Nigeria's production.[4]

Why does international environmental crime exist? Black markets develop in 'environmental' products such as natural resources for the same reasons that they develop in other areas – because individuals or organizations see a chance to generate profits from their sale. There are several contributory factors behind their emergence and growth:

- **Differential costs or values**. Illegal activities may be driven by environmental regulations (e.g. taxes), which raise the cost of legal products; a black market may then arise in illegal, and therefore cheaper, products. Similarly, environmental regulations may ban or constrain the availability of particular products (e.g. endangered species of wildlife), but demand for them may continue if substitutes are not available or not accepted, and also by a lack of concern for the reasons behind their protection.
- **Regulatory failure**. Illegal activities may also result from a lack of appropriate regulation, including failures to determine and/or protect property rights (open access problems – no one, for example, 'owns' the oceans). Hazardous wastes banned for disposal, for example, may simply be dumped in the ocean. In addition, sometimes the suitability of regulations, which are sometimes so badly drawn that it is almost impossible, or at least very costly, to produce legally, contribute to the problem.
- **Enforcement failure**. Finally, black markets frequently thrive because of problems with enforcement, including the obvious practical problems of policing vast areas of forests, for example, or fishing grounds on the high seas, or detecting smuggled endangered species. These are all often exacerbated by a lack of resources and expertise, corruption, and political and economic disruption.

The reported incidence of illegal environmental activities has undoubtedly grown in recent years, partly because the implementation of new multilateral Environmental Agreements (MEAs) has provided new opportunities for evasion, and partly because greater public and governmental awareness has led to more investigation of the issues.

Other contributory factors include the general trend towards trade liberalization and deregulation, which makes enforcing border controls more difficult (though the same process has probably helped reduce smuggling by cutting tariffs and thus the incentives to smuggle), and the growth of transnational corporations, amongst whom regulations are difficult to enforce. The transformation of the former Soviet bloc, and the difficulties of environmental law enforcement in many ex-Soviet economies, have also contributed to the problem, as has the growing involvement of developing countries in MEAs, but – in many of them – a lack of adequate resources to implement their provisions effectively.

Wildlife

The Convention on International Trade in Endangered Species of Wild Fauna and Flora (CITES) was agreed in Washington in 1973 and came into force in 1975. It currently has 169 parties, and is generally regarded as one of the more successful of the international conservation treaties.[5]

The illegal trade in wildlife, in contravention of the controls established by CITES, is perhaps the highest-profile area of international environmental crime. The poaching and smuggling of commodities such as ivory, rhino horn, tiger bones, sturgeon eggs, bear galls, wild-caught parrots and other luckless wildlife with a high commercial value directly threatens some or all of the populations of these species in the wild. Unfettered trade in derivatives from hundreds of other less charismatic species also serves to further deplete wild populations subject to many other pressures. Because of its diverse origins, multiplicity of products, broad consumer base and innately clandestine, high-value/low-volume nature, it may also be one of the hardest to control. Conversely, it is also the area where enforcement authorities have learnt to cooperate with the most success.

The wildlife trade flows predominantly from less developed to more developed countries (i.e. South to North) and reflects consumption patterns ranging from medical need through to the frivolous. Major sources of demand are the exotic pet and flower trade, ingredients for traditional east Asian medicine, cultural materials (such as ivory for personal *hanko* seals in Japan and rhino horns for dagger handles in the Yemen) and exotic curios and accessories. The clandestine nature of the trade means that live specimens are frequently transported in terrible conditions and many die en route. For example, mortality levels of 80 per cent were associated with the wild-caught bird trade from Africa to Europe in the late 1980s (Defenders of Wildlife, 1992).

Compiling data from various sources, the total global commercial exchange of wildlife has been estimated at between $10 billion and $20 billion, of which some $5 billion may be in contravention of CITES.[6] Smuggling wildlife can be highly lucrative. An African grey parrot exported from Côte d'Ivoire, for example, may be worth $20 at the time of capture, $100 at the point of export, $600 to an importer in the US or Europe and over $1100 to a specialist retailer. Despite the financial value of trafficking in prestigious endangered species, the bulk of wildlife crime is made up of less charismatic species like reptiles, which are traded in far larger volumes.

Fishing[7]

A UK study of 10 developing countries in Africa and Oceania in 2005 estimated that 'illegal, unregulated and unreported' (IUU)[8] fishing was worth an average 23 per cent of the total declared catch (Marine Resources Assessment Group 2005). The study showed a strong inverse relationship between the extent of IUU fishing and the level of fisheries monitoring, control and surveillance in the country, and also its general level of governance. Extrapolating these findings to the whole of sub-Saharan Africa gave an estimated annual value of IUU fishing of 19 per cent of the total legal catch, equivalent to about $0.9 billion. Extrapolating further to a global value resulted in a range from $4.2 billion to $9.5 billion per year.

One of the best-known examples of IUU fishing is that of the Patagonian toothfish, a large, long-lived and slow-growing deep-water fish increasingly in demand as a replacement for overexploited white fish such as cod. In the mid-1990s, estimates from port landings and trade data suggested that the total legal toothfish catch was exceeded in volume by illegal catches. Although toothfish stocks are protected under the Convention on the Conservation of Antarctic Marine Living Resources (CCAMLR), ships operating out of non-CCAMLR states were able to avoid the controls. As convention member states gradually closed their ports to unlicensed landings, the pirate ships switched to transhipping their haul directly to freighters at sea; the catch was then processed on land, often passing through free-trade zones. This demonstrates many of the problems connected with controlling IUU fishing: non-signatory states to the relevant convention, ships flying flags of convenience to escape domestic controls, and the enormous difficulty of tracking illegal activities across a huge area of ocean.

Even in comparatively well-regulated European waters, illegal fishing is rife, created largely by the shrinking quotas (including those set under the EU's Common Fisheries Policy) for commercially valuable human consumption stocks. Misreporting of catches and retention of undersized fish or fish caught over the allowed quotas is common; estimates in the late 1990s suggested that up to 40 per cent of the total catch of the Scottish fleet, for example, was probably 'black fish' (illegal). Financial and contractual pressure from retailers (usually supermarket chains) to supply regular quantities of fresh fish often force the processors to buy from the black market, which in turn undercuts legitimate sales.

Logging[9]

Illegal logging takes place when timber is harvested, transported, bought or sold in violation of national laws. By logging in protected areas (such as national parks) or over the allowed quota, by processing the logs (into plywood, for example, or pulp for paper) without acquiring licences, and by exporting the timber and wood products without paying export duties, companies may be able to generate much greater profits for themselves than by adhering to national laws and regulations. The extent of illegal logging in some countries is so large, and law enforcement is so poor, that the chances of detection and punishment may be very small – and the incentives to operate illegally correspondingly large.

The impacts of these illegal activities are multiple. Most obviously, these are environmental: illegal logging depletes forests, destroys the habitats of endangered species and impairs the ability of land to absorb carbon dioxide emissions, with resultant impacts on climate change. It also has direct economic impacts. Estimates from Indonesia, for example, suggest that the government is currently losing more than $1 billion a year in foregone taxes because of illegal logging (compared to a total government budget, in 2003, of about $40 billion), equivalent to about 60 per cent of the development assistance it receives. World Bank studies in Cambodia in 1997 suggested that illegal extraction was at least 10 times the size of the legal harvest; if that level of extraction continued, the country would be logged out within 10 years, removing a valuable source of employment and export revenues for the future.

Illegal logging also undermines respect for the rule of law and of government, and is frequently associated with corruption, particularly in the allocation of timber concessions. Judge Barnett's report on the timber industry in PNG in 1989, for example, described companies 'roaming the countryside with the assurance of robber barons; bribing politicians and leaders, creating social disharmony and ignoring laws' (Marshall, 1990). In some cases, including Cambodia, Liberia and DRC, the substantial revenues from illegal logging have funded national and regional conflict.

Finally, as illegally logged timber is invariably cheaper than legitimate products, it distorts global markets and undermines incentives for sustainable forest management. A study published by the American Forest & Paper Association in 2004 estimated that world prices were depressed by between 7 and 16 per cent (depending on product) by the prevalence of illegal products in the market, losing US firms at least $460 million each year in forgone sales (American Forest & Paper Association et al, 2004). As the World Bank observed in 1999, 'widespread illegal extraction makes it pointless to invest in improved logging practices. This is a classic case of concurrent government and market failure' (World Bank, 1999, p40).

By definition, the scale of illegal logging is difficult to estimate, but it is believed that more than half of all logging activities in the most vulnerable forest regions – south-east Asia, central Africa, South America and Russia – may be conducted illegally. Worldwide, estimates suggest that illegal activities may account for over a tenth of the total global timber trade, representing products worth at least $15 billion a year.

Different resources, different policies

Different resource endowments affect conflict and illegal behaviour in different ways. Firstly, the location of the resources makes a difference. If they are spread throughout the country, or centred on the capital, or offshore, then conflict may focus over control of the state; if they located in one province of the country, then their existence may well lead to a secessionist conflict, as was the case in Bougainville Island.

The amount of investment necessary to extract the resource is another key variable. Anyone can wield a chainsaw and chop down trees but, clearly, developing the infrastructure necessary to access deep-water oil reserves, for example, is beyond the ability of rebel groups – which means that rebellions in countries with oil reserves tend to manifest as coups d'état, or be driven by anticipation of future revenue flows ('booty futures') rather than the actual exploitation of the reserves.

The supply-and-demand dynamics of the marketplace also have a major effect on a commodity's conflict profile. Diamonds probably have a highly elastic demand – they are luxury items and as such susceptible to sanctions or consumer boycotts (the fear of which helped to drive the Kimberley Process); oil is extremely inelastic – everyone needs it – which means that effective consumer and marketplace interventions are less likely. Demand for minerals may be reasonably elastic – excessive supply of coltan to world markets in the early 2000s, for example, led to price drops, which in turn led to a damping down of the conflict in DRC. The portability of the resource is also a factor – timber is relatively easy to detect and interdict, while diamonds are much harder.

These parameters can lead to some conclusions on the best way to address specific resource problems. Table 4.1 analyses three commodities: diamonds, timber and oil. Possible 'weak links' in the commodity dynamics are circled; this is where intervention may be best targeted. For example, conflict diamonds are easily smuggled and transported to world markets, but elasticity of demand is high, so interventions may best be made in consumer markets. Oil revenues are huge but critically dependent on international financing and capital to access the reserves, so it may be more efficient to target the initial investment stage – in other words, targeting extractive companies and financial sector behaviour (see further in Chapter 5). For timber, although access to the resource is easy, logs are hard to transport, so interventions like sanctions may be effective.

This table could of course be extended to other commodities. For example, the parameters for coltan would seem to be medium, low, low, medium, so interdicting the product would make sense (as it is hard to smuggle), as would regulating the trade via a certification process. In the case of coltan, there are very few processors, so targeted action at that point in the commodity chain (processing) could make good sense.

These ideas about resource dynamics provide a few pointers to where interventions may have the most leverage; in practice, the international community needs to create a coherent and overlapping set of laws and procedures that will deter conflict-resource exploitation.

Table 4.1 *Dynamics affecting three natural resources and their relationship to conflict*

	Revenues receivable	Investment required	Portability of product	Elasticity of demand
Diamonds	High	Medium	Very High	Very High
Timber	Medium	Low	Low	Medium
Oil	Very high	Very high	Medium	Low

Tools: Sanctions

Sanctioning conflict resources

Sanctions are the natural weapon through which to deny conflict resources a market – and the one most often used. That said, the history of sanctions is a chequered one; this section reviews lessons learned and suggests improvements to the current global system, including the creation of an international expert panel mechanism to examine sanctions busting, the imposition of punitive measures on sanctions violators, and the mandating of UN peacekeepers to monitor sanctions violations where they are deployed. States also need to criminalize sanctions busting and to make it an extraterritorial crime, so that individuals who violate sanctions can be punished no matter where they are based.

Article 41, Chapter VII of the UN Charter allows the UN Security Council to impose restrictions on the economic relations of UN members with specified countries or groups to maintain or restore international peace and security. The implementation of such sanctions is watched over by sanctions committees within the Security Council; they receive reports as to what measures states have taken to implement sanctions, recommend measures for their implementation and report to the Security Council.

Before the 1990s, UN sanctions were applied sparingly, client regimes of the superpowers generally being protected by liberal use of the veto. When they were employed, they punished an entire state economically, as in Rhodesia in 1966 and, later, Iraq. The concept of applying sanctions to particular resources associated with particular parties in a conflict zone has only really taken hold in the past 15 years, with varying degrees of success. Table 4.2 lists such 'smart sanctions' (i.e. sanctions on specific commodities that should impact on a particular group of belligerents rather than the entire country).

A UN report on sanctions busting in Angola, set up in May 1999, reported that Togo, Burkina Faso and Belgium, amongst other countries, were breaking the sanctions on UNITA diamonds. It was estimated that $350–420 million worth of Angolan diamonds were smuggled into neighbouring countries in

Table 4.2 *UN sanctions on conflict commodities*

Country	Resolution	Year	Commodity sanctioned
Cambodia	S/RES/792	1992	Timber
Angola	S/RES/1173	1998	All diamonds not certified by the government
Sierra Leone	S/RES/1306	2000	All rough diamonds pending the creation of a certification scheme
Liberia	S/RES/1343	2001	All rough diamonds
Liberia	S/RES/1478	2003	Timber
Côte d' Ivoire	S/RES/1643	2005	Rough diamonds

Source: Adapted from Le Billon, 2003

2000 – approximately half Angola's diamond production (Fleshman, 2001, p15). Liberia's continual violation of the sanctions on diamonds from Sierra Leone (which exported approximately $300 million in 1999 when its own productive capacity did not even reach $10 million (GlobalWitness, 2001b))[10] led to the imposition of sanctions upon its own diamonds as well (which later led to the paradoxical situation of Liberian diamonds being smuggled through Sierra Leone after sanctions on the latter were lifted). Timber sanctions on Liberia were more effective, as logs are harder to smuggle than diamonds. Although sanctions have had some impact – one UNITA lobbyist told one of the authors that thanks to diamond sanctions in Angola, he had had to go out and get a proper job – UN smart sanctions on natural resources have not been wholly effective.

Where the UN has sought to impose sanctions on belligerents, their implementation has been left to individual member states, and attempts to enforce them have only been made sporadically. Whilst all UN member states have (as part of their UN Charter commitments) agreed to accept and carry out the decisions of the Security Council, there is no effective means of monitoring and ensuring compliance. The sanctions committees within the Security Council are only meant to review submissions by member states on how sanctions are being implemented and, despite routine laundering of conflict commodities, there has been widespread reluctance to impose secondary sanctions upon states that violate the original sanctions (Le Billon, 2003).

A proxy strategy has developed, though, of using reports by ad hoc 'panels of experts', in which a panel of technical experts is convened to report publicly on areas specified in their mandate (normally, sanctions violations) – that is, to 'name and shame' violating countries. Panels of experts have been formed for DRC, Angola, Sierra Leone and Liberia, amongst others, and have provided the Security Council with in-depth information about the situation on the ground.

Although their reports have done much to bring the debate about conflict resources to the Security Council, each panel is created as is needed and is then disbanded, meaning that there is little continuity or development of institutional knowledge within the UN, and also that each panel is costly and time-consuming to create from scratch. Coordination is lacking between the different panels, and thus there is no means of pooling information gathered on individuals by different panels.

Panels have relatively restricted mandates – either to examine sanctions busting, as was the case with the First Panel on Angola, or to examine resource exploitation, as was the case with the First Panel on DRC. In DRC, only a weapons embargo was imposed upon the country, with the panel being given a wide remit to expose which individuals and companies were exploiting natural resources in a manner which benefited from, or helped to fuel, the conflict.

This proved controversial later on, when the DRC panel named a host of companies alleged to have broken international law and violated the OECD Guidelines on Multinational Enterprises, but provided little evidence on how these conclusions had been reached. While the panel's work led to the disengagement of several companies operating in the region, controversy about its 'naming and shaming' strategy meant that it subsequently chose to provide details of violations in a sealed submission, which was only made available to Security Council members.

Controversy over the credibility of the panel's findings relating to individual companies also overshadowed the recognition and documentation of the role of 'mass scale looting' and 'the systematic and systemic exploitation of natural resources' in DRC's war, and may have hindered stronger international action on that front (UN, 2001, pp8–9). The need for a more professional and systematic set of guidelines for panel operations was also highlighted by the flawed and opaque process through which some companies' cases were suddenly declared 'resolved' by the panel without any clear parameters or explanation being provided.

UN smart sanctions on natural resources, whilst not wholly ineffective, are failing to achieve the impact that they could. This is because the machinery involved in applying sanctions and then monitoring them is ad hoc, inconsistent and incoherent, as well as being subject to the whims of the permanent members of the Security Council. Also, conflict diamonds, in particular, are notoriously easy to smuggle. If freebooters and others are going to be deterred effectively from pursuing natural resource wealth through recourse to violence, and if those who are already doing so are to be punished effectively, the mechanisms through which sanctions are currently implemented need to be reformed to make them more proactive, professional, coordinated and impartial.

Of course, trading partners do not need to wait for the UN; unilateral trade sanctions (and, to a lesser extent, sanctions imposed by regional organizations) can also be applied. These are often quicker than following the UN route and, since they are voluntarily imposed by a trading partner through a sovereign political decision, tend to be better implemented. The wider international community can also encourage bilateral trading partners to take action. The

US Congress FY95 Foreign Operations Act, for example, which threatened to cut off aid to Thailand if it continued to assist the Khmer Rouge, led to the closure of the Thai–Cambodian border and so cut off the illegal timber business, which in turn contributed to the end of the hostilities.

Reforming UN sanctions

Numerous recommendations have recently been produced on how to reform UN sanctions, including the Stockholm Process, which looked at how to make targeted sanctions effective, the UN Security Council's own reports, and those of the Secretary-General's High-Level Panel on Threats, Challenges and Change.

Generally, sanctions have been more successful where their goals have been modest, targeted commodities were clearly specified, the target country was economically weak, politically unstable and smaller than the country imposing sanctions, and the sender and the target conducted substantial trade and were otherwise 'friendly [i.e. cooperative] toward one another'. The impact was maximized by imposing sanctions quickly and decisively, and where the sender avoided high costs to itself (Le Billon, 2003).

Recommendations for improving the UN system have generally focused on reforming the sanctions committees, which work with limited time and resources, do not coordinate with each other or effectively disseminate information – and have called for a standard mandate for sanctions committees, as well as a permanent sanctions coordinator to improve their coherence and coordination. Although these proposals are aiming in the right direction, they are in reality merely tinkering with a system that is primarily run on a part-time basis by states' representatives to the UN, rather than by professionals with a strong practical and theoretical knowledge of how best to apply and monitor sanctions.

Sanctions committees and the ad hoc panel mechanism would benefit from being brought together under a panel process mandated to keep the Security Council informed of developing conflicts in which conflict resources were a factor, and then to monitor states' compliance with existing sanctions regimes. This permanent panel could have a small secretariat with a large number of experts available to call on as necessary. Expertise and speed of response are crucial to effective sanctions, given that sanctions work best when targets are clearly defined and decisively applied to starve the conflict of revenues near the start, rather than part-way through, when belligerents have already built up significant materiel and capital.

By creating a permanent capacity within the Security Council, not only would there be continuity and coordination in examining natural resource-related conflict and sanctions, there would also be capacity for the panel to keep the Security Council informed on conflicts that would otherwise not have been brought to its attention. Furthermore, it would be able to continue the role of reporting on sanctions violators, a function that is currently only used sporadically, when the Security Council considers it necessary. At the present time, the sanctions committees do not monitor sanctions violators, but rather collate the data given to them by member states, who are required to police themselves; a permanent panel of experts would be able to discover for itself what violations were actually occurring on the ground, and thus which individuals and states needed to be punished and what needed to be done to prevent further violations. Sanctions committees could be effectively abolished, with the permanent panel advising the Security Council directly.

The current UN system also lacks any real punitive element. Although being named and shamed may be problematic, given the huge potential profits from sanctions busting more credible deterrents are necessary. Naming and shaming needs to be complemented with measures such as travel bans and asset freezes. To be effective, these need to be entered into national domestic legislation, and sanctions busting properly criminalized, thus giving law enforcement officials a clear mandate. Often by the time that a sanctions buster has been found to be operating in a certain jurisdiction and the authorities have scrabbled round to work out what powers they have to act, the person has fled and the money has disappeared.

States should set about making the violation of UN sanctions a crime with extraterritorial jurisdiction, so that sanctions violators identified by the permanent panel of experts can be arrested and tried, providing a major deterrent to those individuals – the middlemen and brokers – who seek to continue making money from conflict resources even after sanctions have been applied.

UN peacekeeping or observer missions could also be used to enforce sanctions as part of their mandate and be required to report sanctions violations to the UN expert panel. This has occurred on occasion: military observers in Cambodia attached to the UN Transitional Authority were posted at certain border crossings to monitor the timber sanctions, though they were not empowered to interdict the illegal exports they reported, even though those violations that they were reporting would ultimately make their job of keeping the peace more difficult.

Together, these four reforms – better targeted sanctions, a permanent panel of experts to oversee sanctions implementation, criminalizing sanctions busting and allowing UN peacekeepers to enforce sanctions – would greatly enhance the effectiveness of sanctions as a response to the conflict resource problem. There is also a need for more coordinated monitoring of Security Council decisions, more debate in their initial drafting, and perhaps even a specific 'UN Security Council-Watch' organization.

By having a definition of conflict resources that is easy to apply as a 'red flag' for commodities coming from conflict zones, the permanent panel would be able to bring to the Security Council instances when a natural resource was being used to fund conflict, and to demonstrate objectively how this was the case. This would allow the Security Council to apply sanctions almost automatically, without partisan feelings coming into play. Combined with set secondary sanctions, and penal measures to punish those the permanent panel of experts believed to be violating sanctions and efforts by the UN, regional organizations and states to monitor trade flows out of the sanctioned state, this would help sanctions genuinely to deter military–political entrepreneurship.

Tools: Licensing systems

Blanket restrictions on trade, such as the UN sanctions on conflict resources examined above, are clearly inappropriate where the domestic government is struggling to cope with illegal behaviour, or where economic and social development may well depend on the legitimate exploitation of the resources in question, or where the conflict resources may be smuggled into neighbouring countries (unless those countries' governments are themselves colluding in the smuggling). A more targeted solution is to develop systems to identify and license resources produced free of conflict, or legally, which then allows importing countries to bar entry to unlicensed – and therefore presumably conflict-related or illegal – products.

In this section, we examine licence or permit systems in operation or under development for one conflict resource (diamonds) and three natural resources produced illegally (wildlife, fish and timber).[11] We also look briefly at voluntary certification and labelling schemes.[12]

Conflict diamonds: The Kimberley Process

The Kimberley Process on conflict diamonds came into operation on 1 January 2003, and now involves 45 countries as full participants.[13] The process was initiated by a number of southern African countries who decided, in early 2000, to take action to stop the flow of conflict diamonds to the market while at the same time protecting the legitimate diamond industry – in the wake of the limitations of UN Security Council sanctions, including controls on the import of rough diamonds from Angola and Sierra Leone.

The system revolves around the certification of exports. Producer countries control the production and transport of rough diamonds from mine to point of export. Shipments of rough diamonds are sealed in tamper-resistant containers and a forgery-resistant Kimberley Process certificate is issued for each shipment. Importing countries inspect the seal and the certificate (and sometimes the contents) at the time of import, and prohibit the import of rough diamonds not accompanied by a certificate issued by a Kimberley Process participant. Similarly, transit countries ensure that only rough diamonds accompanied by a Kimberley Process certificate are permitted to enter the chain of transactions from import to export. Imports from and exports to non-participants in the process are prohibited, though in fact process participants currently account for 99.8 per cent of global rough diamond production.[14]

Participants undertake to establish internal systems to implement and enforce the certification scheme, including establishing suitable penalties for transgressions. The Process Participation Committee examines each country's national regulations to see if they meet the required minimum standards; if they do not the country is excluded from the process. The first round of scrutiny resulted in 20 out of 58 countries being excluded, of whom 10 have now been readmitted.

Participants also undertake a series of regular review visits to examine the operation of national regulations on the ground, and also specific missions in response to indications of non-compliance. As a result of one such mission, in July 2004 the Republic of Congo became the first country to be expelled from the process, after it persisted in certifying diamonds as originating in Congo when it was clear that it was exporting far more than it was capable of producing.

Simple examination of production, import and export data can also reveal discrepancies. The process recommends, amongst other things, that the names of individuals and companies convicted of breaches of the certification scheme should be made known to all participants. In January 2003 the diamond industry introduced a system of self-regulation to support the process, involving a system of warranties (for all diamonds, not just rough diamonds) underpinned through the verification of individual companies by independent auditors and supported by internal penalties set by the industry. The effectiveness of the system is not monitored, however, and several breaches of it have been exposed.

Although the Kimberley Process certification scheme has only been in existence since 2003, the indications are that it has had some success in excluding conflict diamonds from world markets. It very rapidly developed to cover the vast majority of rough diamond production and trade, seizures of smuggled rough diamonds have increased in number, and anecdotal evidence suggests that non-certified stones are becoming steadily harder to sell.[15] Its inspection scheme for certificates is stricter than CITES, for example (see below), and the participation of industry is helpful. The general problem of corruption and lack of enforcement in all diamond-exporting conflict zones, however, renders enforcement more difficult; rough diamonds can be smuggled out of conflict zones into process participant countries, and thereby 'laundered' into the legitimate trade. It may be possible to introduce full monitoring of the chain of custody from mine to export ('internal controls' in process terminology). The limitation of the scheme to rough diamonds may also lead to many more diamonds being processed in order to be traded outside the system.

Wildlife: CITES

CITES aims to protect endangered species from over-exploitation by controlling international trade, under a system of import and export permits. Almost 33,000 species are listed on different appendices to the treaty, depending on the degree to which their survival is in danger, and trade is only permitted under a system of export and import permits issued by national management authorities; trade in the most endangered species, for example, need both export and import permits (Reeve, 2002).

A key weakness of CITES (and potentially of any licensing system) is that the export and import permits effectively acquire a value, opening up possibilities for fraud, theft and corruption in issuing them, or tampering (such as changing the numbers of specimens covered) while in use. Falsification of CITES permits is a common problem, particularly for high-value products such as caviar. Theft and sale of blank documents similarly undermines the system. In theory, for an export permit to be issued, the management authority of the exporting state must be satisfied that the specimen was not obtained in contravention of the state's laws for the protection of fauna and flora. In practice, however, this is often not observed, thanks to a lack of capacity, or corruption.

Other weaknesses lie in the cross-checking of the documents against each other, and against what is actually in the shipment; there are obvious problems in correctly identifying species, out of the huge number listed in the appendices. Some countries lack the capacity to operate the system correctly, with insufficient numbers of inadequately trained and paid staff, and a lack of basic equipment.

Even in highly developed countries it is clear that the CITES permit system is subject to abuse. An analysis of mahogany imports into the US in 1997–98 (mahogany is the most commonly traded timber species listed under CITES) estimated that at least 25 per cent of sawnwood imports (worth more than $17 million a year) was illegal; the figure did not include trade unreported to US Customs, and the true magnitude was therefore likely to be much higher (Blundell, 2000).

Nevertheless, despite all these problems, CITES has proved reasonably successful. Its secretariat provides training and (limited) capacity building, and coordinates review missions to parties. Trade measures can – and have – been used very effectively against countries failing to implement CITES controls. Most importantly, perhaps, no species listed on CITES' appendices has ever become extinct.

Fish: The CCAMLR Catch Documentation Scheme

The Convention on the Conservation of Antarctic Marine Living Resources (CCAMLR) regulates activities associated with the rational utilization and management of marine living resources in the Southern Ocean. The CCAMLR Catch Documentation Scheme for the Patagonian toothfish, a heavily (and frequently illegally) fished deep-sea species, became binding on all parties in May 2000.[16] The scheme is designed to track the landings and trade flows of toothfish caught in the convention area and, where possible, in adjacent waters, and to limit catches to the national allocation of catch areas and sizes. CCAMLR members are required to ensure that all of their flagged vessels fishing for toothfish are specifically authorized to do so, and complete catch document forms for all catches landed or transhipped; document forms are not to be issued to non-authorized ships. Non-members of CCAMLR are entitled to join the scheme if they fulfil the same requirements.

All landings or transhipments of toothfish catches at CCAMLR members' ports are only permitted if they are accompanied by a valid form, and any export or re-export of toothfish must also be accompanied by the form countersigned by a responsible government official. Where shipments are split, as is often the case, the paper trail is maintained. Customs authorities often carry out cross-checks of weight of fish against the data included in the documents.

The CCAMLR secretariat holds the central register of all completed catch document forms, and satellite monitoring technology has been used for verification. There is interest in moving towards a completely electronic rather than paper-based system, with a central database maintained by the secretariat, and a trial system recently came into operation. If extended to all countries, however, this would probably create capacity problems for some; many customs offices are small and poorly equipped, and may not possess computers or internet access.

Attempts to evade the scheme have included some incidences of document fraud, but at a fairly low level, representing perhaps about 500 tonnes out of a total annual catch of 30,000 tonnes.[17] Forms could be simply photocopied and used for multiple shipments; eventual collation of the documents would spot the fraud, but only several months later. Introduction of a fully electronic system should deal with this problem, and is seen as a more effective measure than making the forms themselves more tamper resistant. It would also help in expediting clearance of shipments where there is some doubt over the documentation; for obvious reasons, suspect shipments cannot be held indefinitely. There is also the possibility of vessels simulating GPS signals to mislead the satellite tracking technology.

The scheme has had a clear impact on the price of toothfish, with a 20–30 per cent price differential developing between illegal and legitimately caught fish (Agnew, 2002). Its main problem to date is the non-participation of two major importing countries, Canada and China; the latter in particular, with a large and growing processing capacity, may pose a significant problem in the future.

Timber: The EU FLEGT initiative

No global agreement regulates forestry and the timber trade (though a small number of tree species are listed under CITES). In the absence of a suitable multilateral framework, and spurred by G8 and other discussions on illegal logging, the EC published its Action Plan on Forest Law Enforcement, Governance and Trade (FLEGT) in May 2003. Its centrepiece is a new timber licensing system, which will require the presence of an export permit, or legality licence, to accompany exports from FLEGT partner countries to any part of the EU; products lacking such a licence will be refused entry, and possibly confiscated by EU customs authorities. The necessary legislation to establish the import controls was adopted in late 2005, and negotiations are currently under way with key timber-producing countries for the 'voluntary partnership agreements' needed to bring it fully into force.

In order for the scheme to function properly, the licences granted under it need to guarantee that the products have been produced and processed legally right along their chain of custody, including their origin, land or concession ownership, and whether harvesting and processing (e.g. at the sawmill), transport and export have all been carried out in conformity with the laws of the country of the origin, including payment of taxes, charges and export duties. There is no shortage of model systems available; in several countries, private surveillance and certification companies have been retained by governments to carry out functions such as collecting export duties or monitoring production, and many of their systems are easily adaptable to verifying legality of production.[18]

Questions over the potential role of independent monitors in acting as an external check on the validity of the system, or over a possible 'whistle-blowing' function for NGOs and local communities, remain to be resolved. Given the lack of enforcement capacity and the extent of corruption in many producer countries, the principle of independent verification of the licensing system is an important one.

Clearly there will be costs associated with the establishment of the licensing system, although experiences with similar systems suggest that they are not likely to be very high – in the region of $1–3 per cubic metre for a third-party control system, compared to export prices for tropical logs and sawnwood of $150–250 and $450–600 per cubic metre (EC, 2004). Financial assistance for the new system is expected to be a feature of the partnership agreements, and in any case their running costs may well be repaid through improved tax collection. There will also be some costs at the EU end, in terms of additional resources for customs agencies, but again these do not seem likely to be very high; European customs authorities are well used to operating licensing systems, and the main ports through which timber from the likely partner countries enter are relatively few in number.

The obvious weakness of the proposed licensing system is that some producer countries may choose not to enter into partnership agreements, in which case no controls will be applied to their exports to the EU. This in turn may provide a relatively straightforward means of transhipping illegal products from partner countries through non-partner countries, effectively 'laundering' them into legitimate markets. It is also not yet clear to what extent partner countries will be required to regulate their own imports to exclude illegal material; as timber is often produced in one country, processed in another (increasingly, China) and then exported to consumer markets, this is an important matter to be resolved.

It should be remembered, however, that the licensing system is not intended to operate in isolation. It should be reinforced by other components of the FLEGT initiative, in particular the use of government procurement policy to source legal timber, from whatever origin (see 'Tools: Procurement') and the possible adoption of additional national or EU legislation to allow more effective action against imports of illegal timber.

Voluntary systems

Government-run internationally agreed licensing systems are not the only means of identifying legal products in trade. For some natural resources, a series of voluntary schemes, including product labelling and certification, have been established to provide additional information to consumers to encourage them to purchase sustainably managed products – which generally means legally produced as well.

Timber

The number of forest certification initiatives has more than doubled since 1996, and there are now over 40 schemes under development in more than 30 different countries (Rugge, 2000). These schemes are intended either to designate products that have been produced in accordance with a set of criteria and indicators of sustainable timber production – perhaps the most well-known is that run by the Forest Stewardship Council (FSC) – or to classify an organization or company in terms of its ability to manage all aspects of its business in an environmentally sound manner – such as the European Eco-Management and Audit Scheme, or the ISO 14000 series.

'Sustainably produced' is of course not the same as 'legally produced' timber; to obtain a sustainability or stewardship certification, a much wider range of criteria must be met. The award of an FSC certificate, for example, requires 10 principles and 56 specific criteria of good forest management to be met. Nevertheless, many schemes denoting the 'sustainability' of their products also possess the requirement that production takes place within the law of the country concerned. For example, the award of an FSC certificate is predicated on adherence to all applicable laws of the country, including international agreements to which the country is a party, requires all prescribed fees, royalties, taxes and other charges to be paid, and forests under approved management must be protected from illegal harvesting, settlement or other unauthorized activities. As with the FLEGT licence, the validity of the system requires effective chain of custody control from the forest to the point at which the product is labelled. Certified wood has to be kept separate from uncertified wood at all phases of transportation, production, distribution, sale and export.

There are five main operational forest certification schemes covering timber and wood products in international trade: FSC, the Programme for the Endorsement of Forest Certification schemes (which covers many separate national schemes), the Canadian Standards Association's Sustainable Forest Management Standard (CSA), the American Sustainable Forestry Initiative and the Malaysian Timber Certification Scheme. An assessment for the UK government's timber procurement policy concluded that all five were adequate to guarantee legality of production, according to the criteria specified by the government.

In practice, however, certified forests represent a small (though rapidly growing) proportion of the world's forests; some important regions, such as

Africa, possess very few certified areas. As of May 2005, the total area of forests certified worldwide was approximately 241 million hectares, or about 6.2 per cent of the world's forests – an increase of more than a third since 2004 (UNECE/FAO, 2005, p85). In western Europe, approximately half of the total forest area is certified, compared to about one third in Canada and the US and no more than 1 per cent in developing countries.

Fisheries

The use of certification or catch document schemes is encouraged in several international agreements, such as the FAO's International Plan of Action on IUU Fishing, and similar systems are applied widely at the national level, including the USA's Certification of Origin of Tuna and Tuna Tracking and Verification Systems, Japan's reporting requirements (including area of capture) for all imports or transportation of tuna into Japan by boat, and the EU's labelling of all fish products (including area of capture).

The best known voluntary certification system aimed at the final consumer market is probably that of the Marine Stewardship Council (MSC), established in 1997 to promote environmentally responsible stewardship of the world's fisheries. The MSC has developed an environmental standard for sustainable and well-managed fisheries, based on the FAO Code of Conduct for Responsible Fisheries, and uses a product label to reward environmentally responsible management and practices. Fisheries anywhere can apply to be independently assessed against the standard, by independent certification bodies approved or accredited by the MSC – along the same lines as the FSC. Once certified, companies wishing to use the MSC products undergo chain-of-custody certification that guarantees traceability of MSC-labelled seafood, ensuring that it has been separated from non-certified product at every stage of the production from the boat to the plate.

The MSC covers only a tiny proportion of world fisheries, though it is growing rapidly. By the end of 2005, 300 products from 14 fisheries had been awarded the MSC label. Like timber certification, it is not primarily designed to identify the legality of a product, though that is a side effect.

Conclusions

Import and export licensing systems are not uncommon in international trade. In addition to those examined above, licensing, permit or 'prior informed consent' schemes are included in the Montreal Protocol on ozone-depleting substances and the Basel Convention on transboundary movements of hazardous waste, and will be introduced under the Cartagena Protocol on biosafety (controlling trade in genetically modified products) and the Rotterdam Convention on hazardous chemicals and pesticides in international trade, which have both recently entered into force. All of these have been introduced to regulate the trade in specified products, and to exclude from international markets products that are deemed undesirable for some reason – often because they have been illegally produced.

Existing licensing systems, however, tend to suffer from a number of problems:

- A reliance on paper certificates to accompany the traded goods in question opens up possibilities for fraud, theft and corruption in issuing them.
- There is (usually) no independent verification of whether the products that are licensed have been obtained in accordance with the relevant regulations.
- Movement documents are often not adequately cross-checked against each other (e.g. export against import permits) or against the goods they are accompanying.
- Products can be moved across borders without monitoring (e.g. at unregulated crossing points) or can be concealed or disguised as legal material.
- Coverage of only some categories of products (e.g. rough diamonds in the Kimberley Process) can lead to processing of products to avoid the controls.
- Non-participation of key countries can undermine the system.

Equally, though, there has been substantial experience in operating licensing systems, tackling these problems and coming up with innovative responses. Lessons can therefore be drawn for the introduction of new systems, and the improvement of existing ones, as can be seen from the descriptions of ongoing developments above.

When are licensing systems preferable to sanctions? Clearly, sanctions are most effective when products originating from a limited and clearly defined area – one experiencing conflict – are to be excluded from external markets. A licensing system is more desirable when a particular category of products originating from many countries – for example, illegally produced products – are to be excluded. In this case sanctions are impracticable because they are too blunt a weapon: they would block the export of legitimate as well as illegitimate products, and in any case cannot realistically be applied against a large number of countries.

The two tools are not, however, mutually exclusive, and licensing systems can also be effective as a back up to sanctions. As the section on 'Tools: Sanctions' made clear, sanctions can often be relatively easy to evade, through smuggling the sanctioned products from the conflict zone into neighbouring countries, and then into international commerce. There is then no real alternative to a licensing system – for example, the Kimberley Process – to exclude the undesirable products from world markets.

Do such licensing systems have to be applied on a product-by-product basis, or is there a case for a general licensing system aimed at excluding all illegal products, or all conflict resources? The volume of world trade – even just in natural resources – is so large, and the range of products covered so wide, that it seems completely impracticable to establish a licensing system covering all of them. World trade proceeds on the assumption that the normal documents accompanying traded products (manifests, bills of landing, etc.) are in most cases an adequate indication of legality. Adding an extra layer of documentation on top, together with the associated costs of verification and monitoring, is only justified either where there is convincing evidence of widespread evasion of laws (e.g. in timber) and/or where particular (e.g. irreversible) damage may be caused where the trade is not regulated in this way – say, in endangered species, or GM products.

Certification systems like the FSC, MSC and others have value in promoting the sale of sustainably – and legally – produced timber and fish products, and in piloting the use of the kind of tracking and verification mechanisms necessary to guarantee legality. By themselves, however, they cannot hope to capture a significant share of the market; there will always be importers willing to undercut them with uncertified – and almost always cheaper – products. It was partly an awareness of the shortcomings of certification systems in ensuring legal imports into the EU (to be fair to them, of course, this is not what they were designed to do) that led to the FLEGT initiative for a timber licensing system.

Tools: Procurement

The counterpart of excluding illegal products from consumer markets is building markets for verified legal products. This can be achieved through public procurement policy, which covers government purchases, and private sector action to secure its supply chains.

Public procurement

The use of government procurement policy offers a promising route to building markets for legal products; it is estimated that the public sector accounts for about 20 per cent of purchases in most developed countries, and thereby can exert substantial influence on the market.

The EU FLEGT initiative (described above) encourages all EU member states to use public procurement policies to promote markets for legal timber and timber products. Five EU states – Belgium, Denmark, France, The Netherlands and the UK – have all recently introduced systems that require proof of legal origin for central government purchases of timber and wood products, and a number of others are considering them.

There is a danger, of course, that the development of different criteria for procurement policies in different parts of the European single market could create barriers to enterprises in producer countries exporting into the EU, and it may be that some coordination of the schemes will occur in due course. All of the five countries listed above differ in their criteria and definitions. The French and Dutch policies are aimed primarily at sourcing sustainable timber; such timber should of course be legal, but this is a side effect rather than the main aim. The Danish and British systems have both been designed to procure legal *and* sustainable timber, recognizing that while sustainable timber is desirable, it may not always be available in sufficient quantities, and therefore a minimum standard of proof of legality should be required for all purchases.

Similarly, those four countries use different definitions of 'sustainably produced'. One particular area of disagreement is the question of whether social criteria over and above those legislated for in the producer country itself – for example, international health and safety standards amongst the logging workforce, or land tenure rights of indigenous communities – can be included.

Whatever the criteria they choose, all these countries have to face the question of how to operationalize their policies – how in practice can they make sure that government purchasers are buying products that meet the criteria. The UK has achieved this through the establishment of a Central Point of Expertise on Timber (CPET), set up to evaluate the extent to which the main certification systems met UK criteria, and also to evaluate alternative documentation that might show legality and sustainability where products are not covered by any of the certification schemes. (EU procurement rules do not permit member states to specify simply products covered by particular schemes; they have to rest on criteria.) CPET also carries out training and awareness-raising exercises and monitors the implementation of the policy amongst government departments.

In most of these countries, the procurement policy is too new for its impacts yet to be measurable. However, UK policy has already had an observed impact. A regular survey of price premiums for verified legal and certified sustainable timber in the UK market, commissioned by the UK Timber Trade Federation, revealed that certified products now dominate a large section of the UK softwood trade, though due to plentiful supply do not command a premium. In contrast, distribution channels for certified hardwood are still poorly developed, availability is restricted, and premiums are still widely demanded, in some cases as high as 30 per cent (Oliver, 2006).

Central, regional and local governments throughout the developed world already possess or are developing a variety of 'green' procurement policies. Many local authorities, for example, encourage the use of sustainably produced timber in building projects, and authorities at all levels often promote the use of recycled paper. In principle, it should not be too difficult to incorporate criteria for the legality of timber and wood products into these policies, and often no new primary legislation is needed. The experience of the EU member states currently implementing such policies provides useful lessons for other countries.

Of the natural resources considered in this chapter, timber (and wood products) is the only one purchased extensively by government, so the use of public procurement policy to exclude illegal products seems likely to be restricted to this sector. The definitions used in the various EU states' policies should all exclude conflict timber, so again public procurement policy is of value in this regard.

Private sourcing

In addition to public sector activities, the private sector can take action to ensure that its own supply chains are free of illegal, unsustainable and/or conflict-related products. In the timber sector, many companies and trade associations have already taken action to source legal timber, partly as a response to government regulation, current and anticipated, but also to a growing understanding of the role of illegal logging in undercutting markets for legal (and sustainable) products, and also to direct consumer and NGO pressure.

In the EU, many companies have responded to government procurement policy, but also to the expectation of the FLEGT licensing system coming into force. A number of industry associations have developed codes of conduct for their members and begun to work directly with suppliers in producer countries, encouraging – and in some cases assisting – them to ensure that their raw materials derive from legal sources.

For example, the UK Timber Trade Federation's Indonesia Action Plan, initiated in mid-2003, included independent legality audits of 16 sawmills across that country, and revealed that all of them had problems meeting the most basic legality requirements. However, it was estimated that they could take action to resolve these problems over perhaps two or three years, and the Federation has begun to work with these sawmills on developing individual action plans for improvements. It is also hoping to establish a common auditing framework for similar work in the future.

As noted earlier, an important driver for the development of the Kimberley Process has been the involvement of the diamond industry through the World Diamond Council. This experience shows how private sector activity can help encourage public policy development, as the responsible portion of the industry lobbies for government action to ensure that its own products are not undercut by illegitimate – and cheaper – products.

WTO implications

Trade controls of the type considered above in this chapter – including sanctions, licensing systems and public procurement policies – bring about at least the potential for conflict with WTO rules. Whether a conflict would really arise is entirely speculative – but this has not stopped opponents of trade controls (for whatever reason) raising the spectre of a clash as a reinforcement to their position.

There has never been a WTO dispute involving CITES or CCAMLR (or any other MEA, including licensing schemes), and the application of these licensing systems within multilateral frameworks makes it unlikely, as there is nothing in WTO rules to allow it to override commitments reached in other international agreements.

The Kimberley Process has, however, been discussed explicitly within the WTO: in late 2002, a number of participating states applied to the WTO

General Council for a waiver from their WTO obligations in this regard, and the waiver was duly granted in February 2003, to extend to 31 December 2006. Most process signatories, however, did not support this move, implying as it did that the process contravened basic WTO disciplines, which they did not accept. It can be argued that a waiver is unnecessary because of the terms of Article XXI(c) of GATT, which exempt from GATT requirements a WTO member taking 'any action in pursuance of its obligations under the UN Charter for the maintenance of international peace and security'.

The potential interaction of the EU's FLEGT timber licensing scheme has also been discussed, though not particularly within the WTO. Japan has raised the general issue of illegal logging and the possibility of trade controls within the WTO Committee on Trade and Environment (probably because, with an extensive history of trade protectionism, the Japanese government now tends to bend over backwards to demonstrate how opposed to protectionism it is), but without generating any useful debate or conclusions. The introduction of the EU scheme through a series of bilateral agreements rather than as part of a multilateral framework does raise rather different questions, but it seems highly unlikely that any of the countries involved in the agreements – which will be the only ones affected by the trade restrictions – would ever open a dispute within the WTO. WTO rules will, however, constrain the EU's adoption of additional measures to control imports of illegal timber from non-partner countries (currently under discussion) – though at least one possible outcome, the adoption of legislation to make the possession or handling of timber produced illegally overseas illegal in the EU, is not a border measure and should not raise any WTO implications.

Nevertheless, considering previous WTO jurisprudence, it is possible to reach some tentative conclusions about the design of policy instruments, which may affect trade:

- The less trade-disruptive the measure involved, the lower the chance of a successful challenge under the WTO – a requirement simply for labelling, or government procurement policy, would be less likely to fail than an import ban.
- The more it can be shown that less trade-disruptive measures – such as preferential tariffs – have been attempted and have not proved effective, the greater the chance more trade-disruptive measures have of being found acceptable. This possibly even extends to non-trade-related efforts, such as capacity-building assistance to the exporting countries concerned.
- The more precisely targeted the measure, the less the chance of a successful challenge. An embargo applied against a country's entire exports of a particular natural resource because some of them were believed to be illegal would be more vulnerable to a WTO challenge than an embargo applied only against products that could be proved to be illegal, or not shown to be legal. In the latter case, adherence to an internationally accepted means of determining legality in this context – for example, a requirement for

chain-of-custody documentation audited by an independent third party – would also help to justify the measure.

- The less discriminatory the measure is, the lower the chance of a successful challenge. A very strong case could be made under the WTO if a country was applying more restrictive measures (e.g. a requirement for legality identification) to imports than it was to its own production.
- The greater the effort to ensure that a measure is multilaterally acceptable, the less it is likely to be challenged. Recent WTO dispute cases suggest that even unilateral measures applied while a multilateral agreement is in the process of being negotiated may be acceptable.

With the exception of the instances noted above, the general topic of exclusion of undesirable products from international trade has never been discussed within the WTO, even though the facilitation of trade promoted by the organization cannot help but make trade in illegal and conflict-related goods easier too. WTO negotiators' inbuilt bias towards trade liberalization and hostility towards any discussion of trade restrictions, however, and their general lack of knowledge about environmental policy in general and environmental crime in particular, must create doubt over whether any broader discussion would generate any useful outcome. It is possible, of course, that the issue may be forced upon the WTO by a trade dispute, but at the moment that seems quite unlikely. Most of the measures are being adopted by multilateral agreement, none of them yet affect very substantial proportions of world trade, and most countries are likely to be reluctant to be seen to trying to use the WTO to force possibly illegal or conflict-related goods on to unwilling consumers in foreign countries.

It seems far better for measures to control the flow of illegal and conflict-related trade in natural resources to be developed and implemented within forums that understand their purpose and operation. As long as these instruments abide by the general WTO principles of non-discrimination, transparency and predictability – and there is no reason why they should not – the matter of their interaction with the WTO should remain, as it now is, speculative.

Conclusions and recommendations

The purpose of this chapter is to examine the various policy tools that can be used to exclude conflict resources and illegally produced resources from international markets, and thereby to deny revenue to those exploiting the resources in breach of national laws and international treaties, and/or where exploitation in a context of violent conflict contributes to, benefits from, or results in, the commission of serious violations of human rights, international humanitarian law or violations amounting to crimes under international law.

Earlier sections of the chapter have outlined the circumstances in which particular tools may be most appropriately used. To summarize:

- Sanctions are appropriate where the origin of the products is geographically limited and easily defined; they will also be more effective where the products are difficult to disguise (timber will be more easily interdicted than diamonds, for example).
- Licensing systems are appropriate where the origin of the products is not geographically limited (e.g. for most illegal products) and where the products can be smuggled relatively easily (e.g. diamonds).
- Sanctions and licensing systems can work well together where products from one region are subject to sanctions but are being laundered into international trade through neighbouring regions.
- Voluntary certification schemes can help to exclude illegal and conflict resources, but are unlikely ever to be very effective in this aim, as they are never likely to cover the whole of a particular market (because they are voluntary).
- Procurement policy can also help to establish and protect markets for legitimate products (legal and/or conflict-free), particularly in government purchasing but also in private sector sourcing. Action by the private sector can be triggered by the expectation of government action (procurement, licensing) but can also in turn lead to more pressure for government regulation (as in the Kimberley Process).

Extensive experience now exists in the exclusion of undesirable products from international markets through all of these policy tools, and lessons can and should be drawn for the future development of such measures. It should be remembered that in principle almost any natural resource (including important industrial resources, such as coltan, zinc or uranium, as well as the more high-profile resources such as diamonds) can be vulnerable to illegal exploitation; exploitation that can lead to conflict. Policy-makers should therefore stand ready to deploy the kind of measures described in this chapter with the aim of building markets that exclude illegitimate products and provide guaranteed returns for legitimate ones.

Notes

1   The authors would like to thank Christopher Edwards and Sofia Goinhas of Global Witness for their input to this chapter.
2   All references for this section are from Martin Evans, 'Ni paix ni guerre: the political economy of low-level conflict in the Casamance', Background Paper for HPG Report 13, February 2003, ODI.
3   For more detail on this topic, see Duncan Brack and Gavin Hayman, *International Environmental Crime: The Nature and Control of Environmental Black Markets* (Chatham House, 2002), www.chathamhouse.org.uk/pdf/research/sdp/Environme ntal%20Crime%20Background%20Paper.pdf
4   See, for example, 'Reforming the nearly unreformable', *The Economist*, 5 August 2004.

5   See Ros Reeve, *Policing International Trade in Endangered Species: The CITES Treaty and Compliance* (Chatham House, 2002) for a good summary of CITES-related issues.

6   This best guess is ubiquitous, although nobody seems certain of its origin. One of its first 'official' uses was in a UNEP press release after the 1994 CITES Conference of the Parties in Fort Lauderdale, USA. The figure may have been an extrapolation to the total commercial value of the wildlife trade based on earlier reports that one quarter of all the trade in parrots across the US–Mexican border was illegal.

7   See the website www.illegal-fishing.info for a wide range of documents, briefings and news stories on all aspects of the debate around IUU fishing.

8   In UN terminology, illegal fishing takes place where the fishery is against the law; unreported fishing takes place where legal instruments are in place to control the fishery, but no requirements for reporting, or penalties for non-reporting, exist; and unregulated fishing occurs where legal instruments are not required, not applied, or not adequate.

9   See the website www.illegal-logging.info for a wide range of documents, briefings and news stories on all aspects of the illegal logging debate.

10 Holbrooke, Ambassador R. (2000) 'Statement in the Security Council during the Exploratory Hearing on Sierra Leone Diamonds', United States Permanent Representative to the United Nations, 31 July 2000 cited in Global Witness (2001b). Some of this excess supply may be accounted for by Russian diamonds, smuggled to avoid taxes.

11 For more detail on all these licensing systems, see Duncan Brack, *A Licensing System for Legal Timber* (Chatham House, November 2004), www.illegal-logging. info/papers/Licensing_system_for_legal_timber.pdf).

12 In practice there is no real difference between 'licensing' and 'certification' schemes – they all aim to provide proof, in the form of a licence or certificate or permit, that the product in question has been produced in accordance with particular standards (e.g. of legality, or sustainability, or free of association with conflict). In practice, 'licensing' tends to mean government-run systems and 'certification' voluntary, industry- or NGO-led systems, but this is not a hard and fast distinction (the Kimberley Process, for example, runs a certification scheme).

13 The process defines 'conflict diamonds' as 'rough diamonds used by rebel movements or their allies to finance conflict aimed at undermining legitimate governments, as described in relevant United Nations Security Council (UNSC) resolutions insofar as they remain in effect, or in other similar UNSC resolutions which may be adopted in the future, and as understood and recognized in United Nations General Assembly (UNGA) Resolution 55/56, or in other similar UNGA resolutions which may be adopted in future' – Kimberley Process Certification Scheme Section 1.

14 See www.kimberleyprocess.com:8080/site/

15 See Chair's Report to Plenary Kimberley Process Plenary Meeting, Gatineau, Canada 27–29 October 2004, www.kimberleyprocess.com:8080/site/www_docs/plenary_meetings20/chair_report_to_plenary.pdf

16 See www.ccamlr.org/pu/e/cds/intro.htm

17 David Agnew (Imperial College), personal communication.

18 For more discussion, see ERM, *Feasibility of and Best Options for Systems for the Identification, Verification, Licensing/Certification and Tracking of Legality of Timber and Related Products for Imports into the EU* (May 2003), www.illegal-logging. info/papers/EC_LEGAL_TIMBER_FINAL_REPORT.pdf

References

Agnew, D. (2002) 'The drivers behind black markets: Illegal and unregulated fishing', Paper to RIIA workshop on International Environmental Crime, May 2002

American Forest & Paper Association, Seneca Creek Associates and Wood Resources International (2004) *Illegal Logging and Global Wood Markets: The Competitive Impacts on the US Wood Products Industry*, www.illegal-logging.info/papers/afandpa. pdf accessed in 2006

Bell, T. (2004) 'Soldiers and rebels struggle to control the trade in "Himalayan Viagra"', *Daily Telegraph*, 14 August 2004

Blundell, A. (2000) *Mahogany: Unregulated Trade*, Washington DC, US Environmental Protection Agency

Defenders of Wildlife (1992) Wild Bird Conservation Act, www.defenders.org/wildlife/ birds/04/wbca.html accessed in 2006

Ellis, S. (1999) *The Mask of Anarchy: The Destruction of Liberia and the Religious Dimension of a Civil War*, New York, New York University Press

European Commission (2004) *Impact Assessment of the EU Action Plan for Forest Law Enforcement, Governance and Trade (FLEGT)*, Brussels, EC Directorate General for Development T/2004/002

Evans, M. (2003) 'Ni paix ni guerre: The political economy of low-level conflict in the Casamance', Background Paper for HPG Report 13, London, Overseas Development Institute

Fleshman, M. (2001) '"Conflict diamonds" evade UN sanctions', *Africa Recovery*, vol 15, no 4, p15

Global Witness (1998) 'A rough trade: The role of diamond companies and governments in the Angolan conflict', report, London, Global Witness

Global Witness (2001a) 'Liberia – Strategic Commodities Act', www.globalwitness.org/ campaigns/forests/liberia/downloads/act_strat-com-liberia.htm accessed in 2006

Global Witness (2001b) 'The role of Liberia's logging industry on national and regional insecurity', report, London, Global Witness

Global Witness (2004a) 'Time For transparency: Coming clean on oil, mining and gas revenues', report, London, Global Witness

Global Witness (2004b) 'Same old story: A background study on natural resources in the Democratic Republic of Congo', report, London, Global Witness

Human Rights Watch (2005) *The Curse of Gold*, New York, Human Rights Watch

Integrated Regional Affairs Network (2001) 'Mortality rates remain high', Integrated Regional Affairs Network, 3 September 2001

Integrated Regional Affairs Network (2002) 'UNICEF appeals for $18 million', Integrated Regional Affairs Network; 11 January 2002

Keen, D. (1998) *The Economic Function of Violence in Civil Wars*, Adelphi Paper, no 320, New York, Oxford University Press

Le Billon, P. (2003) 'Getting it done: Instruments of enforcement', in Bannon, I. and Collier, P. (eds), *Natural Resources and Violent Conflict*, Washington DC, World Bank

Marine Resources Assessment Group (2005) 'Review of impacts of illegal, unreported and unregulated fishing on developing countries: Final report', www.passlivelihoods. org.uk/site_files/files/reports/project_id_274/Appendix%204%20MRAG%20Revie w%20of%20IUU%20Fishing%20Impacts.pdf accessed in 2006

Marshall, G. (ed) (1990) *The Barnett Report: A Summary of the Report of the Commission of Inquiry into Aspects of the Timber Industry in Papua New Guinea*, Hobart, Asia-Pacific Action Group

Oliver, R. (2006) 'Price premiums for verified legal and sustainable timber', UK Timber Trade Federation, www.illegal-logging.info/documents.php#177 accessed in 2006

Reeve, R. (2002) *Policing International Trade in Endangered Species: The CITES Treaty and Compliance*, London, RIIA/Earthscan

Renner, M. (2002) 'The Anatomy of Resource Wars', *World Watch Paper 162*, Washington DC, Worldwatch Institute

Ross, M. (2005) 'Booty futures: Africa's civil wars and the futures market for natural resources', manuscript, www.polisci.ucla.edu/faculty/ross/bootyfutures.pdf accessed in 2006

Rugge, I. (2000) *Progress in Timber Certification Schemes Worldwide*, London, Forests Forever

SAMFU (2002) *Plunder: The Silent Destruction of Liberia's Rainforests*, Monrovia, Save My Future Foundation

UN (2001) *Report of the Panel of Experts on the Illegal Exploitation of Natural Resources and Other Forms of Wealth in the Democratic Republic of Congo*, S/2001/357, New York, UN

UN Panel of Experts (2000) *Report of the Panel of Experts Appointed Pursuant to Security Council Resolution 1306 (2000)*, UNSC S/2000/1195, New York, UN

UNECE/FAO (2005) *Forest Products Annual Market Review, 2004–05*, Timber Bulletin, vol LVIII, www.unece.org/trade/timber/docs/fpama/2005/fpama2005a.htm accessed in 2006.

World Bank (1999) *Forest Sector Review*, New York, World Bank

Chapter 5

Promoting Conflict-sensitive Business in Fragile States: Redressing Skewed Incentives

Karen Ballentine

Introduction

One of the central challenges facing the international community today is to reconcile the forces of economic globalization with the achievement of sustainable peace and development. The liberalization of global trade and investment has led to an unprecedented surge in foreign direct investment (FDI) worldwide, including in emerging markets and the developing world. In the aggregate, increased investment has been positively correlated with reduced conflict risk and increased national economic growth, creating jobs and raising living standards.[1] However, and contrary to the confident expectations of ardent globalizers, increased FDI has not delivered these benefits evenly or everywhere. Indeed, in many parts of the developing world, globalization has not only failed to deliver, it has actually served to perpetuate the vicious cycle of conflict and underdevelopment.

This is particularly true in sub-Saharan Africa. Although the region's share of global FDI continues to be modest in absolute terms, on a per capita basis it is significant, not only in strict economic terms but also with regards to its wider impact. Tellingly, the vast share of the region's FDI inflow is directed towards the extractives sector in countries such as Nigeria and Angola. Despite this, these countries continue to rank poorly in terms of political stability, good governance, per capita wealth and other indicators of development and human security.[2]

In explaining the linkages between natural resource dependency, under-development and conflict, much attention has been paid to the economic agendas of criminal groups, warlords, and corrupt elites operating on or beyond the margins of law. However, the focus of this analysis is the otherwise legitimate extractive companies and financial institutions who are the central agents of global trade and investment. Their activities in fragile and war-torn states are problematic not only because they may violate established norms, as some do, but also because they often operate beyond the reach of current normative and regulatory frameworks.

Changing the behaviour of extractive companies, and of market actors generally, requires changing their calculation of value and risk. This means not only changing corporate cultures and business practices but also the broader incentive structure in which they operate. As described in the second part of this chapter, the current structure of opportunity is shaped by a governance deficit that is good for extractive company and investor profit but bad for the wider peace and prosperity of developing countries. Remedy lies in realigning the gross imbalance in costs and benefits. In the section on 'The spectrum of regulatory responses: Ad hoc, uneven and incomplete', I identify three major approaches in the emerging spectrum of regulatory responses: voluntary self-regulation by companies, mandatory regulation by states, and mixed forms that supplement regulation with market rewards. All three are examined in terms of their ability to alter the conduct of particular companies as well as the prevailing incentive structure. Here, I argue that approaches that focus only on the behaviour of extractive companies is to mistake the symptom for the disease. Like other market actors, extractive companies do not operate in a vacuum but in a web of incentives and risks that define the market context in which they operate. Where elites are 'corrupt', rebels 'greedy' or companies 'indifferent' to the externalities they perpetuate, fault also lies in the structure of economic opportunity, not just the particular agent's moral failings, however egregious. If the goal is to reduce the negative developmental, conflict and human rights impacts of natural resource extraction, then efforts that focus on the conduct of particular companies need to be supplemented with policies that address the wider marketplace. I conclude by offering some recommendations of how this might be accomplished.

The global market for natural resources: A permissive playing field for a race to the bottom

It is taken as conventional wisdom that companies and investors prefer a business-friendly environment: one in which national authorities are stable and legitimate, security risks are low, property rights secure, and regimes of taxation and trade favourable. Indeed, the absence of these conditions is a central reason why FDI inflows to manufacturing and tertiary sectors in areas like sub-Saharan Africa remain so small.[3]

Yet, in many fragile states, where administrative capacity and rule of law is weak or absent, even where violent conflict rages,[4] some market actors remain undeterred. These include a range of opportunists – arms traders, private security firms and black marketeers – whose raison d'être is to seek profit from anarchy. Likewise undeterred, however, are multinational extractive companies and their affiliates, who, alongside national governments, are a central focus of this discussion.

The global marketplace for natural resources is shaped by an incentive structure that is highly permissive of aggressive, often predatory, resource exploitation, even in otherwise high-risk settings. Increasingly, the last untapped reservoirs of lucrative and strategic natural resources upon which the extractive industries depend are in regions of the developing world experiencing instability or even violent conflict.

Given the seemingly insatiable global demand for resources, and oil and gas in particular, this trend cannot but continue. In Africa alone, international oil companies are set to invest $50 billion over the next decade in resource-rich developing countries such as Nigeria, Angola, Equatorial Guinea, Gabon, Sudan, Cameroon and São Tomé e Príncipe. Cumulatively, this is the largest investment in African history and one that is estimated to double the continent's oil production over the next decade (Gary and Karl, 2003, p1). The entry of China in the scramble for Africa's oil and gas reserves has added a new sense of urgency to an already intense inter-state competition.[5] While the financial, security and reputational risks to companies are high, they are outweighed by the prospect of enormous profits.

These market factors help explain why multinational extractive companies and their affiliates go where other companies fear to tread. Alone, however, they do not explain why it is that the otherwise 'legitimate' behaviour of these companies often exacerbates corruption, instability and violent conflict. Here, the critical variable is poor governance. Where market regulation is weak, there are few barriers to untrammelled profit seeking. Company competition for lucrative natural resources drives a race to the bottom, both in encouraging the further lowering or evasion of regulatory standards and in enhancing the negative externalities that society bears. This regulatory deficit is manifest at all levels: company, state and inter-state.

Company conduct and misconduct and violent conflict

There can be little doubt that extractive companies invested in fragile parts of the developing world, whether public or private in name, routinely – and often egregiously – engage in self-regarding, even predatory economic activities.[6] There are a variety of ways in which the financial and operational decisions of extractive companies have perpetuated instability and conflict. Some have been the unintended but problematic consequences of legal activities, some the result of illegal conduct. In most cases, however, violence and instability have stemmed from company disregard for the conflict risks that attend their activities. First, the lack of full disclosure of the concession payments, royalties and bonuses paid by companies to host governments creates powerful incentives for official corruption, reinforcing predatory elites, while denying affected citizens critical information by which they might better hold their leaders to account. During the Angolan civil war of the late 1990s, for example, this sort of fiscal opacity enabled the Angolan government to divert some $5 billion in public monies from the state budget (Global Witness, 2004b). In some instances, signature bonuses paid to the Angolan government were used for covert purposes, including suspicious arms deals and elite self-enrichment, all of which severely undermined accountability, civilian security and human rights (Human Rights Watch, 2004, pp28, 50).

Second, in war-torn countries, where the security of plant and personnel are obvious priorities, but local law enforcement is weak or non-existent, companies may seek security however they can get it. In some cases, this has entailed making protection payments to local warlords or rebel groups. In so doing, companies secure a semblance of safety, but at the cost of sustaining combatant capacity to fight. More commonly, companies may contract private security companies or local security forces without screening out those with dubious human rights records and/or a volatile relationship with local communities that may engender further abuse and violence. In one fateful instance, Occidental Petroleum's use of Colombian military forces to secure its pipeline from rebel attacks resulted in a raid on a civilian community in 1998 that left 19 civilians dead.[7] While such arrangements may be technically legal and required by host governments, companies that undertake them risk supporting security forces they can neither control nor hold accountable.[8]

Third, core business activities can also have untoward effects at the operational level. For example, in Bougainville, PNG, the establishment of a major mining operation in a remote and ill-governed region generated a significant inflow of ethnic outsiders seeking jobs, at the same time as its activities degraded the local environment and disrupted traditional livelihoods. These impacts, which were neither anticipated nor compensated for, upset the existing balance within Papuan society and fed into existing grievances. The result was a spiralling cycle of violence in which the company become a proxy target for anti-government protest and a reluctant party to repressive government countermeasures (Regan, 2002, pp133–166; Zandvliet, 2005, pp185–206). It is worth noting that even well-intended efforts to secure a social licence to operate can fuel rent-seeking and violence (BBC, 2004). The practice of providing direct monetary compensation to affected communities for land use or environmental damage has proven particularly harmful.[9]

Numerous reports have made clear that otherwise legitimate companies have engaged in questionable business deals with corrupt and repressive governments and elites who abscond with national wealth and perpetrate massive human rights violations, often in the context of armed conflict (International Crisis Group, 2002; BBC, 2004). More troubling, there have also been documented cases of companies dealing in what one analyst has dubbed 'booty futures'; that is, the direct company financing of rebel groups in return for future exploitation rights once military victory is achieved (Ross, 2002).

One of the most striking examples of this sort of investment occurred in Congo Brazzaville, the details of which were brought to light by a high-profile trial in France. During the 1997 civil war, the French national oil company

Elf-Aquitaine used its assets and influence to provide Sassou Nguesso, the final victor, with military assistance from Angola in return for the future rights to Congo's substantial oil reserves. At the same time, Elf executives also organized an oil-backed loan (mortgaging future oil production at high rates of interest for up-front money) for Sassou's opponent President Pascal Lissouba, with which he could purchase arms.[10] Financing both sides of the conflict to secure 'booty futures' on Congo's oil was part of Elf's so-called 'Africa System', a long-standing arrangement to protect oil profits and extend influence in Africa through kickbacks and pay-offs to trusted African leaders. In so doing, Elf was at least partially responsible for a civil war where systematic rape was prevalent, thousands died and hundreds of thousands more were displaced.

The absence of host-state governance

The willingness of some companies to engage in these more dubious sorts of enterprise is not only a function of the profits to be had, but also of a weak regulatory environment in which the costs and penalties for misconduct are few and the rewards perversely high. One part of this weak regulatory environment concerns host states. Often they are politically indifferent or too institutionally weak to prevent or mitigate the negative economic, environmental and social impacts of natural resource extraction. The very resource dependence of these countries has 'cursed' them with an increased vulnerability to price shocks and lopsided investment. Resource windfalls also beget corruption and rent-seeking, and a temptation to disregard the social contract between the government and the governed, all of which may generate powerful social grievances.[11] In the context of sub-Saharan Africa, resource wealth has reinforced patrimonial rule and emboldened repressive regimes, even while stripping state capacity to maintain basic order and public services.

For these reasons, many host governments are ill-equipped to manage their countries' natural resources responsibly, let alone ensure responsible conduct of multinational companies on whom a considerable portion of their revenues depend. Even where appropriate regulatory frameworks exist, the incentives and means to implement, monitor and enforce them may be weak, particularly in remote and ill-governed hinterlands, where mining and drilling operations are typically located. For example, with the assistance of the IMF and the World Bank, the DRC government introduced a new Mining Code in 2003. As Human Rights Watch has reported, while in many respects a model code, implementation has been slowed by lack of resources and enforcement capacity, especially in mineral-bearing regions, where violent contests over resources continue. The code has also been thwarted by continued practices of political patronage that bypass the mines ministry, and ignore the law, in the awarding of concessions. In the worst cases, contests over title to resource concessions and revenue distribution have contributed to violent conflict and extensive human rights abuse (Human Rights Watch, 2005). In effect, the potential for larger social harm is so great because the domestic constraints against harmful business activities are so few.

Globalization without governance

Poor governance at the national level is compounded by a deficit of global governance. While globalization has opened up a wide range of decentralized, transborder opportunities for trade and investment, governance is still viewed as the domain of states and remains chiefly limited to activities within their sovereign borders. The global regulatory architecture provided by the WTO and the OECD exists to facilitate unencumbered trade and investment. These arrangements are not designed to address, let alone remedy, the negative non-commercial externalities – borne largely by marginalized populations in the developing world – that cross-border transactions routinely incur. Likewise, home governments, who remain preoccupied with maintaining global competitiveness, have been reluctant to exert meaningful regulation over their internationally operating companies. Taken together, national and international trade and investment policies have yet to address meaningfully the corrosive effects of natural resource extraction in fragile and war-torn states. Indeed, until recently, the various forms of risk mitigation and protection (including export credit assistance, overseas investment insurance and project finance) provided to extractive companies by national export credit agencies (ECAs) and multilateral lenders such as the International Finance Corporation have ignored conflict and human rights impacts (Goldzimer, 2003; Gary and Karl, 2004; Hildyard, 2005, pp235–262). As such, financing agencies have served to reinforce the already permissive incentive structure.

The spectrum of regulatory responses: Ad hoc, uneven and incomplete

Like other new areas of global governance, efforts to address the negative security and developmental impacts of trade and investment have been prompted by NGO advocacy campaigns. As discussed elsewhere in this volume, NGOs such as Global Witness, Partnership Africa Canada, Human Rights Watch and Amnesty International have led the way in exposing the conflict trade in timber, gold, diamonds and other lucrative minerals, as well as the linkages between oil and gas extraction, corruption and poor governance (see Chapters 3 and 4). Their investigations, backed by public 'naming and shaming' and threats of consumer boycotts of implicated companies and sectors, have pressed companies that value reputation to adopt more responsible business practices, while keeping the spotlight on the unethical activities of those who continue to regard operations in weak and war-torn states as 'business as usual'.

NGO policy research and advocacy has also played a critical role in placing these issues more prominently on the policy agendas of home and host governments and international organizations, including the UN, the African Union, the EU, the OECD and the World Bank. NGOs have also played an important and continuing role in developing global governance in this area through their participation in a number of multi-stakeholder initiatives, including the UN Global Compact, the Voluntary Principles on Security and Human Rights, the Kimberley Process for the certification of rough diamonds, and the Extractive Industry Transparency Initiative. Their decision to engage with companies represents a departure from traditional NGO advocacy policy of keeping distance from those whose practices they deem complicit in human rights abuse and underdevelopment. It may also represent their awareness of the abiding limitations of 'naming and shaming' in altering the powerful global market incentives in which business actors are, for better and for worse, still embedded.

NGOs have also been in the forefront of developing a new paradigm of conflict-sensitivity through which companies operating in fragile states can better manage the security and developmental impacts of their activities. The term 'conflict-sensitive business practices' – like the term 'conflict-sensitive development', from which it was adapted – underscores the fact that no intervention is neutral (Anderson, 1999). Private investment, like donor assistance, can even trigger unanticipated harm. Broadly speaking, conflict-sensitive business practices refer to proactive and responsive efforts to ensure that routine company investments and operations in weak states, including those at war and those emerging from conflict, do not contribute to ongoing violence, corruption or human rights violations. They also include positive efforts by companies to contribute actively to peace-building, human security, and sustainable development. While the full range of such practices is still being explored, they include efforts to stem the illicit conflict trade; the use of conflict-impact assessments that anticipate ways in which investments and operations may exacerbate instability; proactive engagement with affected populations; a responsible use of security services; and a commitment to transparent and accountable business dealings with host governments and communities (International Alert, 2005).

The current regulatory landscape is still a long way from embedding conflict-sensitive business practices into routine trade and investments. What regulation exists has emerged largely from ad hoc responses to specific challenges and opportunities. As such, it is an uneven patchwork of issue-driven, problem-focused initiatives that vary widely in terms of their objectives, the actors and activities addressed, and the strategies for doing so. For example, the Kimberley Process for certifying rough diamonds and EU efforts to regulate tropical timber were undertaken in response to specific instances of violent conflict, particularly in Sierra Leone and Liberia, in which the unregulated trade in lucrative commodities was identified as a barrier to conflict resolution. By contrast the current focus on transparency of natural resource revenues, although informed by specific conflicts, has also been shaped by parallel international efforts to tackle the debt crisis, reduce aid dependency, and promote accountability and good governance.

While commodity controls have been targeted at curtailing illicit exploitation and trade (particularly by non-state armed groups and transnational criminal networks), transparency initiatives are aimed at reducing the development and security risks of otherwise of legal business actors in the extractive sector.

This accounts for the diversity of regulatory approaches employed: from the prohibition of 'criminal' and 'rebel' actors to voluntary self-regulation through multi-stakeholder engagement and consensus building with 'otherwise legitimate' companies.

This differential treatment of market actors may be justified as an effort to distinguish and protect legitimate trade and investment from criminal activities. However, it has been criticized as an unacceptable double standard, one that protects the powerful and well-connected – chiefly multinational companies in the developed world and key host governments in the developing world, while often criminalizing comparable economic activities conducted by actors already condemned as 'rogues' for strategic or political reasons. Differential treatment of this sort may lead to policies that address only a part of the problem.

The classic case in point is the definition of 'conflict diamonds' adopted by the UN. From an ethical point of view, conflict diamonds might be classified as 'all diamonds that are extracted, traded, marketed or consumed in violation of internationally recognized labour and human rights standards and in ways that exploit, profit from, or contribute to violent conflict, whether for pecuniary and strategic gain' (Winer, 2005, pp71–72). From a strict legal perspective, they might be defined as 'all diamonds that have been extracted, traded, marketed or consumed in violation of the laws and customs regimes of at least one of the countries in which they move' (Winer, 2005).[12] However, the UN adopted an even narrower definition of conflict diamonds as 'rough diamonds used by rebel movements or their allies to finance conflict aimed at undermining legitimate governments' (UN, 2001). By this standard, rough diamonds that are extracted by state actors – regardless of whether done legally or in violation of law and regardless of whether the proceeds are used to finance armed conflict – do not qualify and would not be, indeed have not been, subject to UN Security Council sanctions. By making the critical element one of agency rather than activity, this sort of regulation may target some of the most egregious offenders but it leaves unaddressed the fuller dimensions of conflict trade.

Very often, discussions of regulatory responses to conflict-promoting business activities are cast in terms of a 'voluntary versus mandatory' dichotomy. While the distinction is analytically useful, the dichotomy is not (Lunde and Taylor, 2005, p318). For one, it obscures a number of promising hybrid initiatives that combine market inducements with legal sanction, such as the Kimberley Process, which though voluntary, has binding effects throughout the diamond trade (Smillie, 2005, pp52–53). More important, however, where the objective is to change the incentives that enable conflict-promoting business activity, then what matters is not whether the approach is voluntary or mandatory, but whether it can promote positive change among market actors.

As will be detailed below, although voluntary codes and other forms of industry self-regulation do suffer from self-selection and weak enforcement, they have provided important guidance and even a market niche for progressive companies seeking to improve business practice in challenging operating environments. By the same token, while mandatory or legal regulation is essential to the creation of a level playing field for conflict-sensitive business and for addressing the most egregious conduct, it cannot remedy the many conflict-promoting yet still legal market activities. At present, there is little normative consensus among key stakeholders as to what sorts of activities are unacceptable, let alone those that should be prohibited by law. And even where relevant international and domestic legal norms do exist, they too may suffer from weak or selective enforcement.

As other analysts have stressed, efforts to curtail the negative impacts of unregulated trade and investment in fragile and war-torn states confront a 'malign problem structure', in which a heterogeneous set of actors operating across jurisdictions have strong incentives to evade regulation, and where the costs and benefits of regulation are asymmetrical (Lunde and Taylor, 2003). However, just as different market actors have varying sensitivities to risk and opportunity, their receptivity to different forms of regulation is also highly variable. For this reason, efforts to promote conflict-sensitive business need to take advantage of the full spectrum of regulatory options.

Voluntary codes and industry self-regulation: Necessary but not sufficient

That one can even speak of progressive companies today signifies an important change from the past. Pressed by advocacy groups, shareholder activism, and UN efforts to address the economic dimensions of armed conflict, an increasing number of extractive companies, particularly large multinationals, are embracing the notion that good corporate citizenship extends beyond the boardroom and the company gate (Haufler, 1995).

For progressive firms operating internationally and concerned with their reputational capital, obtaining a 'social licence to operate' among local and national stakeholders in host countries is now seen as an essential component of sound business planning. Fiscal transparency, positive community relations, environmental protection, and sponsorship of health and education initiatives have already become standard elements of today's corporate social responsibility (CSR) agenda. More recently, some companies have begun exploring ways to extend traditional CSR to embrace conflict sensitivity, and thereby to address broader issues of peace, security, human rights and sustainable development, particularly in war-affected settings in which they operate. This change was prompted in part by the difficult security risks some companies have encountered when operating in conflict-affected countries. It has led these companies not only to adopt conflict-sensitive codes of conduct but also to join in broader industry and multi-stakeholder efforts to prevent and manage conflict.[13] Among such initiatives are the Voluntary Principles on Security and Human Rights, the UN Global Compact's Dialogue on Private Sector Actors in Conflict Zones, and the Extractive Industry Transparency Initiative. These initiatives have the advantage of providing sustained engagement of key stakeholders: local and international NGOs, human rights advocates, governments and international organizations (including IFIs), and companies. They have helped to build some badly needed confidence, legitimacy and consensus, and to target attention to practical and policy challenges.

While these codes remain mostly aspirational benchmarks, a few companies have started to commit resources and personnel to match them with meaningful implementation and to make public reports on progress.[14] They have also transformed the way these companies conceptualize and assess the risks posed by doing business in unstable or war-torn countries. In addition to traditional risk assessments that focus on the threats to company operations and investments, some companies are now seeking to identify the possible security and welfare risks posed by their own operations to surrounding communities, and to undertake appropriate preventive measures. In moving to incorporate some elements of conflict-sensitive business practices, such as revenue transparency or responsible security, corporate codes of conduct have the potential to set rudimentary benchmarks, sensitize the internal corporate culture to the value of conflict prevention and to help build skills and capacity for improved policies on the ground.

While the benefits of voluntary initiatives are important, they tend to be obscured by criticism of their shortcomings. These shortcomings are real and consequential. One weakness is the partial, self-selective nature of voluntary self-regulation. The few companies that elect to endorse them are typically large multinationals based in OECD countries that value reputation and their 'social licence to operate' and are easy targets for advocacy groups.[15] Small, 'junior' companies and independently operating entrepreneurs are less visible, and are thus better insulated against naming and shaming. As such, they have few, if any, incentives to sign on. This asymmetry of reputational risk leaves progressive multinational companies vulnerable to undercutting by more numerous rivals less committed to responsible, conflict-sensitive practices and human rights norms.

As documented by the UN Panel of Experts on the Illicit Exploitation of Natural Resources in the DRC, this undercutting is precisely what occurred during the DRC conflict: large multinationals were effectively squeezed out by less visible, less scrupulous junior companies unconcerned by reputational or security risks or by the corrosive effects of their activities on the safety and well-being of the Congolese people.[16] Many fear this pattern will be replayed on a larger scale where large and politically insulated state-owned companies from non-OECD countries such as China, India and Malaysia are heavily involved in resource extraction.[17]

Industry-driven efforts have thus far proven to be unable to affect the behaviour of state-owned, junior and rogue companies. This problem has been compounded by the reluctance of some multi-stakeholder initiatives to engage with problematic companies. For example, the founding participants of the Voluntary Principles on Security and Human Rights, eager to protect the integrity of the initiative and undecided about membership criteria and performance obligations, resisted the inclusion of Talisman Energy in the process.[18] This reluctance stemmed from Talisman's controversial role in the

Sudan conflict, although Talisman had by then undertaken several good-faith efforts to improve its CSR profile. While formal exclusion of companies from the process does not prevent them from endorsing and implementing the principles unilaterally, as Talisman now does, it risks slowing their broader adoption and reduces the opportunities for companies to share best practices. Indeed, six years after the establishment of the Voluntary Principles (VP), only 16 companies are signatories.[19]

A second shortcoming is that company and industry self-regulation has led to a proliferation of voluntary codes for responsible conduct, none of which have global reach and authority. For some companies, the bewildering array of codes has led to confusion and to code-fatigue, as well as to concerns of continually moving goalposts, all of which undermine their efforts to set and operate by clear, predictable expectations. Company-adopted voluntary initiatives may also lack credibility if they do not rely upon internationally adopted standards to establish clear benchmarks for distinguishing good performers from non-compliers.

Third, self-regulation often lacks transparent reporting and reliable performance requirements, without which voluntary codes remain unenforceable. Indeed, voluntary initiatives, whether company, industry or multi-stakeholder-based, are subject to varying levels of implementation, while performance assessments depend largely on self-reporting that cannot be verified. Even where non-compliance is reported, however, companies incur no penalty beyond damage to reputation, which may or may not be a matter of concern.

The credibility and effectiveness of voluntary codes and standards could be greatly improved if companies that have adopted them were to commit themselves to the creation of clear, common and verifiable performance obligations. Strengthened self-enforcement not only would demonstrate a serious commitment to conflict-sensitive business practice and human rights norms but would also enable more reliable assessments of actual progress. Not least, it would help identify non-compliers, thereby enhancing the reputational, and possibly financial, rewards to those companies with demonstrated records of sound corporate conduct. Recently, these criticisms have prompted the UN Global Compact to take steps toward establishing meaningful benchmarks and reporting mechanisms.[20] New measures have been adopted that include the prospect of sanctioning non-compliers through public suspension or exclusion of non-complying member companies. While promising and needed, these efforts remain untested, and in any event will still fall short in affecting companies that remain insensitive to reputational risk.

Fourth, voluntary efforts to 'do good' by individual companies may be undercut not just by other less scrupulous companies, but by host governments unconcerned by, or unable to address, issues of corruption, criminality and conflict. The first obligation of a company is to abide by the laws of their host countries. In vulnerable and war-torn states, however, where rule of law is compromised and government capacity is weak, there are strong incentives for corruption and economic criminality.

In such settings, companies that seek to be law-abiding have been unable to exert their influence to redress the many egregious economic activities of partners and competitors that exacerbate violent conflict. As some companies have observed, their ongoing efforts to promote transparency in dealings with host governments have been stymied by host country perceptions that transnational companies were unilaterally imposing alien norms or interfering in the sovereign affairs of state. This was the case for British Petroleum (BP) when, pressed by international NGOs, it published documentation of a signature bonus paid to the government of Angola. The Angolan authorities retaliated with threats to revoke BP's concessions, a threat made credible because of the presence of other companies willing and able to play by Angola's rules. As much as one may think that large multinational extractive companies have leverage over their host partners, the truth of the matter is that, acting alone, they do not. The problems of collective action and the ability of host governments to play companies against each other are abiding constraints.

In sum, however useful they have been in reforming internal corporate culture and establishing some useful benchmarks, voluntary business initiatives for socially responsible and conflict-sensitive conduct have not coalesced into a cumulative, systemic impact on the ground. At best, they may reflect the changing incentives of individual companies that adopt them. But they do little to alter the actual rewards and penalties of the overall marketplace.

Mandatory regulation: Towards binding rules and a level playing field?

Given the many inherent shortcomings of industry self-regulation, there is a strong case to be made for more robust forms of regulation, at both the national and international level. Unlike voluntary codes, mandatory regulation governing corporate activities in weak and war-torn states holds the promise of altering the incentives of the wider marketplace, while creating a level playing field.

Ideally, national governments should be the primary agents of regulation of extractive activities that are undertaken within their sovereign borders, ensuring that these activities are transparent, socially responsible and environmentally sound. Increasingly, a number of host states in the developing world have undertaken to strengthen the appropriate legal and institutional capacities, by adopting new anti-corruption laws, reforming mining codes, and by improving environmental oversight.[21] Nigeria and Indonesia, for example, have taken legal action to hold extractive companies accountable for environmental damage.[22]

However, in most vulnerable and war-torn states, where rule of law is weak or absent and where regime survival is at a premium, state authorities have neither capacity nor resources, nor often the political will, to pursue effective regulation. The result is market failure, often of a most egregious kind. For this reason, as well as because of the transnational nature of extractive activities, those seeking remedy have looked to some form of international governance.

A common set of authoritative and legally enforceable global rules would accomplish several things. First, rigorous sanctions would make accountability of economic actors meaningful and curtail the current climate of impunity. Second, common rules would reduce the collective action and free-rider problems that currently impede the extension of improved corporate conduct to the broader set of market actors, while also injecting clarity and predictability into what is currently an unwieldy and confusing array of voluntary corporate codes. Third, having rules with global coverage would end the current jurisdictional double-standard that allows companies to conduct themselves abroad in ways that would never be permitted at home. Less obvious, perhaps, an international legal framework for responsible business conduct abroad would make companies less vulnerable to retaliation by unaccountable host-country partners, and perhaps, too, increase their leverage to promote host-country accountability (Petrasek, 2002).

Thus far, however, neither governments nor international organizations have committed themselves to address the global regulatory deficit by undertaking to build such a regime. This is hardly surprising, given the prevalence of economic liberalism and its attendant suspicion of all things regulatory, particularly among the industrialized countries that are the main beneficiaries of market-driven globalization and the chief consumers of natural resources. But sovereign economic self-interest is not the only obstacle. Indeed, a central and still unmet challenge is to define the normative content of such a regime.

As the recent debate over the UN *Norms on the Responsibilities of Transnational Corporations and Other Business Enterprises with Regard to Human Rights* has dramatized, beyond the recently agreed international prohibition on corruption, there is little consensus among governments, corporations, and civil society on the precise scope of unacceptable economic activities in fragile and war-torn states or on the extent to which business entities should be legally obliged to refrain from them.[23]

A company operating in repressive, weakly governed or war-torn states might have a duty of heightened care, but the legal implications of this duty are far from clear. Should companies be disbarred from investing or operating in all conflict-torn states? Specifically, should there be an international moratorium on resource exploitation in countries where warfare or corruption has effectively destroyed domestic regulatory capacity? Should conducting transactions with known rebel and insurgent groups be criminalized? Should there be different standards governing those invested in a stable country that descends into war as opposed to those seeking entry into known war-zones? How would such provisions be reconciled with state sovereignty and what would be their humanitarian impacts? It is precisely these sorts of thorny issues that make the creation of clear international norms on the wider responsibilities of business entities in war-torn states so problematic yet so urgent.

The strengthening of mandatory regulation does not, however, rely exclusively on the creation of a full-blown international regime, nor does it have to proceed from scratch. As several studies have recently demonstrated, there is a range of existing and emerging international norms and national legal instruments that could provide the building blocks for a more coherent global framework (International Peace Academy and Fafo, 2004; Open Society Justice Initiative, 2005). Here the challenge lies in extending their coverage and strengthening their enforcement.

Current remedies under international law

Under current international law, there are few provisions that directly address economic activities that profit from or promote conflict. While designed for other purposes, anti-corruption and anti-bribery measures offer a second area in which existing international and national regulatory mechanisms could be better deployed against conflict-promoting extractive industry activities. As has been widely reported, and as many court cases have proven, in fragile states transactions between extractive companies and unaccountable host governments are widely accompanied by bribery of public officials, money laundering, tax evasion, and outright theft.[24] Many of these are recognized as crimes, duly codified in domestic law and in a number of international conventions.[25] Despite several prominent court cases and a growing number of legal investigations of alleged wrong-doing by corporations by some home jurisdictions, legal convictions against companies for corruption offences have been rare.[26]

While political interference is one reason for poor enforcement of this legal remedy, another lies in the technical, legal and jurisdictional hurdles involved in prosecution. Technically, opaque accounting rules and complex bank secrecy laws can impede the collection of evidence, while high legal thresholds, such as the US Foreign Corrupt Practices Act's requirement of proof of intent to commit bribery, are difficult to meet (Open Society Justice Initiative, 2005, p21). The UN Convention against Corruption goes some length to address these problems by requiring signatory governments to criminalize a wider range of bribery-related offences, to render mutual legal assistance in the collection and transfer of evidence for use in court, and to undertake measures to assist asset recovery including the tracing, freezing and confiscation of proceeds of corruption. As with the more established OECD Anti-Bribery Convention, however, the UN convention suffers from a lack of robust oversight and monitoring, a weakness that hampers efforts to reduce the current climate of impunity.

Because international criminal law, international humanitarian law, and international human rights law have been extensively codified, have comprehensive international coverage, and enjoy broad international consensus, they provide another, arguably more reliable, basis for concerted action to hold economic actors accountable, thereby increasing the costs and reducing the impunity of conducting business in host countries where domestic protections are lacking. Despite the broad acceptance of international human rights norms, just whether and how these translate into obligations for companies and other non-state actors remains a matter of contention (Clapham, 2006).

Within the business community, the fact that these statutes have been designed by and agreed among states has often led to a mistaken belief that they cover only offences committed by state actors. While it is true that states have the primary responsibility for preventing crimes against humanity, for observing the laws of war, and for promoting and protecting human rights, individual non-state actors can be held accountable for these offences.

Under these norms, there are no provisions that directly address economic activities that directly cause or promote instability or conflict. As such, the mere presence of a company in a fragile or war-torn state is not an actionable offence. These norms do, however, include provisions that directly address certain economic activities that profit from conflict. The Rome Statute of the International Criminal Court defines pillage, plunder and spoliation as actionable war crimes. While company executives have been prosecuted under these provisions in the past, the narrow scope and high legal thresholds of these offences will continue to make such prosecutions rare.

Company executives and employees can, however, be held accountable where they are found to be complicit in the perpetration by others of war crimes, crimes against humanity, and other grave violations of human rights such as genocide, ethnic cleansing, torture, forced detention, use of child soldiers, slavery and extra-judicial killing (International Peace Academy and Fafo, 2004). While the concept of complicity is subject to differing interpretations in different jurisdictions, a common legal definition has been codified in the Rome Statute (article 25). This subjects individuals to prosecution for war crimes and crimes against humanity if that person purposefully aids and abets the commission of such crime, including providing the means for its commission. Complicity in such international offences has been further extended by the notion of 'joint criminal enterprise' invoked in indictments by the International Criminal Tribunal for Yugoslavia and the Sierra Leone Special Court, under which even remote accomplices to an offence committed by others can be held accountable where the acts committed were a foreseeable outcome of the conspiracy.[27]

As yet, there have been no international criminal prosecutions against economic actors for aiding and abetting war crimes and crimes against humanity. However, the chief prosecutor of the International Criminal Court signalled that such prosecutions are within his remit, while the Special Court of Sierra Leone has issued indictments that explicitly charge former Liberian president, Charles Taylor, and his associates of complicity in the 'joint criminal enterprise' of waging war to gain control of Sierra Leone's diamond wealth.[28]

Current remedies under national law

Holding companies liable for actions that aid and abet violations of international criminal and human rights law is also within the power of national governments. Several cases are now pending in France, Belgium, The Netherlands and the US that seek to prosecute individual businessmen and large multinational corporations for their complicity in offences committed by others abroad. Most of these are civil suits brought against large extractive companies in US courts under the Alien Torts Claims Act (ATCA), a statute that explicitly provides civil redress in American courts for violations of 'customary international law' committed abroad.

Both Unocal and Total were sued by Burmese plaintiffs for aiding and abetting forced labour and forced displacement of civilians by the Burmese military in connection with their joint-venture pipeline project. In other cases, suits have been brought against companies for their complicity in murder, torture and false imprisonment committed by host-country security forces in their employ and for the provision to government forces of plant and assets that were then used in the commission of ethnic cleansing and other acts of aggression against civilians.

While the Unocal and Total cases were settled out of court, and while no ATCA case has yet resulted in a conviction, interim court decisions have helped to clarify actionable standards of complicity liability of companies for grave human rights abuse.[29] To cite one such judgement, a lower federal court found that Unocal's involvement met the standard of providing 'knowing practical assistance ... that had a substantial effect on the perpetration of a crime' by the Burmese military, suggesting that doing business with others who commit atrocities, where such an outcome was plainly predictable, does expose companies to complicity liability (Hoffman, 2005, p404).

These suits have also signalled to companies operating in fragile and war-torn states and partnering with abusive host governments that they will face expensive and reputation-battering court cases for their failure to exercise prudence in their investment and operational decisions. Indeed, while companies continue to protest publicly that they have no legal duty to promote and protect human rights in the countries in which they are operating, the prospect of protracted legal trials has prompted an increasing number of companies to become more proactive in adopting human rights and conflict-sensitive principles and altering their practices accordingly.[30] More robust legal sanction may therefore be enhancing the appeal and strengthening the scope and effectiveness of voluntary codes and standards.

Ultimately, the effectiveness of legal forms of regulation should not be judged by the number of cases pending nor the convictions achieved. Indeed, if an increased incidence of prosecutions and compensation settlements after the fact were all that was accomplished, the harmful security and development impacts of extractive companies in weak and war-torn states would not have been prevented in the first place.

The real value of legal prosecution is to clarify minimum standards of unacceptable economic activities and to reduce the incentives to companies for entering into transactions where the risk of involvement in violations of those standards is present and unavoidable. The fact that bringing civil or criminal action against companies for offences committed abroad continues to face a host of daunting jurisdictional and procedural challenges offers companies (and their well-heeled counsel) a variety of risk-reducing stratagems, including transferring legal incorporation to more lax jurisdictions and using foreign-based corporate subsidiaries, that add more obstacles to efforts to pierce the corporate veil. In short, while legal action can have profound and reformative effects on the incentive structure of some market actors, these effects are likely to be incremental and uneven.

Mixed forms of regulation: Making markets responsive

While voluntary and mandatory forms of regulation have differing strengths and weaknesses, they do share a common shortcoming: a lack of market inducements that reward companies that adopt meaningful conflict-sensitive business practices. From an extractive company perspective, voluntarily scaling up due diligence of foreign business partners, signing on to implement emerging best practices in revenue transparency, anti-corruption, human rights and conflict prevention, devoting the human and financial resources needed to sustain engagement in the plethora of voluntary multi-stakeholder and community engagement initiatives on these issues, while also tasking lawyers to track the emerging complicity liability risks, are both a costly and uncertain investment, the benefits of which have yet to be felt.

It is particularly expensive for the small-scale prospecting companies that are typically the first to enter fragile states, which may be one reason why this category of companies has such a poor track record of socially responsible business practice (Sherman, 2002; Balch, 2005). But these costs remain a concern for major multinational extractive companies as well, particularly as they find themselves competing against more insulated state-sponsored rivals from weakly governed jurisdictions, such as China, India and Malaysia. These costs can be prohibitive, even to progressive companies with a demonstrated commitment to responsible business practices. Likewise, while legal prosecution does impose economic costs, both direct legal costs and indirect reputational costs that may translate into lost investor confidence, its salutary effects are undercut by the lack of positive inducements. Given this fact, and given the enormous profits to be had from natural resource exploitation, some companies – especially those protected politically – may reckon that it is more profitable to take the liability risk and continue 'business as usual' than to expend resources and efforts on developing responsible conduct, the bottom-line benefit of which appears neither immediate nor certain.

Arguably, company participation in industry-wide or multi-stakeholder initiatives can help reduce the overall costs to companies, by pooling resources and by allowing newcomers to share best practices developed by others. The greater challenge, however, is to supplement these initiatives and regulatory prohibitions designed to mitigate negative company impacts with economic inducements that reward good business practice. While promising steps have been taken, those in a position to proffer such rewards, namely government, international financial lenders and regulators, shareholders and consumers have yet to deploy their full political, regulatory and financial influence accordingly.

Strengthening market inducements through supportive public policy

The most notable example is the Kimberley Process Certification Scheme (KPCS). Established in 2003, the KPCS seeks to regulate the previously uncontrolled global trade in rough diamonds, and to curtail the opportunities for illicit trade that have financed insurgent groups. The product of an inclusive, multi-stakeholder process, the KPCS is a voluntary agreement among industry actors, financial institutions, NGOs and governments in diamond producing and trading states. It provides common standards and a requirement for participating members to supply certificates testifying to the legitimate origin of the rough diamonds they trade, together with an auditable chain of warranties from origin to destination, and a system for peer monitoring to ensure the integrity of these measures. Participants have committed to trade only with other members of the process and to reject the importation of diamonds that lack the required certification. While initially weak, the monitoring and enforcement provisions have steadily improved (Global Witness, 2004a). Notably, these measures have required participating governments to undertake domestic legislation to provide penalties for non-compliance. Although implementation on the ground in diamond producing countries continues to face technical and political challenges, the measures undertaken through the KPCS have significantly reduced market access of non-participants as well as participating non-compliers. While the KPCS is technically a voluntary arrangement, its requirement that participants trade only with other members of the process, and its ability to suspend non-complying members, has radically altered the balance of incentives governing the international diamond market. Indeed, for those who seek to trade in this market, its effects are essentially obligatory. Indeed, by late 2004, some 43 countries, representing 98 per cent of the diamond trade, had signed on to the scheme.[31]

In the area of money laundering, positive dynamics have been generated by the OECD Financial Action Task Force (FATF). Launched in 1989 by the OECD to help combat the rising threat of the global trade in illicit drugs, the FATF was initially targeted at identifying and correcting vulnerabilities in the international banking system that enabled drug cartels to launder their ill-gotten gains. It was later amended to address money laundering associated with a wide range of serious crimes, including terrorist financing. The centrepiece of the FATF is a set of 40 recommendations that set standards that require governments to criminalize the laundering of the proceeds of such crimes, including legislation to seize and confiscate them, and obliges financial institutions to identify all clients, report suspicious transactions, and keep records of their transactions.

Like the Kimberley certification scheme, the FATF is based on a voluntary agreement and relies on a cooperative system of technical assistance and mutual monitoring. And like Kimberley, it derives its effectiveness from provisions that threaten the denial of market access to non-complying jurisdictions. Since 2000, the FATF has done this by publicly blacklisting 'non-cooperative' jurisdictions, including those outside the OECD that lack adequate legislation to ensure that their financial institutions have the needed due diligence measures in place. Blacklisted countries are liable to a number of countermeasures, the most notable of which is the suspension of banking transactions with other FATF members. As these members are OECD states, this sanction effectively threatens to cut off critical access to major financial centres, thereby posing serious economic consequences.

Although such measures have not yet been imposed, the mere threat of market loss has proven sufficient enough an incentive for targeted countries to undertake the necessary reforms. Indeed, of the 23 jurisdictions designated as 'non-cooperating' in 2001, only three remain so.[32] The progress of both the KPCS, in regulating the global trade in rough diamonds, and the OECD FATF against money laundering, demonstrate that voluntary agreements to implement a core set of regulatory standards can effect positive change when supported by effective oversight, transparent performance assessments and meaningful market inducements, particularly the denial of market access to non-compliers.

Strengthening market inducements through shareholder activism

Tying good performance to the threat of market loss is one way that economic inducements can be deployed in support of conflict-sensitive business practices. Another avenue for increasing financial support for conflict-sensitive business is through a targeted leveraging of investor influence. Where companies are publicly held, shareholder associations, pension funds and institutional investors have significant leverage that can be brought to bear to improve business conduct in vulnerable and war-torn countries. As socially responsible investment has become more popular, there has been a steady increase in the number of shareholder actions to press companies to improve their conduct and limit their non-commercial risk vis-à-vis the environment, community impacts and human rights, particularly in war-torn or repressive states.

The most common objective is 'avoidance', that is shareholder and institutional investors that pressure company boards to avoid investments that have undesirable impacts. This sort of shareholder activism played a critical role in effecting the withdrawal of the Canada-based Talisman Energy from its problematic pipeline project in war-torn Sudan, as well as in Talisman's subsequent strengthening of its CSR profile. More recently, shareholders of major extractive companies including ExxonMobil and Freeport MacMoran have tabled resolutions that seek to address negative human rights impact of their operations in Indonesia.

Investor activism has also put pressure on companies from the outside, through the leverage of capital markets. In 2000, in protest against PetroChina's poor labour, environmental and human rights record, a diverse coalition of NGOs joined forces with institutional investors to block PetroChina's gaining listing on the New York Stock Exchange. While the Initial Public Offering (IPO) went ahead, the disciplined boycott cost PetroChina some $7 billion in expected public investment (Social Funds, 2000). In the US, this sort of targeted investor activism has been echoed by the policy and legislative changes in several state-run public pension funds that bar these funds from being invested in companies with problematic projects in troubled places, in some cases requiring divestment.[33]

Companies have been less than comfortable with shareholder activism for socially responsible investment, particularly those resolutions that would impose significant costs, like the costs of wholesale divestment. However, shareholder and investor demands for improved accountability have also taken the form of informal engagement, whereby investors and shareholders work with companies not only to mitigate risks but to identify and adopt practical standards to promote and ensure conflict-sensitive investment practices. In several cases, this sort of push has led companies to adopt conflict-sensitive principles, such as the Voluntary Principles on Security and Human Rights and the revamped International Finance Corporation (IFC) safeguards, to participate in the UN Global Compact, and to support other policy processes such as the Extractive Industries Transparency Initiative (EITI), all of which do much to strengthen the credibility and efficacy of these tools, as well as to broaden their reach. As socially responsible investment becomes more widespread, and provided that these standards can be translated into meaningful change on the ground, investor support of conflict-sensitive business holds real promise, not only for identifying and penalizing non-compliers, but also for identifying and rewarding top performers.

The financial leverage of shareholders and institutional investors can alter the economic incentive structure in which some companies operate, but can do little to level the still uneven global playing field. For one thing, these actions remain largely limited to the level of individual companies and funds. For another, the opportunities for shareholder activism vary from country to country, and in some places are non-existent. This was the case with Talisman, where shareholder pressure compelled the company to sell off its problematic Sudanese assets to India's National Oil Company – a company more insulated against such pressure. What worked to reform one company's policy and practice therefore did little to change business as usual in war-torn Sudan (Mansley, 2005, p220).

Making project insurance and financing a reward for good conduct

Shareholders and institutional investors are not the only, or even the primary, source of financing for the extractive industry. Particularly with high-risk infrastructure and extractive projects, those projects most implicated in conflict, the support of the private-sector financing arms of multilateral development banks, such as World Bank's IFC and Multilateral Investment Guarantee Agency (MIGA), and national export credit agencies (ECAs), is critical. These agencies provide companies various forms of risk mitigation and protection, including export credit assistance, overseas investment insurance and project finance. Though modest in absolute terms, this financing adds a vital margin of safety for company operations in unstable places. And by increasing investor confidence, this support has a multiplier effect by opening up new avenues for companies to obtain larger amounts of private financing that would otherwise not be forthcoming.[34]

As recently detailed in a study by International Alert, however, these bodies have been slow to develop meaningful environmental and social standards, and even slower to make conflict-sensitive business practices a systematic feature of their lending and oversight policies (Crossin and Banfield, 2006).

Overall, their approach to political risk still prioritizes risks to operations and investment posed by challenging contexts, while insufficiently addressing the conflict and human rights risks posed by extractive operations themselves. As part of the World Bank, both the IFC and MIGA share its broader mandate to reduce poverty and promote sustainable development. However, as recently as 2006, an internal investigation into a troubled IFC-backed gold mining project in Guatemala found that the IFC had no policy on conflict assessment and failed to take into consideration the local human rights and security impacts of the project. Similarly, MIGA came under intense NGO criticism in 2006 for approving a $13.3 million political risk guarantee to Anvil Mining for a project in the still-volatile Katanga region of the DRC, despite Anvil's problematic role in an October 2004 massacre by DRC troops and concerns about fiscal improprieties with local authorities (*The World Today*, 2005). As with the IFC, MIGA was faulted for its failure to require companies it supports to conduct rigorous, independent conflict-risk assessments in the screening phase and for failing to undertake due diligence to verify company commitment and capacity to do so meaningfully. Without such conditions, not only do these lenders fail to ensure that the projects they back 'do no harm', but – by providing loans irrespective of conflict risk – they perpetuate disincentives for companies to take the necessary steps to avoid exacerbating conflicts.

Largely in response to NGO criticisms, and the World Bank's own Extractive Industries Review in 2004, both the IFC and MIGA have recently undertaken steps to extend their standards beyond environmental and social risk assessments and to address the conflict and human rights risks posed by extractive companies to the communities in which they operate. The IFC Safeguards[35] and Guidance Notes, for example, were recently amended to explicitly address the security risks associated with extractive projects, in particular by requiring companies to undertake due diligence of security agents they employ.[36]

Meanwhile, an audit of MIGA's due diligence in the Anvil case – and of extractive projects more generally – criticized MIGA's failure to ensure that the company was actually fulfilling its stated commitment to the Voluntary Principles on Security and Human Rights. The audit also contained a series of useful recommendations to strengthen MIGA standards for security and human rights, for more thorough and reliable diligence at the screening and underwriting stage, and to proactively engage with companies to ensure compliance with these requirements.[37] It remains to be seen whether MIGA will take on these recommendations.

But as some NGOs have noted, despite a long consultative process, the IFC standards fall short of requiring companies to undertake a full-spectrum conflict assessment, including prior consultations with affected communities and the determination of criteria for no-go areas. Nor do they offer clear and verifiable benchmarks for compliance. Given the wide discretion the IFC maintains on implementation, and on what course of action would ensue if a company failed to comply, the IFC standards are still far away from making conflict-risk assessment a hard condition for the provision of World Bank risk insurance, guarantees and project support (International Alert, 2005, p18). This said, both the revised IFC safeguards and the MIGA recommendations are positive and important first steps to bringing the Bank's weight to bear on improving the conduct of companies it supports.

As International Alert has stressed, given the size of ECA financing, and given that ECAs are funded by the taxpayer, ECAs should be obliged to ensure that they are underwriting socially responsible trade and investment, particularly where their governments have otherwise strong foreign policy commitments to sustainable development and international security (International Alert, 2005). Overall, however, ECAs have an even weaker profile than the IFIs on promoting sustainable and conflict-sensitive business practice or integrating explicit standards into their lending procedures.

There are numerous case examples of ECA-backed projects that have had negative social and environmental impacts, including those that have fuelled corruption and exacerbated violent conflict.[38] In part this is due to the narrow mandate of ECAs, which is to promote and protect their countries' trade and investment activities abroad. In a handful of countries, such as Canada, Norway and, to a lesser extent, Switzerland, some steps have been taken to integrate social impacts into their due diligence processes, and to link up ECA activities with broader aid and conflict management policies. In most countries, it is still the case that a company that obtained its concession through rebel groups or corrupt side-payments to host officials, or that routinely employs security staff with poor human rights records, or that disregards community and environmental security, has as good a chance at getting ECA backing as does a company that has signed onto and shows commitment in implementing CSR standards.

Given that ECAs compete with each other much as companies do, however, those undertaking unilateral reform initiatives face losing investment opportunities to less reformist ECAs. As with individual company initiatives, unilateral ECA policies in support of improved sensitivity to non-commercial risks, like instability and conflict, are unlikely to alter conditions on the ground. The much welcomed current review of the OECD Common Approaches for ECAs has some potential to make the guidelines more sensitive to conflict issues, but given the consensual nature of the OECD and its narrow remit on these issues, meaningful change of ECA policies will require additional push and commitment by governments.

Recommendations: Globalization with governance

The economic forces that underpin armed conflict are deeply embedded in the prevailing international economic order. As such, addressing conflict-promoting economic activities through improved national governance in affected countries of the developing world, though essential, will accomplish little unless the global regulatory deficit is also addressed. Policy makers seeking to devise regulatory and policy mechanisms to reduce the pernicious, conflict-promoting effects of commerce confront what some analysts have described as a 'malign problem structure'. It is a structure that consists of a heterogeneous set of market actors with strong incentives to evade regulation, a lack of empirical and normative consensus as to which activities are legitimate and which illegitimate, competing and ill-defined regulatory jurisdictions and frameworks, and asymmetrical costs and benefits of regulation. The multi-dimensionality of the problem also means that there is no obvious, single and authoritative international forum or agency that could provide a 'policy home' in which diverse initiatives could be brought together (Lunde and Taylor, 2005, pp330–337).

To date governments, particularly those of the developed world, have relied on voluntary codes to address the problem, thereby relying on an ideal of enlightened corporate self-interest that does not yet widely exist. To be sure, company and industry self-regulation have added value by making corporate cultures more sensitive to the reciprocal nature of the risks of doing business in fragile states; by building guidance from best practices; and by building confidence between multiple stakeholders.

However, initiatives like the Voluntary Principles on Security and Human Rights and the Extractive Industry Transparency Initiative cannot remain aspirational: governments, NGOs, the UN and international financial institutions need to ensure that they are backed up by clear criteria for participation, transparent and measurable performance obligations, transparent reporting, independent monitoring and enforceable provisions for suspending or expelling non-complying members. As the case of the Kimberley Process demonstrates, and as the UN Global Compact has learned, doing so would not make them any less voluntary. But it would make them credible.

Given the fiercely competitive nature of the global market for natural resources, it cannot be expected that improved conduct will naturally trickle down from progressive companies to laggards. Indeed, as long as the playing field remains as uneven and ungoverned as it is, there is a greater likelihood of backsliding. These structural impediments are currently exacerbated by two contingent factors. First, the windfalls to host governments from the historically high prices of oil, gas and gold may make them less receptive to undertake needed improvements in the management of their natural resource wealth, whatever incentives or penalties may be proffered.

Second, the increased role in extraction by state-owned companies from non-OECD countries, such as China, whose terms of trade and investment are indifferent to the non-commercial negative impacts on host countries, may erode the position and influence of progressive companies, no matter their current market size and influence. Taken together, these factors underscore the collective action problems that can lead to 'market failure' in the provision of peace and sustainable development. They also point to the critical need for improved inter-state frameworks that discourage operations and financial flows that may contribute to or prolong conflict, while also promoting investment that encourages recovery from conflict.

A central impediment to improved global governance of market actors operating and investing in weak and war-torn states is the lack of normative consensus on the sorts of activities that need to be regulated. For some, the controversial history of the aforementioned UN Norms on the Responsibilities of Transnational Corporations might be taken as an object lesson in the difficulty of building such consensus, particularly in the absence of some galvanizing crisis. Arguably, however, what made the UN Norms so problematic was the ambitiousness of their scope and their uncritical inclusion, alongside core rights, of economic and social rights that are still far from being widely accepted by governments, let alone by private sector actors. As such, this debate makes clear the need to begin by focusing on core norms, as embodied in international criminal and humanitarian law and on ratified international conventions. On core issues, such as anti-corruption and transparency, environmental protection, community empowerment and welfare, responsible company security policies and protections against the most egregious violations of human rights, there may in fact be more multi-stakeholder consensus than the critics concede.

This is not to say we should abandon the search for internationally agreed, authoritative standards that can assist governments to govern companies operating in fragile states. In an era of global interdependence, where economic development is led by private sector actors, achieving a universal framework on the rights, responsibilities and liabilities of these actors is an essential and much needed antidote to a global marketplace that is currently too permissive towards the social and human costs of profit. Moreover, the continuing absence of clear norms provides less scrupulous actors a convenient cover for equivocation and evasion. For these reasons, it is imperative that affected communities, NGOs, companies and governments continue to work through the UN, regional organizations, IFIs and other international bodies on building these core norms.

As discussed above, however, mitigating many of the negative impacts of extractive and other companies in the developing world need not await the creation of a brand new framework; progress can be and is being made through the extension and clarification of existing legal and regulatory frameworks and their applicability to market actors, while also improving their implementation and enforcement. Here, there are a variety of practical steps that can and should be taken.

First, more must be done by governments in the developed world to create robust criminal and civil mechanisms to hold companies based in their jurisdictions accountable when found complicit in violations of international humanitarian law, environmental and anti-corruption conventions. The current muscularity of the US Alien Tort Claims Act and of other extraterritorial legal mechanisms elsewhere for providing redress to victims, while holding companies accountable for their actions has proven to be an effective way of signalling to companies and the investment community that they cannot operate with impunity abroad. No less important, these legal actions have helped clarify the legal standards of complicity liability of companies in a way that no international treaty could. States that demur from replicating these legal remedies in their own jurisdictions may find their home companies being brought to bar in the US or elsewhere and their own sovereignty compromised.

As for improved enforcement of existing treaty obligations, signatory states must ensure meaningful implementation. They must provide adequate resources, not only to strengthen their own capacities to monitor and curtail, for example, private sector complicity, money laundering and bribery, but also to strengthen the same capacities in the developing world. One practical step would be to increase the resources available for the investigation of corrupt practices under the OECD's 1999 Convention on Combating Bribery of Foreign Public Officials in International Business Transactions and the more recent UN Convention against Corruption. Doing so might help to increase the possibility of successful prosecutions of corrupt practices in developing countries by companies headquartered in the developed world, if only by reducing the not unjustified perception in poor countries of double standards on corruption that favour rich countries.

Second, national and international financial institutions that currently set the rules for global economic development need to take far bolder steps to ensure that globalization has truly global benefits. The recent and positive steps of IFI private sector financing arms to address some of the negative environmental, social, human rights and conflict impacts of the companies that they finance need to be given added momentum. Ensuring due diligence of measures to mitigate these impacts is a start but, in the absence of clear benchmarks and sanctions, it is only a start. The provision of project financing should be made conditional on a demonstrable adherence by recipient companies to observe established standards, such as the Voluntary Principles for Security and Human Rights.

At a minimum, companies should be required to undertake conflict and human rights impact assessments and demonstrate due diligence with regard to partners and suppliers. Doing so would provide additional investor leverage over a larger range of companies, particularly state-owned enterprises that seek increased access to shareholder financing. This kind of conditionality could be extended by integrating broader CSR performance requirements into the listing rules of securities and exchange commissions and the assessment criteria of private rating agencies.

IFIs and national export credit agencies need to be guided by policies that effectively link their policies and practices to broader agendas of sustainable development and conflict prevention. This can be promoted through improved intra-agency coordination, both within donor governments and between them and IFIs. Specifically, these critical allies of extractive industry projects in the developing world need to adopt leading standards of conflict risk and human rights impact assessments and make clear that companies that fail to adhere will not receive their risk insurance, guarantees or project finance.

At the same time, these lenders could enhance incentives for compliance by setting up a public 'white list' of good performers and rewarding them with preferential terms of lending. As international donors routinely use the services of private banks for the management and disbursement of public monies, they could create standards by which to 'white list' those banks that have demonstrated their adherence to basic transparency standards and integrity safeguards. By giving accredited banks preference in providing financial services to governance and multilateral organizations, such an arrangement would create significant market leverage for improved compliance of private banking institutions with national and international prohibitions against money laundering and terrorist financing. Such white listing could also be applied to the selection criteria of government procurement programs.[39]

There is much that extractive companies can and should do to make their financial and operational activities truly conflict sensitive. Alone, however, even successful company efforts can do little to alter the conduct of less scrupulous competitors, let alone improve the security and welfare of citizens of fragile states. Achieving these outcomes requires more dedicated government action. Even in a highly globalized world, where non-state actors – be they NGOs, corporations, or criminal and terrorist networks – have greater influence than ever before, national governments remain the essential sources of power, legitimacy and influence. This is particularly true of governments in the developed world, whose countries are the chief consumers of the world's natural resources. For too long, these governments, even those otherwise committed to sustainable development, the protection of human rights and the prevention and resolution of violent conflict, have hidden behind the corporate veil, behind sovereignty, behind flaccid inter-governmental processes, and behind company assurances that they are doing well and doing good. Fostering demand for improved business conduct in fragile states is the responsibility of governments. On an uneven playing field, they remain the only authoritative referees.

Notes

1　For analysis of the conditions that facilitate investment to promote economic growth, employment and other benefits, see Dollar et al (2004).

2　Nigeria has earned $300 billion in oil revenues over the last 25 years, yet per capita income remains below $1 per day (Gary and Karl, 2004).

3　In 2004, Africa's share of global FDI inflows was 3 per cent; most of these inflows were in natural resource exploitation (UNCTAD, 2005).

4　The concept of 'fragile state' has various definitions. Core features include: loss of territorial control, low administrative capacity to provide basic security and public goods, neo-patrimonial politics, arbitrary and repressive rule, and weak legitimacy. For a fuller discussion see Torres and Anderson (2004).

5　Twenty-five per cent of China's current oil imports come from African countries, notably Algeria, Angola, Chad and Sudan, and increasing stakes in Equatorial Guinea, Gabon and Nigeria (Bajpaee, 2005).

6　A recent survey by the UN Special Representative on Business and Human Rights notes that of 65 cases of alleged company misconduct regarding human rights in 27 countries, two thirds involved oil, gas and mining companies, all concerned low and low-middle income countries, all of which scored poorly on standard indicators of good governance, and two thirds of which were experiencing violent conflict or emerging from it. As the survey was based on recent NGO reports, and may have selection bias, it is broadly suggestive of the salience of the problematic impacts of the extractive sector in weak and war-torn states. See 'Promotion and protection of human rights: Interim report of the Special Representative of the Secretary-General on the issue of human rights and transnational corporations and other business enterprises', 22 February 2006, E/CN.4/2006/97, p8.

7   The case has been brought before US courts. See International Labor Rights Funds Submission, http://72.14.203.104/search?q=cache:BmPwLsVggZcJ:sdshh. com/ICLR/ICLR_2003/16_Collingsworth.pdf+ILRF+and+occidental&hl=en&g l=us&ct=clnk&cd=4.

8   See, for example, the controversy stemming from payments made by Freeport–McMoran to the Indonesian military (Global Witness, 2005).

9   For a fuller analysis, see 'Peace and security in the Niger delta: Conflict expert group baseline report', Working Paper for SPDC (WAC Global Services, 2003, p5).

10   Elf played a similar role supporting contending factions in Angola. See Elf Indictment, p84 (Global Witness, 2004a).

11   For further analysis of the developmental consequences of the resource curse, see Karl (1997). In the context of fragile and war-torn states, see Ganesan and Vines (2004).

12   For discussion of these conceptual issues, see also Goredema (2002).

13   For example, the UN Global Compact's Dialogue on the Private Sector in Conflict Zones. See www.un.globalcompact.org

14   For a comparative survey of company performance on revenue transparency, see Save the Children UK (2005).

15   Ironically, too, those who do sign on to CSR codes are often subject to a higher level of continued scrutiny and criticism than those who do not.

16   For the full report, see 'Report on the Panel of Experts on the illegal exploitation of resources and other forms of wealth of the Democratic Republic of Congo', UN Docs. S/2001/357, 12 April 2001, and S/2002/1146, 16 October 2002.

17   In the case of Sudan, allegations of complicity in war crimes and crimes against humanity led Talisman Energy to divest its share in a controversial pipeline joint venture with the Khartoum government. This share was subsequently snapped up by the Indian state-owned oil company, with little perceptible change in the security situation faced by southern Sudanese. See also French, 2004. Indeed, in a recent transparency ranking of oil and gas companies, Chinese and Malaysian state-owned companies ranked lowest. See Save the Children UK (2005).

18   Confidential interview by the author.

19   Thus far, the VPs have also failed to establish clear and enforceable membership, performance and reporting requirements for participating companies. See Amnesty International (2006).

20   The Compact's new governance framework and integrity measures can be found at www.globalcompact.org

21   For example, since 2003 the EITI has been endorsed by 14 countries and implemented by eight countries. See www.eitransparency.org

22   See 'Shell told to pay $1.5 billion damages', Reuters, 24 February 2006; 'Newmont case tests Jakarta's resolve', *Financial Times*, 5 August 2005.

23   See www.oecdwatch.org, and www.ohchr.org

24 See the case study of the case brought against Elf Aquitaine in Open Society Justice Initiative (2005). This report also notes that 36 per cent of all the US Securities and Exchange Commission enforcement actions under the Foreign Corrupt Practices Act since 1977 have involved bribery related to natural resource extraction.

25 These include the UN Convention against Corruption, the OECD's 1999 Convention on Combating Bribery of Foreign Public Officials in International Business Transactions, and various domestic laws, such as the US Foreign Corrupt Practices Act.

26 According to a study conducted by US law firm Shearman and Sterling, the number of criminal and civil investigations for potential violations of the US Foreign Corrupt Practices Act has risen from 7 in 2002 to 16 in 2004. Criminal prosecutions are still rare and none have yet been brought against US companies operating in foreign jurisdictions (Open Society Justice Initiative, 2005).

27 For a discussion, see Schabas (2005), pp427–428.

28 See International Criminal Court, 'Communications received by the office of the prosecutor of the ICC', press release no pids.009.2003-EN, 16 July 2003, pp3–4, www.icc-cpi.int; see also the indictment of the Sierra Leone Special Court against Charles Taylor, Case No. SCSL 2003-03-I, Indictment, 7 March 2003, paras 20–23, www.sc-sl.org.

29 For a fuller discussion of the ATCA cases, see Hoffman (2005), pp395–424 and International Peace Academy and Fafo Institute for Applied International Studies (2004), pp24–26.

30 For example, though established in 2000, the Voluntary Principles on Security and Human Rights had not developed beyond the declaratory stage until 2004–5. See www.voluntaryprinciples.org. For a sample of such protests, see company testimonies critical of the UN Draft Norms on The Responsibilities of Transnational Corporations and Other Business Enterprises With Regard to Human Rights at www.ohchr.org.

31 For more, visit www.kimberleyprocess.com

32 See the OECD Financial Action Task Force, *Annual Report 2004-2005*, p12, www.fatf-gafi.org. For a fuller analysis of the FATF, see Winer (2002).

33 In response to the ongoing slaughter in Darfur, several US states adopted legislation that prohibits pension funds from supporting any company with an investment connection in Sudan. In so doing, they have closed a loophole by which some US companies have sidestepped the 1997 US sanctions against direct US company investment. 'How states are aiming to keep dollars out of Sudan', *New York Times*, 29 February 2006.

34 Post-conflict support makes up approximately 13 per cent of MIGA's portfolio, and between 1988 and 2003 it issued 56 guarantees worth $1.5 billion for investments in 16 conflict-affected countries. For the year ending 30 June 2005, MIGA supported 12 projects in conflict-affected countries, including its first project in the DRC (MIGA, 2005, *Annual Report*, www.miga.org). According to Gary and Karl, 'The amount of investment that ECAs support globally is significantly greater than the total amount of lending from the World Bank, IMF, and other multilateral institutions combined, according to the IMF. In 1998, ECAs supported exports totalling $391 billion or eight percent of total world exports. Export credit agencies have been instrumental backers of extractive industry projects in developing countries, including oil projects in Africa' (Gary and Karl, 2004, p21). Every dollar provided or supported by an ECA can attract two or more dollars of purely private financing (Maurer and Bhandari, 2000, p4).

35   The IFC safeguard policies were created to address social and environmental risks in co-financed development projects in high-risk settings. They have become internationally recognized benchmarks and were subsequently integrated into the Equator Principles.

36   In effect, they have incorporated key provisions of the Voluntary Principles on Security and Human Rights. See 'IFC performance standards on social and environmental sustainability', Performance Standard 4: Community Health, Safety and Security, www.if.org.

37   See CAO (2005). This audit is available at www.cao-ombudsman.org/html-english/documents/DikulushiDRCfinalversion02-01-06.pdf.

38   See, for example, the official complaint to the IFC's Compliance Advisor/Ombudsman regarding the Baku–Tbilisi–Ceyhan (BTC) Main Oil Export pipeline project, CEE (Central and Eastern European) Bankwatch (2004), www.bankwatch.org.

39   For further elaboration of this recommendation, see Winer (2003).

References

Amnesty International (2006) 'Voluntary principles for security and human rights', www.web.amnesty.org/pages/ec-voluntaryprinciples-eng accessed in 2006

Anderson, M. (1999) *Do No Harm: How Aid can Support Peace – or War*, Cambridge, MA, Collaborative for Development Action

Bajpaee, C. (2005) 'Sino–US energy competition in Africa', *Power and Interest News Report*, www.pinr.com/report.php?ac=view_report&report_id=378&language_id=1

Balch, O. (2005) 'Small business and corporate responsibility', *Ethical Corporation*, 15 November, London, Ethical Corporation

BBC (2004) 'Shell admits fuelling corruption', British Broadcasting Corporation, 11 June

CAO (2005) 'CAO audit of MIGA's due diligence of the Dikulushi copper-silver mining project in the Democratic Republic of the Congo: Final report', Office of the Compliance Advisor/Ombudsman International Finance Corporation/Multilateral Investment Guarantee Agency

Clapham, A. (2006) *The Human Rights Obligations of Non-state Actors*, Oxford, Oxford University Press

Crossin, C. and Banfield, J. (2006) *Conflict and Project Finance: Exploring Options for Better Management of Conflict Risk*, London, International Alert

Dollar, D., Hallward-Driemeier and Mengistae, T. (2004) 'Investment climate and international integration', Policy Research Working Paper 3323, Washington, DC, World Bank

Donnan, S. (2005) 'Newmont case tests Jakarta's resolve', *Financial Times*, 5 August

French, H. (2004) 'China in Africa: All trade, with no political baggage', *The New York Times*, 8 August

Fried, C. (2006) 'How states are aiming to keep dollars out of Sudan', *The New York Times*, 19 February

Ganesan, A. and Vines, A. (2004) *Engine of War: Resources, Greed and the Predatory State*, Washington DC, Human Rights Watch

Gary, I. and Karl, T. (2004) *Bottom of the Barrel: Africa's Oil Boom and the Poor*, Baltimore, Catholic Relief Services

Global Witness (2004a) 'The Kimberley Process gets some teeth: The Republic of Congo is removed from the Kimberley Process for failing to combat the trade in conflict diamonds', press release, London, Global Witness

Global Witness (2004b) 'Time for transparency: Coming clean on oil, gas and mining revenues', report, London, Global Witness

Global Witness (2005) 'Paying for protection: The Freeport Mine and the Indonesian security forces', report, London, Global Witness

Goldzimer, A. (2003) 'Worse than the World Bank?: Export credit agencies – the secret engine of globalisation', *Backgrounder*, vol 9, no 1, Oakland, CA, Institute for Food and Development Policy

Goredema, C. (2002) 'Diamonds and other precious stones in armed conflicts', Occasional Paper #57, Pretoria, Institute for Security Studies

Haufler, V. (1995) *The Public Role of the Private Sector*, Washington DC, Carnegie Endowment for International Peace

Hildyard, N. (2005) 'Export credit agencies and corporate conduct in conflict zones', in Ballentine, K. and Nitzschke, H. (eds), *Profiting from Peace: Managing the Resource Dimensions of Civil War*, Boulder, CO, Lynne Rienner Publishers

Hoffman, P. (2005) 'Corporate accountability under the Alien Tort Claims Act', in Ballentine, K. and Nitzschke, H. (eds), *Profiting from Peace: Managing the Resource Dimensions of Civil War*, Boulder, CO, Lynne Rienner Publishers

Human Rights Watch (2004) *Some Transparency, No Accountability: The Use of Oil Revenue in Angola and Its Impact on Human Rights*, Washington DC, Human Rights Watch

Human Rights Watch (2005) *The Curse of Gold*, Washington DC, Human Rights Watch

International Alert (2005) *Conflict Sensitive Business Practices: Guidance for the Extractive Industries*, London, International Alert

International Criminal Court (2003) 'Communications received by the office of the prosecutor of the ICC', press release no. pids.009.2003-EN, The Hague

International Crisis Group (2002) 'God, oil and country: The changing logic of war in Sudan', *Africa Report*, no 39, Brussels

International Peace Academy and Fafo Institute for Applied International Studies (2004) *Business and International Crimes: Assessing the Liability of Business Entities for Grave Violations in International Law*, Oslo, IPA/Fafo

Karl, T. L. (1997) *The Paradox of Plenty: Oil Booms and Petro-States*, Berkeley, UC Press

Lunde, L. and Taylor, M. (2003) 'Commerce or crime: Regulating economies of conflict', Fafo Report no 424, Oslo, Fafo Institute for Applied International Studies

Lunde, L. and Taylor, M. (2005) 'Regulating business in conflict zones: Issues and options', in Ballentine, K. and Nitzschke, H. (eds), *Profiting from Peace: Managing the Resource Dimensions of Civil War*, Boulder, CO, Lynne Rienner Publishers

Mansley, M. (2005) 'Private financial actors and corporate social responsibility in conflict zones', in Ballentine, K. and Nitzschke, H. (eds), *Profiting from Peace: Managing the Resource Dimensions of Civil War*, Boulder, CO, Lynne Rienner Publishers

Maurer, C. and Bhandari, R. (2000) 'The climate of export credit agencies', *Climate Notes*, Washington DC, World Resources Institute

OECD Financial Action Task Force (2005) *Annual Report 2004-2005*, Paris, OECD

Open Society Justice Initiative (2005) *Legal Remedies for the Resource Curse: A Digest of Experience Using Law to Combat Natural Resource Corruption*, New York, Open Society Justice Initiative

Petrasek, D. (2002) *Beyond Voluntarism: Human Rights and the Developing International Legal Obligations of Companies*, Geneva, International Council on Human Rights Policy

Regan, A (2002) 'The Bougainville conflict', in Ballentine, K. and Sherman, J. (eds), *The Political Economy of Armed Conflict: Beyond Greed and Grievance*, Boulder, CO, Lynne Rienner Publishers

Reuters (2006) 'Shell told to pay $1.5 billion damages', Reuters, 24 February

Rights and Accountability in Development (2004) *Unanswered Questions: Companies, Conflict and the Democratic Republic of Congo*, Oxford, RAID

Ross, M. (2002) 'Booty futures: Africa's civil wars and the futures market for natural resources', manuscript, 18 December

Roy, E. (2005) 'World Bank to investigate Anvil Mining', *The World Today*, Australian Broadcasting System, 23 August

Save the Children UK (2005) *Beyond the Rhetoric – Measuring Revenue in the Oil and Gas Industries*, London, Save the Children UK

Schabas, W. (2005) 'War economies, international actors and international criminal law', in Ballentine, K. and Nitszchke, H. (eds), *Profiting from Peace: Managing the Resource Dimensions of Civil War*, Boulder, CO, Lynne Rienner Publishers

Sherman, J. (2002) *Options for Promoting Corporate Responsibility in Conflict Zones: Perspectives from the Private Sector*, IPA Conference Report, New York, International Peace Academy

Smillie, I. (2005) 'What lessons from the Kimberly certification scheme?', in Ballentine, K. and Nitzschke, H. (eds), *Profiting from Peace: Managing the Resource Dimensions of Civil War*, Boulder, CO, Lynne Rienner Publishers

Social Funds (2000) 'PetroChina IPO raises social concerns', *Social Funds*, 6 April, www.sofialfunds.com/news/article.cgi/211.html

The World Today (2005) 'World Bank to investigate anvil mining', *The World Today*, Australian Broadcasting System, 23 August

Torres M. M. and Anderson, M. (2004) 'Fragile states: Defining difficult environments for poverty reduction', Poverty Reduction in Difficult Environments Working Paper 1, London, UK Department for International Development

UNCTAD (2005) *World Investment Report 2005: Transnational Corporations and the Internationalization of R&D*, New York and Geneva, United Nations

United Nations (2001) 'The role of diamonds in fuelling conflict: Breaking the link between the illicit transaction of rough diamonds and armed conflict as a contribution to prevention and settlement of conflicts', resolutions adopted by the General Assembly A/RES/55/56 and A/Res/56/263

United Nations (2002) *Report on the Panel of Experts on the Illegal Exploitation of Resources and Other Forms of Wealth of the Democratic Republic of Congo*, UN Docs S/2001/357 and S/2002/1146

United Nations (2006) *Promotion and Protection of Human Rights: Interim Report of the Special Representative of the Secretary-General on the Issue of Human Rights and Transnational Corporations and Other Business Enterprises*, UN Doc E/CN.4/2006/97

WAC Global Services (2003) 'Peace and security in the Niger delta: Conflict expert group baseline report', Working Paper for SPDC, WAC Global Services

Winer, J. (2002) 'Illicit finance and global trade', Fafo Report no 380, Oslo, Fafo Institute for Applied International Studies

Winer, J. (2003) 'Globalizing transparency: Implementing a financial sector white list', Fafo Paper 7, Oslo, Fafo Institute for Applied International Studies

Winer, J. (2005) 'Tracking conflict commodities and finance', in Ballentine, K. and Nitzschke, H. (eds), *Profiting from Peace: Managing the Resource Dimensions of Civil War*, Boulder, CO, Lynne Rienner Publishers

World Bank (2005) *World Development Report 2005: A Better Investment Climate for Everyone*, Washington DC, World Bank

Zandvliet, L. (2005) 'Assessing company behaviour in conflict environments: A field perspective', in Ballentine, K. and Nitszchke, H. (eds), *Profiting from Peace: Managing the Resource Dimensions of Civil War*, Boulder, CO, Lynne Rienner Publishers

Chapter 6

Managing Revenues from Natural Resources and Aid

Richard Auty and Philippe Le Billon

Introduction

Natural resources and foreign aid revenues can play a crucial role in improving the security of populations in poor countries. Many commodity prices, especially oil and minerals, as well as aid in the form of debt relief and ODA rebounded in the mid-2000s, after more than a decade of decline. If well managed, these financial flows could help improve the lives of some of the poorest and most conflict-affected populations in the world. If mismanaged, however, these revenues could once again trigger economic growth collapses, feed grievances and sustain repressive regimes or armed groups. Iraq or Africa's Great Lakes region clearly illustrate the dramatic costs of revenue mismanagement – at the individual, regional and international levels.

This chapter examines the research evidence on revenue management in mostly low-income countries, exploring how resource and aid revenues can improve or undermine the security of local populations through economic and political channels. Examples of unsuccessful revenue deployment, such as Algeria and Iraq, are contrasted with more successful cases such as Botswana and Mozambique. Drawing from the lessons of the past and current policy debates, we then discuss in the section on 'How resource and aid revenues can undermine or improve security' the main ways in which revenue management can be improved in terms of transparency, accountability, revenue sharing and income stabilization. The concluding section discusses some of the main challenges to improved revenue management and provides a number of recommendations.

How natural resource and aid dependence can undermine the economy

Starting in 1973, severe primary commodity price shocks brought an end to the so-called 'Second Golden Age of Economic Growth' experienced by most low-income countries after World War II.[1] Resource-rich countries tended to be among the most adversely affected. Whereas, in 1960, per capita income in resource-rich countries was typically 50 per cent higher than in the resource-poor countries, by the late 1990s it had fallen significantly below the resource-poor level (Auty, 2001, p5). The severe terms of trade shocks (commodity price swings) and economic recessions (or growth collapses) of the period 1974–85 were associated with increased risk of civil strife, particularly in the case of oil countries (Rodrik, 1999; Collier, 2000). The growth collapses were also accompanied by increased dependence on foreign aid, which was intended to speed economic recovery (Boone, 1996, pp290–291). During the 1990s, however, evidence emerged to suggest that foreign aid could have adverse impacts similar to those associated with abundant natural resource revenues (Burnside and Dollar, 1997; Svensson, 2000; Easterly, 2001; Van de Walle, 2005). In short, reliance on natural resource revenues and aid as sources of income resulted in major distortions of both the economy and the political systems.

Economic theory demonstrates that with appropriate policies, revenues from natural resources and foreign aid, which are forms of rent,[2] can accelerate economic growth and support specifically targeted poverty alleviation programmes (World Bank, 2001, p48). Higher aggregate national income accompanied by lower levels of poverty are major factors in reducing the risk of armed conflict and improving the security of individuals. Rents can accelerate growth because they support higher rates of investment and fund the imports required to restructure the economy, lift productivity and sustain rising incomes. Natural resource revenues can also fund the pro-poor provision of public services and expand employment opportunities. Similarly, if well coordinated and tightly targeted, aid programmes can expand social and economic infrastructure, and also transfer assets to the poorest to help them to improve both their skills and income-earning abilities.

Economic policies, however, are not shaped only by economic theory and ideals of equitable economic growth. Political dimensions also matter a great deal in shaping policies, and especially so in resource and aid sectors, where revenue flows are often tightly controlled by governmental actors (Gelb and associates, 1988). As a result, rent from natural resources and aid can prove counter productive by distorting the economy away from its underlying comparative advantage, as well as by feeding corruption. Resource revenues also have an impact on politics and on the quality of governance, with oil, for example, tending to hinder democratization (Ross, 2001; Murshed, 2004).

Taking an economic *and* political approach focusing on rent-driven growth can help explain why, in recent decades, resource and aid dependent countries have been prone to growth collapses and vulnerable to civil strife (Ross, 1999). When combined with hard-won developmental experience, a political economy approach suggests not only which economic policies can avoid such adverse outcomes, but also the coalitions that must be formed between government, businesses and social movements in order to implement such policies within the context of different types of political state.

The 'staple trap'

The vulnerability of rent-rich countries to growth collapses can be explained through the 'staple trap' model. In brief, economic dependence on a resource (or staple) can undermine the required competitive diversification of the economy so that it becomes progressively weaker. Since revenues from most resources (and aid) are volatile, such weakened economies are vulnerable to growth collapses if commodity prices abruptly fall. More specifically, the staple trap is the result of interacting economic and political processes.

First, high-rent countries face pressure to spend the proceeds from natural resource windfalls quickly, particularly on behalf of powerful interest groups eager to see tangible benefits. However, the rapid domestic absorption of the commodity revenue can distort the economy and trigger so-called 'Dutch disease' effects. The sudden expansion in domestic demand stokes inflation in the price of non-traded goods, which face little international competition, strengthening the domestic currency so that sectors that are traded like 'non-boom' agriculture and manufacturing cannot compete internationally and contract, destroying many labour-intensive jobs in the process. This process reverses the diversification of the economy that is required to sustain economic development and leaves it vulnerable to recession.

Second, in the presence of high 'windfall' commodity revenues, governments find more immediate and lucrative rewards from capturing and redistributing commodity revenues (including to themselves) than from encouraging wealth creation – which they tend to neglect. This is because high commodity revenues offer the prospect of immediate enrichment for those in power whereas the rewards from expending revenue on long-term wealth creation are far more distant, and therefore more uncertain. Such conditions tend to nurture predatory political systems, in which elites have a strong financial interest in staying in power, even if it is through repressive and authoritarian means. Revenue windfalls also affect the relationship between rentier states and taxpayers by undermining the political representation and accountability requirements associated with broad taxation.

With diminishing competitiveness in agriculture and manufacturing, along with increasing dependence on a booming resource sector that tends to create relatively few jobs, unemployment becomes a cause of concern for governments, fearful of social unrest. As a result, governments tend to spend some revenue to create jobs by expanding the public sector or forcing industrialization by over-protecting infant industries. A bloated and inefficient public sector and non-competitive industrial sector become an increasing burden on the economy, and particularly on the resource sector that generates their subsidies. If commodity prices fall, governments tend to squeeze even more from the resource sector, weakening its competitiveness while also increasing foreign debt, rather than reining back support for the subsidized sectors. In the absence of economic reform, these distortions eventually lead to a growth collapse, likely to be accompanied by mounting repression in the face of growing opposition. The risk of abrupt and violent political change therefore intensifies.

Resource dependence and price volatility

The extent of a country's dependence on commodity revenues and the price of those commodities are two crucial elements of the staple trap model. The level of dependence assesses the relative importance of the natural resource rent in relation to the overall economy (as percentage of GDP) or to public revenue (as percentage of public revenue). Natural resource rents typically ranged from 9 to 21 per cent of GDP in low-income countries during the mid-1990s (Auty, 2001, p5), with a generally higher level of dependence in terms of public revenue. Levels of dependence can go significantly higher during boom times when commodity prices are high, reaching 92.7 per cent of GDP and nearly all government revenue for the extreme case of Equatorial Guinea in 2005.

Foreign aid has run at 10 to 20 per cent of gross domestic income (GDI) in recent decades, and above 40 per cent of GDI at times in Mozambique, for example (World Bank, 2005), as external intervention increased in response to the growth collapses that occurred in many developing countries during the period of oil price volatility of 1974–85. In addition, government interventions to adjust prices, notably by fixing artificially high exchange rates and by using crop marketing boards to depress domestic crop payments relative to world prices to 'tax' wages and profits in some sectors, constitute a third category of rent (termed 'contrived rent'), which could also amount to 10 to 30 per cent of GDP (Krueger et al, 1992).

In aggregate terms, these three types of rent account for a sizeable fraction of GDP in developing countries – typically around one third. Such high levels of rent dependence have considerable potential to destabilize not only the economy (if the rent is extracted from competitive activities and diverted to non-competitive activities) but also political stability (because large amounts of floating revenues attract political contests for their capture).

Even mature high-income economies with deeply rooted and resilient institutions might experience difficulty in handling such a large and volatile stream of 'loose' revenue. However, given the close positive link between per capita income and the quality of governance (Treisman, 2002), low-income developing countries tend to be singularly ill-equipped to manage such large and volatile revenue streams.

This high level of dependence also exposes the economy to variations in commodity prices and aid provision. Two major dimensions are important with regard to primary commodities: the long-term trend in the price of primary commodities and the volatility of prices around that trend. In short, many commodities have seen a decline of their value relative to other goods and services; by 1999 commodities were one fifth of their value a century earlier (Cashin and McDermott, 2002). As a result, many countries stuck in the staple trap and unable to drastically improve productivity have seen their economic situation worsen over time. Even a resurgence of commodity prices may not rapidly benefit these countries, as they remain out-competed by more efficient and larger producers. The more capital-intensive commodities like minerals require large investments with long lead times before they start to produce. Moreover, oil production sharing agreements, for example, generally allocate most of the revenues in the early years to foreign companies to recoup their initial investments. Oil producing governments often respond by requiring large payments in cash – or 'signature bonuses' – when such agreements are passed.

Not only have many commodity prices declined over the past decades, but the volatility of primary commodity prices has intensified, in terms of both the scale and duration of the resulting price shocks. The terms-of-trade volatility of the regions with the highest share of primary products in their exports was two to three times that of the industrial countries during the years 1970–1992 (Westley, 1995). Such fluctuations in commodity prices can administer substantial shocks to non-diversified economies. When commodity exports are one third of GDP, a 1 per cent decrease in price translates into a 1.5 per cent decrease in national income due to the multiplier effect of second-round spending and indirect employment opportunities (Deaton, 1999). The higher the reliance upon a single primary commodity, the greater the impact on the domestic economy of a change in its price. Low-income countries in sub-Saharan Africa are more vulnerable than their counterparts in south Asia, which tend on average to be larger and therefore have more diversified economies.

The duration of the shock is also important. Mineral exporters have performed especially poorly during the last two decades because of price downswings. As noted above, mining tends to have long lead times for investments and so responds slowly to changes in the market price. High mineral prices will spur new projects, but these will take time to deliver additional volume to markets. High prices can thus depress global economic activity and encourage substitution or conservation. In consequence, demand may lie well below expectations by the time new investments eventually come on stream, ushering in an extended period of surplus capacity and consequently low prices. This phase of depressed prices deters new capacity expansion while stimulating demand, thereby setting up the next cycle of price boom and bust. In the case of oil for instance, the frequency of the long-run cycle appears to be around 25 years, with around eight years of high prices giving way to a longer period of relatively depressed prices.

If policy makers could predict price trends, then commodity revenues could be managed to smooth their impact on the domestic economy. Unfortunately, there are fluctuations or sub-cycles within this long-run cycle, which complicate predictions. More generally, commodity price volatility is bad for economic growth not only because of falling prices, but also because rising prices tend to lead to increased expenditure, which in the public sector tends to result in overspending and poorly planned investments. Such increased public expenditure often acquires a momentum that renders it difficult to cut back during downswings. This leads to the accumulation of debt, which merely postpones the necessary fiscal expenditure adjustment so that the eventual cutbacks are much more painful.

Interestingly, there is evidence that whereas governments tend to react as if the increased income associated with a commodity boom is permanent, private actors exhibit greater caution (Bevan et al, 1987). Consequently, private firms and institutions tend to save more for future downturns and thereby slow the rest of domestic expenditure. Where governments permit, their responses include investing overseas, which helps to further retard domestic absorption and so limit the Dutch disease effects so that the risk of locking the economy into a staple trap is diminished.

Besides orienting windfalls towards savings, trade policy also appears important. The negative impacts of price volatility increase with growing dependence on a small number of natural resource exports (Combes and Guillaumont, 2002). A closed economy would in theory prevent exposure to price volatility shocks. In practice, however, closed economy policies remain selectively open to key primary commodity exports. Such a selectively closed economy policy thus tends to magnify a lack of economic diversification, notably by reducing investments, and to aggravate commodity price instability effects. It thus appears that open trade policy increases the resilience of primary commodity exporters, even if such exports also increase their exposure to shocks in the first place.

Overall, heightened commodity price instability has slowed per capita GDP growth significantly in the developing countries since the 1960s, except for industrializing east Asia and, to a more modest degree, the larger south Asian countries. To sum up, dependence on either natural resource or aid revenue requires matching public expenditure to the absorptive capacity of the domestic economy and also promoting the diversification of the economy away from slow-growth commodity dependence.

How resource and aid revenues can undermine or improve security

The staple trap development trajectory is not inevitable. Rather, it points to a pattern of behaviour among many resource and aid dependent countries. The pattern has become so pronounced in relation to natural resources that the term 'resource curse' is commonly used to describe the somewhat paradoxical negative effects of resource wealth. The cases of Algeria and Iraq each illustrate how resource or aid dependence can undermine the security of local populations.

Algeria: Inefficient industrialization, growth collapse and civil war

After a devastating war for independence the Front de Libération Nationale (FLN) government opted to take a lead role in directing revenues from the oil and gas industry. It nationalized this sector in 1972 and promoted resource-based industrialization as the principal vehicle for restructuring the economy, with state-owned enterprises given the dominant role.

Although GDP growth was rapid through the 1970s and into the 1980s, the government neglected social infrastructure and also unemployment, which reached 18 per cent by the late 1980s. By then, the neglected agricultural sector, which prior to independence had fed the country and produced a surplus for export, employed one quarter of the total workforce but produced only one quarter of the country's food. Moreover, the new industrial sector proved inefficient, and could not sustain economic growth when oil revenues declined through the 1980s (Nashashibi, 1998).

In the context of rapid population growth and rising unemployment, sharply lower oil prices cut the oil rent per capita from the peak of $1200 (in 1990 dollars) in 1981 to $200 in 1986, thereafter fluctuating between $200 and $400 through the 1990s (Aissaoui, 2001, p30). Locked in the staple trap, the Algerian government failed to respond promptly when oil prices collapsed in 1985. It curbed public expenditure and rationed goods, but failed to prevent recurring budget deficit, which accounted for 13.7 per cent of GDP in 1987. External debt topped 100 per cent of GDP and the deteriorating economic situation and rising unrest undermined the position of the FLN government. By the late 1980s, the opposition Front Islamique du Salut (FIS) gained widespread popular support by denouncing the failure of the Algerian government's petroleum-driven economic model of state-led industrialization and a 'socialist market'.

In 1989 civil unrest led to the adoption of a new constitution allowing for multi party elections. Despite the manipulation of electoral rules by the ruling party, the opposition FIS dominated the election results (winning 47 per cent of the vote in local elections in 1990; 54 per cent in the national elections of 1992). Unwilling to accept this result, the military intervened and the Supreme Court prevented the FIS from assuming power on the grounds of its alleged links to terrorist activity (Nashashibi, 1998, pp2–3). This triggered civil war that persisted for almost a decade at the cost of an estimated 100,000 lives.

Rather than follow the IMF's economic reforms, the weakened Algerian government sought to maintain a consensus-based approach between the army, unions and businesses with regard to basic decisions on national resource allocation. Such inclusive political mechanisms maintained both formal and informal efforts to limit destitution in the face of the post-boom economic and civil war related hardships and to sustain a minimum of social cohesion in a context of civil war. Income inequalities eased from the mid-1980s to the mid-1990s (Adams and Page, 2001), but this was mainly because more people were getting poorer. In fact, the proportion of the population living in poverty doubled during the 1990s.

Table 6.1 *Structure of GDP and employment in Algeria, 1999*

	Value added (% GDP)	Private sector share of value added (%)	Employment (million)	Sector share of total employment (%)	Private employment in sector (%)
Agriculture	11.4	99	1.490	25	99
Hydrocarbons	29.5	1	0.135	2	2
Manufacturing	9.6	35	0.690	11	37
Construction	11.6	55	1.110	18	56
Services	25.4	75	1.190	20	74
Public administration	12.5	0	1.435	24	0
Total	100.0	41	6.050	100	52

Source: Aissaoui, 2001, p291

The essential restructuring of the economy was constantly postponed and unemployment reached 30 per cent of the workforce in the early 2000s. The state sector still dominated the economy (Table 6.1), and the hydrocarbons sector in particular, with 30 per cent of GDP, 60 per cent of government revenue and 95 per cent of exports, but barely 2 per cent of employment (Nashashibi et al, 1998, p2). However, the unexpected oil price increases of the mid-2000s provided the Algerian state with a revenue windfall, which it plans to invest in infrastructure projects and to moderate some economic reforms (Beaugé, 2005). This increased public expenditure may help improve the life of many Algerians anxiously awaiting improvements after more than a decade of civil war. Yet such a rapid expansion in public expenditure also risks making wasteful investments and entrenching corruption, calling for strong accountability to prevent this.

Iraq: Dictatorship, repression and military adventurism

Oil has been a major driving force behind insecurity in the Persian Gulf, and most notably in Iraq's internal, regional and international conflicts. The creation of Iraq by the British after World War I had the somewhat ironic objective of securing the control of oil reserves in that region. A pattern of institutionalized corruption in part motivated several attempted coups d'état against the British-supported Hashemite monarchy, which was finally brought down in 1958.

Successive military regimes, including that of Saddam Hussein after the Ba'ath party seized power in 1968, achieved dominance through a pattern of populist patronage and coercion. Oil only came to dominate the economy after nationalization of the petroleum sector between 1961 and 1972, and the 1974–78 oil boom. Annual economic growth averaged 14 per cent in the 1970s and by 1979 Iraq was the second largest OPEC oil exporter behind Saudi Arabia. Oil windfalls made populist economic policies more affordable to the Ba'athist regime. This wealth was also used, however, for a massive arms build-up and for funding the private interests of the Ba'ath party regime's cronies.

In 1979, Iraq launched an opportunistic and disastrous war against the new Islamic Republic of Iran that bankrupted the country. The economy contracted by 6 per cent per year during the 1980s. Financially bankrupt but still militarily strong, the Hussein regime sought to avert a political and financial crisis by invading Kuwait in 1990. Although this choice sustained Hussein's rule for 13 more years, drastic blanket sanctions were imposed that aggravated the country's economic collapse. By 1994, when the sanction regime was still in full force, Iraq's per capita real GDP was estimated close to that of the 1940s (Alnaswari, 1994).

This situation was somewhat improved under the UN's Oil-for-Food programme (see Box 6.1), but the state withdrew from many basic social and economic services, while corruption sharply increased in scale and breadth. The control of smuggled goods, including oil, and kickbacks from oil sales became the central economic focus of an Iraqi regime that had lost its formal control over the main economic sector of the country. By 2000, after a decade of war and a decade of international trade sanctions, Iraqi incomes had fallen to less than one fifth their 1980 level, with most Iraqis dependent upon the government, either directly for food or, in the case of the 2.25 million civil servants that comprised one third of the country's formal workforce, indirectly for employment (Economist, 2003). The US-led invasion of Iraq in 2003 led to massive looting and appropriation of state assets by political factions, and ordinary Iraqis, which further undermined the capacity of the state, while the ongoing insurgency in many areas of the country has retarded a rapid recovery and left large parts of the population highly insecure.

Escaping the resource curse

Not all resource-dependent countries experience growth collapses, as illustrated by revenue management in Norway and Botswana. Norway was already an industrialized country with strong institutions by the time oil revenues flowed in. Careful revenue management, relatively slow oil development and strong domestic absorption capacity, as well as saving part of the oil revenues through an oil fund, were key to this success.

Success was not immediate, however. When oil prices were high during 1973–85, the real costs of Norwegian non-oil producers rose 15–40 per cent more than the costs of their competitors; manufacturing output and exports stagnated, public sector employment rose by 70 per cent during 1970–91 and social welfare jumped to 17 per cent of GDP by the early 1990s – thereby absorbing the bulk of government oil revenue.

When oil prices finally crashed in the mid-1980s, Norway experienced a recession that lasted from 1986 to 1993. This led, among other things, to a self-defeating acceleration in oil extraction during a period of over-supplied markets

Box 6.1 The UN Oil-for-Food programme in Iraq

In operation between 1996 and 2003, the United Nations Oil-for-Food programme generated $64.2 billion dollars from Iraqi oil sales, of which $34.5 billion were allocated to a humanitarian programme for Iraq. In effect, the programme was one of the largest international aid projects in recent decades, but also one of the most controversial.

UN sanctions reduced Iraqi oil exports by 90 per cent between 1990 and 1995, with a terrible toll on its population. After obtaining discretionary control over oil pricing and the selection of purchasers of its oil exports, and humanitarian (and oil industry spare parts) imports, the Iraqi regime finally agreed to a revised sanctions regime. Although this new regime eased the plight of the population, it also opened the door to massive misuse of the programme by the Iraqi government.

The illicit income received by the Iraqi government from manipulating the Oil-for-Food programme is estimated at $1.779 billion, comprising $229 million from surcharges on oil sales and $1.55 billion from kickbacks on humanitarian purchases. An estimated 56 per cent of companies purchasing Iraqi oil and 62 per cent of companies providing humanitarian goods contributed to this illicit income.[3] Beyond consolidating the formal patronage capacity of the regime domestically, the Oil-for-Food programme was also politically manipulated internationally, with the regime extending its reward system overseas through oil vouchers provided as gifts, commissions for services, or in payment for goods to foreign companies and influential individuals. Many of the voucher recipients lobbied for an end to sanctions and for the normalization of relations with Iraq.

The Oil-for-Food programme suggests political opportunism (or 'realism') on the part of UN Security Council members, political complicity by the UN Secretariat managing the programme, and widespread collusion on the part of companies. The US and UK sought to maintain the sanction regime by turning a blind eye to practices commercially benefiting Security Council members opposed to the sanction regime – in effect 'buying' their consent. The US also turned a blind eye on oil smuggled to 'friendly regimes' such as Jordan and Turkey. Between 1997 and 2002, illicit Iraqi revenues from oil smuggling (outside the Oil-for-Food programme) are estimated to have been worth between 5.7 and 13.6 billion dollars.

The UN Secretariat itself did not tackle the problem of illicit revenues, considering it a political issue to be addressed by the Security Council. Bureaucratic corruption by the head of the programme, Benon Vahe Sevan, and conflicts of interests on the part of UN Secretary General Kofi Annan's son Kojo, have been demonstrated. Many companies and individuals also benefited from kickbacks orchestrated by Saddam Hussein. The official investigation into the programme under Paul Volcker has recognized the political interference of Security Council members in the running of the programme, but it has also strongly criticized the failure of the UN Secretariat to challenge this interference and to observe its 'own rules of fairness and accountability'.[4] What the Volcker commission may be missing here, or be prevented from saying by its limited mandate, is that it is the sanction regime itself that failed to follow these rules. From the perspective of a high-ranking UN official, the programme had turned into a 'Frankenstein' that escaped the control of its creators.[5] From the perspective of the Iraqi people, however, sanctions were from the onset anything but fair and accountable.

in an attempt to offset lost revenue (IMF, 1998, p8). Burnt by this experience, the Norwegian government established a Government Petroleum Fund in 1990 in order to minimize the economic distortions of oil booms and to stockpile wealth for future generations.

Botswana has also relied heavily on resources revenues since the 1970s. As a low-income country with weak 'modern' state institutions, Botswana could easily have followed a growth collapse path towards the staple trap. Unlike many other primary commodities, however, diamond prices have remained relatively stable as a result of the monopoly power of the De Beers company (one of the world's largest diamond mining companies and the world's largest trader in rough diamonds). The key in this sector is rather for the government to capture, and publicly account for, a sizeable share of diamond revenues.

The Botswanan government was able to access a large part of the diamond revenue through its control of the deep-shaft mines and a business partnership with De Beers. Although Botswana's society remains highly unequal economically, the ruling party maintained strong legitimacy through the broad provision of public services, and a relatively open democratic system. The government sought to ensure that public services could be fiscally sustainable, at least in the medium term, by capping budgetary expenditures and saving most surplus revenues in a long-term reserve fund (called the Pula Fund). In terms of governance, the government placed strong emphasis on meritocracy and integrity in its bureaucracy, initially enrolling foreign expertise to increase its capacity, supporting training and education, and creating a stringent anti-corruption legal framework.

There are also successful examples of the prudent use of overseas aid, where foreign aid disbursements tightly channelled by donors have helped improve the economic situation of the country as a whole. Post-war Mozambique is often cited as an example of successful aid spending in light of the partial economic recovery of the country over the past decade when the level of aid dependence was extremely high. Mozambique shows that the dispersion of aid to geographically and socially diverse groups, and the allocation of aid to health, education and productive economic sectors, lowers the risk of the 'windfall curse'. The inflationary effects of massive assistance in the early 1990s also led the IMF to impose strict limits on the amount of aid available for disbursement by the Mozambican government. Such limits, however, raised issues of political sovereignty loss and reconstruction delays and were progressively relaxed.

Donors targeted foreign aid at investment to rebuild the shattered economic infrastructure of Mozambique, rather than into current consumption, because tangible investments (such as schools and hospitals) are easier for aid agencies to monitor than public expenditure. Although targeting aid on a sectoral basis is sound, assistance was too often implemented through a multitude of unrelated and incoherent projects, fragmenting assistance and undermining the capacity and role of the government. Donors have more recently used direct budgetary support to address these problems, with the hope of maintaining oversight by directly participating in processes of budgetary allocation.

Overall, external assistance appears to have buttressed a democracy that achieved relatively high levels of institutional quality for a country of its per capita income. Corruption and persistent inequalities, however, have tainted the relative successes of the 'economic growth' coalition formed by donor agencies and the Mozambican government around neoliberal policies.

These case studies demonstrate the importance of tackling the volatility of resource prices and improving the management of revenues by governments. In principle, the less volatile and more easily controlled the resource revenue is, the better. The volatility of revenues and high levels of resource or aid dependence highlight the importance of sound macroeconomic policies in smoothing revenue flows and managing adjustment to external shocks such as volatile commodity prices.

The case studies also underline the importance of matching the rate of spending of natural resource and aid rents to the capacity of a country to absorb and make effective use of that spending. Giving more control to governments over these rents is only beneficial if governments deploy them efficiently for pro-poor purposes. As such, the efficient management of these specific revenues often reflects the overall performance of the government. The institutional context in which resources are exploited and revenues allocated is thus crucial to ensure the money is well spent. In this regard, as set out below, key requirements include building transparent, fair and accountable institutions, controlling corruption, stabilizing revenues and tailoring initiatives to the specific contexts of conflict-affected countries.

Improving natural resource and aid revenue management

As discussed above, there are clear incentives for improving revenue man-agement for the sake of security in resource and aid dependent countries. Preventive measures mostly concern the governance of revenues, as well as efforts to stabilize the price of resource revenue and diversify economies (see Curtis, this volume).[6] Some of these measures are also relevant in terms of conflict resolution and post-conflict recovery. Revenue management is not only important for the current generation, but also for future ones. Natural and environmental resource accounting provides a rationale for allocating the natural resource rent between consumption by the present generation and investment for future generations (Auty and Mikesell, 1998). In policy terms, this requires investment of the rent to diversify the production structure of the economy in order to reduce dependence upon the rent stream. Such investment also enhances the resilience of the economy to economic shocks.

Attempts to improve revenue management have been made at both the domestic and international levels, sometimes in combination. At a domestic level, specific regulatory frameworks and institutions define management structures, with resource-revenue management legislation as its foundation. Internationally, transparency benchmarks, reporting rules, initiatives to build accounting capacity and setting up trust funds to help reform failing domestic revenue management and corporate practices are also required. The following sections examine domestic revenue-management laws and international initiatives to improve transparency in the natural resource sectors.

Improving revenue governance: Revenue management laws

Revenue management laws generally address three main areas: the collection, administration and allocation of resource rents. Within each transparency, accountability, representation and equity are major issues in order to avoid rent capture by narrow interest groups, notably political elites, and reduce the risks of (renewed) armed conflict.

Revenue management laws generally first set the principles and objectives defining the management of resource revenues, using principles of transparency, fairness in allocation between producing and non-producing regions, and objectives of poverty alleviation and improvement of public health and education services. These laws also often create specific budgetary instruments, such as stabilization and savings funds (see below), and can set financial benchmarks, such as ratios setting maximum annual withdrawals from revenues or saving funds. Finally, these laws define administrative and oversight bodies in charge of the governance of the sector and its revenues.

A key element for resource management laws is their scope, which needs to be comprehensive and have application to all resource-related revenues, not just some types of revenues from some areas. The law also needs to set precise rules of governance (e.g. responsibilities, accountability and penalties) and insulate oil revenues from political party interests (like patronage and populist policies, political party financing, embezzlement). The revenue allocation principles and mechanisms need to be consensual and representative, must notably include a practical means of informing and consulting populations, and cannot be exclusively reliant on prominent civil society organizations.

Financial transparency in revenue flows should be guaranteed, including frequent reporting in the public media and publicly accessible websites. The asset-management strategy should be coordinated with budgetary policy, and borrowing on resource revenues should be prohibited. The conditions of parliamentary scrutiny and budgetary decision-making should be secured, with a detailed breakdown of accounts. Finally, there should be independent and credible oversight, auditing, and performance evaluation.

Most studies have noted that revenue-management laws can only be effective if they are part of a sound overall fiscal management structure. This should not only ensure that other income streams and expenditure flows are adequately managed, but also that resource revenues are coherently integrated into fiscal policies and budgetary processes. In this regard, there remains some debate about the value of using resource revenue or aid trust funds that aim to deter political interference and insulate the economy from rent distortions (see Box 6.2).

Box 6.2 Revenue management laws in conflict-affected countries

Azerbaijan: Transparency and presidential probity

In the wake of a violent transition from the Soviet Union, the Caucasian republic engaged in a broad set of reforms as international oil companies increased their presence. Since 1999 there has been an Oil Fund under presidential control (through oversight-body nominations and expenditure control), and a new Budget System Law providing for greater parliamentary scrutiny and decision making over oil revenue allocation, as well as public reporting on the executed budget. Although there has been improvement, much of the management rests on presidential decisions, and levels of expenditure have exceeded planned withdrawals – by a substantial margin – during recent high oil prices (Tsalik, 2003).

Chad: Loopholes and frustrations in the Petroleum Development and Pipeline Project

After nearly three decades of civil war, peace negotiations in the mid-1990s made it feasible for oil companies to develop oil fields in southern Chad. The Exxon-led consortium of oil companies asked the World Bank to act as a 'moral guarantor' of the project and to assist the Chad government with revenue management (Horta, 1997). Several oversight committees, including an International Advisory Group, observe and make recommendations on the implementation of the project.[7] The oil revenue management law directs oil revenues into an offshore savings account and towards pro-poor social services (after reimbursement of project-related public debts).[8] While the Chad–Cameroon Project was hailed as a 'new model' for oil development in poor countries and benefited from unprecedented attention and efforts, the project failed to ensure that strong institutions were in place before oil revenues start flowing. This new model of governance has come under strong criticism, notably for its lack of comprehensive coverage and implementation of the International Advisory Group recommendations, inadequate government capacity, and poor oversight of budgetary execution (Gary and Reisch, 2005).

Iraq: Revenue management under foreign occupation

Following the US-led war in Iraq, the UN Security Council directed Iraq's oil revenues and repatriated funds to a Development Fund for Iraq placed under the authority of occupying forces (the US-led Coalition Provisional Authority), provided that the right of the Iraqi people to 'control their own natural resources' be recognized, and that the management of oil revenues by occupying forces 'benefit the Iraqi people' and be adequately audited.[9] Many of the failings of the US-led Coalition Provisional Authority can be accounted for by the massive challenges that it faced, although policy orientations, shifting timetables largely dictated by US domestic political priorities, bureaucratic infighting and red tape, as well as high staff turnover and lack of experience also contributed in major ways (ICG, 2004). Key failures included: a lack of Iraqi policy ownership; a bias in disbursing Iraqi rather than US funds for reconstruction; inappropriate budgetary allocation mechanisms, benefiting well-connected US companies rather than local Iraqi firms and people; lack of transparency, including in shaping future oil policies; and unjustifiable delays in auditing, including by the International Advisory and Monitoring Board for Iraq, created to independently monitor the Development Fund for Iraq (Le Billon, 2005a).

São Tomé e Príncipe: Exemplary legislation and political discord

With two recent coup attempts in 1995 and 2003, and continued political tension within the government, São Tomé e Príncipe's potential oil wealth has raised much concern for the future of the tiny archipelago. The recent Oil Revenue Law, however, provides extensive guarantees in terms of transparency, accountability and governance (Bell and Faria, 2005).[10] The drafting of the law itself benefited from extensive consultation with opposition parties and the public at large, as well as the technical assistance of the Earth Institute of Columbia University. Despite this exemplary framework and process, there remains much tension within the current regime, with the prime minister resigning after denouncing the discretionary power of the president in signing new production sharing agreements without proper consultation, including with the parliament.

Sudan: Revenue-sharing between (former) belligerents

As part of an ongoing peace process, in January 2004 the government of Sudan and the Sudanese People's Liberation Army/Movement signed a wealth-sharing agreement over oil resources, dividing oil revenues between the two parties. The scheme, however, is not independently supervised. Significantly, the agreement leaves aside the issue of ownership of subterranean natural resources (Tellnes, 2005). The agreement places the oil sector under the management of a National Petroleum Commission with representatives from both parties, and allocates revenues equally to the national and regional governments. Stabilization and Future Generation funds are to be established. All funds and special accounts are to be on-budget operated. Oil-collateralized loans are not prohibited. Transparency provisions include the creation of a Fiscal and Financial Allocation and Monitoring Commission (staffed only by officials from both governments), and public accounts subject to public scrutiny and accountability. Auditing is to be performed by regional and national audit chambers, whose members are nominated by the presidency and confirmed by the assembly. Overall, the scheme lacks independent oversight mechanisms.

Timor-Leste: From UN revenue savings policy to Petroleum Fund Act

A petroleum revenue savings policy was established under the United Nations Transition Authority in East Timor, whereby oil tax revenues were allocated to the annual budget, while oil royalties were saved for future use. In 2005, the government established a permanent Petroleum Fund, collecting all petroleum revenues (taxes and royalties), from which budgetary allocations can be drawn within the limit of a sustainable income from total petroleum wealth (current fund and estimated future income from reserves) estimated by the government. Fund withdrawals have to be approved by the national parliament and all fund operations are placed under the oversight of a consultative council of eminent persons and subject to independent audits.[11] Any encumbrance on the assets of the petroleum fund is prohibited. The Petroleum Fund Act also sets transparency as a fundamental principle and establishes accountability rules. Petroleum revenues for this impoverished state, however, are under threat from an Australian government eager to control the lion's share of oil and gas reserves in the Timor Sea.

International initiatives can also promote better revenue management, by supporting domestic policies as well as by helping define and enforce good practice in both the public and private sectors. Yet taken in isolation, such interventions have also proven to be controversial and misdirected. Critics of the IMF and World Bank, for example, argue that forced deregulation and privatization in the resource sectors have constituted damaging forms of political interference (Tan, 2002). Critics of transnational corporations have similarly pointed to their very mixed record in terms of their human rights, revenue sharing and support for repressive regimes (Global Witness, 2004).

Aid and resource revenues were perceived until the 1980s – at least in official international development and security circles – as key ingredients of the consolidation of 'friendly' states on both sides of the Cold War divide. Growing national debt and structural adjustment policies, the decline of Cold

War geopolitics and greater awareness of economic agendas in wars shifted this focus towards 'good' governance and market-oriented priorities (Berdal and Malone, 2000; Bannon and Collier, 2003; Le Billon, 2005b). As a result, there has been a focus on policies to promote transparency, while other policies, like government-led price stabilization mechanisms, have declined. The following sections examine domestic revenue management laws and international initiatives to improve transparency in the resource sectors.

Stabilizing revenues

One way of reducing the adverse effects of commodity price volatility on the domestic economy is for local governments to set up capital development funds. In practice, the rent is placed within a fund managed by the central bank, with sizeable windfalls invested offshore to limit Dutch disease effects until such time as the domestic economy can absorb them productively. Investing a fraction of the rent in alternative wealth-generating assets – capital development or economic diversification – can also ensure that the income-generating capacity of the depleting mineral resource is passed on to future generations (Auty and Mikesell, 1998).

Capital development fund management usually entails setting an expected commodity price and automatically transferring revenues above that price to the fund. A public revenue stabilization fund may also be adopted to smooth the flow of volatile commodity revenues into public finances. Within a transparent fiscal system, such a fund can help to constrain the scope for governments to use revenues earmarked for medium-term and long-term objectives to overcome short-term political problems. Revenues can also be stabilized through a number of financial instruments, such as commodity bonds and derivatives, to hedge exposure to commodity price fluctuations. Finally, a public-sector project-evaluation unit can complement the capital and public-revenue stabilization funds by objectively comparing the economic returns to alternative uses of public expenditure, including the potential returns on overseas investments.

The utility of capital development funds has been challenged, however (Davis et al, 2001). The main criticisms are that such funds:

- may be poorly integrated with the budget and so lose control of public spending;
- encourage off-budget spending that undermines fiscal integrity;
- complicate coordination between fund management and budget management;
- tend to function with even less transparency than the government budget and thereby increase the likelihood of the political deployment of the revenues.

In fact, these problems are all associated with poorly designed funds and are not inherent in the system. Moreover, the examples cited to suggest that funds have failed are drawn from the polarized democracies of PNG and Venezuela, but ignore the positive experiences of consensual democracies like Botswana and Chile (Auty and Mikesell, 1998). As Fasano (2000, p19) concludes from a review of six resource funds, a 'stabilization fund cannot be a substitute for sound fiscal management, and its success or failure can be attributed as much as to fiscal discipline as to the fund's management'. Ironically, resource funds seem to work best only where they are not needed; that is, when sound fiscal policies are already observed and resource revenues represent only a small part of fiscal inflows.

Internationally, the IMF's Compensatory and Contingency Financing Facility provides budgetary support in the form of short-term loans to governments facing low resource revenues that are believed to be temporary. Where a more fundamental structural shift in commodity prices occurs, the IMF can provide loans to extend the period of adjustment to reduced prices, while the World Bank and regional development banks, among others, can provide conditional loans for economic restructuring.

The EU also uses such a system – Stabex, or Flex since 2000 – in order to help ACP countries adjust to unfavourable shifts in their terms of trade. Despite easing the criteria for assistance, Flex remains too selective and characterized by long delays in disbursement that undermine its effectiveness. Such mechanisms can be linked to lower debt service obligations, with a reciprocal arrangement to accelerate debt repayment if revenues are unusually high. More broadly, aid could be related to vulnerability to trade shocks, rising in cases where that vulnerability is substantial, provided that the recipient governments exhibit the ability to make effective use of such aid in terms of target criteria such as economic growth or poverty reduction (Combes and Guillaumont, 2002).

Most attempts to assist governments are tied to economic or political conditionalities. Governments are thus frequently reluctant to accept them, especially when the political cost is high. Governments may actually wait until a point of economic crisis is reached before accepting reforms (Bruno and Pleskovic, 1997). Other potential beneficiaries and stabilization mechanisms with fewer political constraints should also be considered. Using international funds to create an insurance mechanism directly targeted at commodity-producing households and companies may be more effective than allocating funds through governments.

Aid trust funds constitute a financial instrument through which funds are collected from donors and allocated to recipients in a supposedly independent fashion. In practice, however, trust funds have often mirrored resource revenue management funds in terms of political and allocation biases. Trust funds often retain close ties with donor interests, such as political leverage, commercial objectives and preferential home-country contracting (Chatterjee, 1994; Schiavo-Campo, 2003).

Aid trust funds can smooth aid flows and help generate future income, notably by timing the disbursement of funds according to domestic needs and absorptive capacity rather than to donor imperatives. Crises are often followed by donor pledges in part motivated by short-term and visible demand and expected outcomes. Many crises call in fact for a gradual and rising provision of assistance, rather than the boom-and-bust often characteristic of 'CNN-driven' crisis management. As discussed below, the level and allocation of aid flows is an important component of aid effectiveness. Recovery in post-conflict situations, for example, requires large and rising levels of aid during the first half-decade. Part of the donations immediately made after the signature of a peace agreement can be 'saved' for future use as the absorptive capacity of the country increases. Yet aid inflows often remain donor-dependent, and the separation into an investment trust fund and a recurrent cost fund can result in budgetary fragmentation and policy incoherence (Schiavo-Campo, 2003).

Improving public sector expenditure over the long term is related to effective capital development and revenue stabilization funds. External agencies, such as the World Bank, can intervene in this regard not only by promoting savings, but also by jointly building up institutional capacity and using such mechanisms as loan conditionality and incentives to improve transparency and accountability. Within such an institutional framework, macroeconomic policy should seek to create an enabling environment for investment by balancing public expenditure with revenue, maintaining the external (trade) equilibrium balance and correcting market failure through the provision of infrastructure, education, health facilities and environmental policies.

International and domestic revenue transparency initiatives

A lack of transparency increases not only the risks of corruption and embezzlement, but also of inequity, distrust and false expectations. More specifically, in the absence of adequate disclosure, producing provinces and the general population can be financially disadvantaged. Lack of knowledge can also reinforce distrust among stakeholders, most notably between civil society and governments or companies. A lack of clarity on current (and future) revenue flows can also result in rising expectations on the part of populations (and governments), with false hopes of wealth later resulting in grievances, distrust and legitimacy issues. In contrast, transparency can consolidate democratic debate by providing accurate figures upon which stakeholders can negotiate and plan.

Transparency has three main components: revenue disclosure, transparent governance, and auditing and reporting. Disclosure is the basis of transparency and is most often understood as full public disclosure (rather than disclosure limited to business partners and authorities). The objectives of transparency, however, could arguably be achieved through adequate financial governance, auditing and reporting. It may not be as important to know 'how much' revenue is flowing in the resource or aid sector, as to know how well these have been managed and accounted for. Most citizens in the world have little idea of precise budgetary flows, but they do care about the adequacy of the political and bureaucratic processes serving their interests. The public character of information should thus be guaranteed not only by disclosure, but also by the quality of governance. As such, disclosure is particularly important in situations of 'weak' governance (Laffont, 2005), where disclosed information may help to compensate for such weakness and consolidate a transition to more effective and legitimate governance.

Transparency is not only about dollar figures, but also about individuals and interest groups in charge of, or influencing, the management of revenue flows. The governance of financial flows needs to be transparent in terms of who is doing what, and with which potential conflicts of interest. The background and personal assets of decision makers need be made publicly available. For example, a president's nephew may head an NGO and not be a government official, but is unlikely to have an 'arm's length' relationship with the ruling party and should not qualify as a civil society representative on a monitoring board. Reliable and easily accessible information are key elements of transparency. Major challenges in this regard include a lack of credibility about sources due to conflicts of interests or poor expertise, as well as financial flows hidden in obscure and difficult to access or understand documents.

According to Goldwyn and Morrison (2004), any transparency model in oil-producing countries should include the following:

- disclosure of corporate and government revenues (royalties, taxes, signature bonuses and other fees);
- open and transparent processes for bidding on concessions and procurement;
- disclosure of oil-backed loans;
- auditing of national accounts and oil companies (including state oil companies);
- publication of fiscal accounting reports requested by the IMF;
- expenditure transparency in public budgeting;
- legislated access to information;
- independent auditing and public reporting of public finances.

Transparency can be supported at the international level through corporate revenue disclosure rules, and the promotion of international norms of public and private financial governance (through voluntary or mandatory approaches), capacity-building assistance, and international auditing and reporting. The IMF and DAC constitute the two pillars of international transparency for resource revenues and aid, respectively, but they are not enough. The IMF provides valuable information on resource revenues through its Country Reports, the information for which is mostly provided by the country's central banks. Yet such reporting depends to some extent on the goodwill of domestic governments, many figures (or detailed breakdowns) remain confidential and it rarely engages with the most politically sensitive aspects of transparency. The DAC provides statistics on aid flows (and other resources) to developing and transition countries, available on a donor, recipient, grants/loans, and major sectors basis. These figures, however, fail to provide detailed accounts of the use of aid and do not report on many private financial flows.

International financial institutions and auditing companies should (continue to) take on an advocacy and implementing role to promote public disclosure. International media – especially radio and television – should systematically incorporate revenue information in the same way as financial reporting is done on currencies and stock exchanges. International advocacy organizations can play a strong role in analysis and as channels of information to both domestic and international audiences. Their international status and location offer some protection against pressure from domestic authorities, in effect 'taking the heat' of reporting off local civil society organizations.

Three complementary initiatives are now underway to improve transparency in the resource sectors. The British-government-led Extractive Industries Transparency Initiative (EITI) lays out principles of transparency, accountability and prudent management of resources for voluntarily participating countries and companies.[12] It also provides specific revenue reporting guidelines and criteria for participation. In contrast to the Publish What You Pay (PWYP) campaign detailed below, which largely inspired the initiative, the British government stressed the responsibility of host governments on transparency, while the US government also lobbied hard for EITI to follow a voluntary rather than mandatory approach (Goldwyn, 2004). Being voluntary, it is incentive driven, and critics have suggested that the main incentive for joining EITI has been for governments and companies to deflect criticism and gain domestic and international legitimacy.

So far, EITI fails to require that its prescriptions are legislated and that the overall process be formally overseen by a democratic mechanism (although arguably this is a 'non-starter' in many countries where transparency is most needed). However, adherence to EITI principles is now a criterion for access to finance for extractive sectors from many ECAs and other international financial institutions. Supporters believe that EITI may progressively assume widespread international recognition.

Key countries with major domestic or international extractive industries are not yet EITI members, such as the US, Canada and France, as well as China, India and Malaysia. EITI should also be integrated into 'post-conflict' management, notably in Algeria, Angola, Colombia, Iraq, Liberia and Sudan. Critics have suggested that DFID, in consultation with EITI partners, should have a more prescriptive approach to address the 'advice needs' of potential participants (Global Witness, 2005). Although local policy ownership and some flexibility are needed, a common criteria and reporting regime is highly desirable. Finally, EITI should also protect its reputation through reviews of implementation criteria and strong links with accountability mechanisms.

The PWYP campaign launched in 2002 by Global Witness and George Soros' Open Society Institute aims at mandatory disclosure of all payments to host governments by oil, gas and mining companies.[13] The campaign was supported in 2005 by a worldwide coalition of 270 NGOs and major investment funds, as well as a few extractive companies, such as STATOIL from Norway, that published a breakdown of these payments to governments worldwide.[14]

The PWYP campaign argues that corporate disclosure is an important step towards comprehensive accountability in the resource sectors. Campaigners note that voluntary initiatives are proving useful with some countries and companies, but remain unlikely to achieve a global and lasting solution. Most companies have so far resisted disclosure, on grounds of contractual confidentiality and competition (or even irrelevance, in the early days of the campaign). With some of the largest oil companies being non-listed state companies and very few producing countries 'publishing what they get', mandatory disclosure in producing countries is also regarded by campaigners as essential.[15] To achieve this comprehensive transparency coverage, PWYP is advocating 'double book-keeping' by extractive companies and governments, through revenue disclosure laws in both host and home countries. PWYP campaigners have articulated several approaches through key institutions, such as stock markets, IFIs, export credit agencies and accounting standards, but many have yet to come to fruition.

The IMF Guide on Resource Revenue Transparency (GRRT) aims to promote transparency by requesting a clear definition of roles and responsibilities from governments, as well as public disclosure of all resource revenues, financial assets, debts and quasi-fiscal information on state-owned enterprises by governments. The GRRT also calls for open budget preparation, execution and reporting, with clear policy statements and revenue volatility risk evaluation. It also suggests external or independent assurances of integrity, through international accounting, auditing and reporting standards, with national audit office reporting to parliament. The GRRT stresses the diversity of country backgrounds and the need for time, sustained commitment to reforms on the part of domestic governments, companies and donors and 'a close linkage between fiscal transparency assessments, country administrative reform, and carefully designed technical support from international and bilateral agencies' (IMF, 2005, p9).

So far few resource-dependent countries follow the more general IMF Code of Good Practice in Fiscal Transparency and undertake the Reports on the Observance of Standards and Codes (ROSCs) that gives it teeth. The same may be expected with the GRRT, in part because large resource revenues insulate governments from the assistance and demands of IFIs. The IMF should thus attempt to make GRRT implementation mandatory, ensure greater civil society participation, and systematically conduct and publish ROSCs.

An international extractive sectors transparency agreement

Both PWYP and EITI aim to emulate the success of the KPCS on conflict diamonds by enlisting the support of key international institutions, governments and companies. But, in the opinion of several analysts, neither PWYP nor EITI – as they now stand – possess the scope and leverage to succeed; see Table 6.2 (Goldwyn, 2004). PWYP initially failed to cover non-listed companies, while EITI has no hold on unwilling producing countries. EITI also focuses too heavily on 'developing countries' heavily dependent on natural resources, and to some extent overlooks the responsibilities of industrialized countries towards fair, transparent and accountable revenue management both domestically and internationally.[16]

Table 6.2 *PWYP and EITI compared*

PWYP	EITI
Work through company reporting regulated by their home governments (additional to EITI).	Work with individual host governments.
Pros	*Pros*
1 One mechanism can cover all countries in which internationally regulated companies operate. 2 Affords companies protection and a level playing field. 3 Consistent level and availability of information to civil society and investors.	1 Supports national ownership of initiative. 2 Covers all companies operating in the host country.
Cons	*Cons*
1 Home government regulations cover only companies that are registered or raising finance in their territory. 2 Current lack of political will for regulation and global standards.	1 Impossible where host government is unwilling (and where need may be greatest). 2 Slow roll out on a host country by country basis. 3 Reversible on change of host leadership.

Source: Save the Children (2005)

Building on current initiatives and the lessons of the KPCS, an effective international scheme may require a quasi-global participation backed by criteria enshrined into national legislation, with effective sanctions in effect for non-participation (e.g. foregoing vast trading and investment opportunities) and non-compliance (e.g. exclusion) (Mokgothu, 2003). In such a scheme:

- participation would be required from the overwhelming majority of resource importing and exporting countries, and relevant institutions (e.g. backed through a resolution of the UN General Assembly, and possibly UN Security Council);
- participating countries would agree to common standards of resource revenue disclosure and governance (much like the existing EITI and IMF's GRRT) and accordingly enforce appropriate regulations and minimal standards;
- trade and investments in resource sectors outside of the participating countries and institutions may be subject to a review process by a designated authority at the home country level and notification at the international

level[17] (a more stringent regime would require a review process at the international level);

- peer-review monitoring would be conducted to ensure continued compliance of participating members, backed by capacity-building assistance and enforced if necessary through exclusion.

Initiatives for conflict-affected countries

A characteristic of conflicts in low-income countries is to increase dependence on a narrow range of primary commodities and aid while manufacturing and services (such as tourism) contract. Revenue management during hostilities and post-conflict transition can prove decisive to the security of local populations. Three broad types of initiatives can curtail the use of resource revenues by belligerents to finance and profit from hostilities. They are: capturing resource areas from belligerent forces; imposing economic sanctions; and sharing resource revenues between belligerents.

The relative effectiveness of these initiatives appears to respond in part to the characteristics of the targeted resource (Le Billon, P. (2004) 'Natural resources and the termination of armed conflicts: Share, sanction, or conquer?', unpublished manuscript). Resources most easily accessible to rebel forces – such as alluvial diamonds – are best addressed through sanctions (see Chapter 4 on conflict resources), while military capture is most effective in the case of bulky resources controlled by the government, such as oil. Controversially, when illegal resources are financing war, such as narcotics in Burma, sharing arrangements between belligerents have proven to be more effective, but it is arguably a rare official option for governments and even less so for external actors attempting to resolve the conflict. New market regulation schemes, such as commodity certification and transparency schemes, have also improved the control of conflict trade and revenue governance. Resource revenues are not, of course, the only dimension of conflicts, and none of these initiatives provides a comprehensive solution on its own.

Although international financial institutions and donors intervene increasingly early in conflict termination processes, the political economic implications of peace-building have generally been neglected and often left to the initiative of belligerents who can jockey for key economic positions within the new authority or simply embezzle funds to re-arm. Beyond sanctions and global regulatory measures, practical regulatory frameworks can be set up to deprive belligerents of revenues they could use to follow a double agenda of peace transition and rearmament, as has happened repeatedly in Angola, Cambodia, Colombia, Liberia, Sierra Leone and Sri Lanka.

Internationally supervised tax collection and budgetary allocation could seek to ensure that populations and public institutions benefit from resource revenues. Direct payment of resource revenues could be made to the population, as suggested in the case of Iraq (Palley, 2004). This would have the advantage of clearly distributing a 'peace dividend' to the neediest, and it partly addresses the problem of lack of representation and accountability through broad-based taxation that affects the many resource-dependent countries. Spreading the wealth in such a way would have effects that might be counterproductive, however, such as inflation and rising consumption of imported and non-productive consumer goods. Businesses themselves could be deterred from operating outside the scheme through a system of incentives and sanctions. If successful, and in the absence of alternative sources of support, opting out of a peace process would become prohibitively costly for belligerents. Like all instruments of control, the effectiveness of such a scheme would depend in part upon the characteristics of the targeted resource sector and the economic incentives attached.

Conclusions and recommendations

Since the late 1970s, some developing economies, such as Chile, Indonesia and Malaysia, have escaped the staple trap of primary commodity export or aid dependence. Three key factors behind their success include: sound macro-economic management that allowed them to take full advantage of increased opportunities to trade; central control of corrupt rent-seeking behaviour so that illicit imposts are known and not random; and the pro-poor expenditure of some commodity revenues to improve the competitiveness of labour-intensive activity. All successful countries maintained, or eventually shifted towards, increased public accountability as they sought to competitively diversify their economies out of slow-growth primary commodities into higher-growth commodities and a widening array of manufacturing and services (Martin, 2002). The larger economies of Malaysia and Indonesia made a spectacularly rapid transition from resource-based growth to manufacturing-led growth during the 1980s.

There remains, however, a large number of less successful primary commodity export and aid dependent low-income countries that have yet to restore rapid economic growth after the growth collapses of 1974–85. Many are located in sub-Saharan Africa, where their populations face numerous sources of insecurity, from human rights abuses to poor health services. It is imperative that revenues generated by natural resources and aid reach and benefit these populations, notably through strong and legitimate institutions allocating revenues fairly and efficiently. Inappropriate domestic and foreign policy interventions, as well as the poor quality of domestic institutions and political incentives constrain such improvements. It is thus imperative for these priorities to be considered within the broader political and economic contexts in which revenue management is to be addressed.

To achieve this both domestic and international efforts are needed. The literature and case study evidence surveyed in this chapter suggest three policy priorities:

1   Creating an enabling environment within which the private sector can invest efficiently to diversify the economy into competitive and employment-intensive activity.

2   Stabilizing revenue flows from natural resources and aid to ensure that such flows do not out-strip domestic absorptive capacity, and can therefore be applied to secure long-term improvements in social welfare rather than short-term gains for the politically well connected.

3   Controlling corrupt rent-seeking and ensuring that an increasing fraction of revenue goes towards increasing the capacity of the poorest to participate in economic development.

Hopes for improved terms of trade for the commodity producers rest to an important degree upon improving economic performance and thereby reducing the labour surplus that depresses the wages of the poor throughout the tropical regions (Deaton, 1999). In the absence of this advance, international and domestic interventions in supply and/or demand management will struggle. Past interventions through international commodity agreements and domestic commodity marketing boards, for example, have a poor track record. A superior long-term solution is therefore to promote the competitive diversification of the economy out of slow-growth commodities that exhibit declining terms of trade.

A further obstacle to diversification out of dependence upon slow-growth commodities lies in the vested interests that benefit from the corrupt rent-seeking that past policies (notably closure of the economy to create domestic monopolies for the politically well connected) nurtured. The resistance of such elites to top-down reform prompts an alternative strategy that is based upon the establishment of early reform zones, which are geographical areas within which efficient infrastructure, competitive incentives and cost-effective and reliable public services immediately apply. Such zones can accelerate the attraction of domestic and foreign investment into competitive activity that generates employment, taxes and skills and at the same time builds a pro-reform political constituency. China provides a clear example of such a dual-track reform strategy: it set up experimental export zones in the mid-1980s while it postponed reform of the moribund state sector industry until the competitive market economy had grown sufficiently in size and resilience to help absorb surplus labour from the lagging state sector. Elsewhere, Malaysia and Mauritius also deployed a dual-track strategy that nurtured a competitive manufacturing sector able to propel the economy when commodity revenues slowed.

Recommendation 1 *Assess the local viability of early reform zones in specific commodity and/or aid dependent countries*
The most important areas for successful economic diversification reside in international and domestic trade contexts. The conditions of meaningful access to markets by low-income countries are far from being met. One obvious reform priority centres upon dismantling the protectionist trade policies of the leading trading blocks in North America, western Europe and Japan, which subsidize domestic farmers and sunset industries, such as mass textiles, at the expense of low-income developing countries. Reforms in market access,

such as the diffusion of most-favoured-nation status or Europe's everything but arms policy, are well directed but often have only a minor effect on the trade of the poorest countries, including short booms in 'footloose' light manufacturing plants. The questions of production subsidies, tariff escalation, and non-tariff barriers need to be urgently addressed by the dominant markets, notably the USA, EU and Japan, as well as China and India. The influence of large multinationals on producer prices and revenue share also needs to be addressed given the massive corporate concentration of some sectors and weak bargaining position of many producers. Meaningful market access also entails enhancing the trading capacity of low-income countries, which can be advanced through both international assistance in building trade capacity and domestic trade policy reforms.

Recommendation 2 *Systematize the identification of resource revenue allocations in international statistics (e.g. World Bank or IMF databases) to facilitate their use in international negotiations and public debate*
Improving the terms of trade and the share of revenue accruing to producing countries and governments may paradoxically expose them to even greater economic shocks. A further priority is therefore to minimize economic shocks and promote sustainable diversification of the economy to escape the staple trap. Although countries can help stabilize fluctuating rent flows through their own domestic policies rather than by producer action to control commodity prices, they often require international coordination and assistance.

Recommendation 3 *Reinvigorate the debate on measures for commodity price stabilization, beginning with the IMF's Compensatory and Contingency Financing Facility and the voluntary schemes being developed by the fair trade movement. As a priority, income stabilization mechanisms should improve natural resource revenue flows in conflict-threatened areas*
Greater and more stable revenues have little influence on the security of the population if corruption is rife and revenues are unfairly and inefficiently allocated. The third priority is thus to address rent-seeking and revenue allocation by promoting transparency, political accountability, voice and rule of law. Yet any intervention also needs to be carefully tailored to the domestic political economy if it is to succeed. Donors and agencies can also provide technical assistance to host governments in revenue management, resource pricing, accounting, reporting and auditing. This is particularly the case for sound domestic fiscal frameworks, and support of resource stabilization and savings funds.

Recommendation 4 *Build effective revenue management mechanisms that increase the transparency and accountability of natural resource and aid revenues, and promote long-term income stability for natural resource dependent countries*
Recent global initiatives on transparency and accountability in trade and aid transactions have produced promising results, but they are limited by conflicts over national sovereignty and by voluntary rather than mandatory approaches.

Transparency and accountability can be improved by the regulation of financial markets (including banks) and better-targeted international assistance. The repatriation of embezzled funds and debt cancellation can help remedy past mismanagement and help compensate for lost incomes during bust times. Resource exporting and importing countries can agree upon national, bilateral or international extractive sector transparency agreements.

Recommendation 5 *Strengthen the Extractive Industries Transparency Initiative and the IMF Guide on Resource Revenue Transparency. Merge them into an International Extractive Sector Transparency Agreement with common standards of revenue disclosure, independent monitoring and effective compliance measures. Increase capacity building to improve revenue management, resource pricing, accounting, reporting and auditing*

International initiatives can help to bolster domestic responses to many of these priorities and recommendations. As suggested in this chapter, such initiatives are particularly significant in conflict-prone countries. These countries are often affected by a lack of trust between, and within, government and society. This makes the potential role of international agencies significant as independent third parties and guarantors of agreements. Low institutional capacity, poor or unfair regulatory environments, and/or predatory practices also often characterize conflict-prone countries. Capacity-building assistance and strong oversight, addressing issues of impunity, are of major importance. Unless these tasks are seriously addressed at the international level, aid and trade will continue to prove a potential source of insecurity.

Notes

1   However, several countries, including Chile, Ghana, Mexico and India, were already beginning to exhibit signs of economic distress even before the 1974–85 period of heightened primary commodity price shocks, due to the cumulative misallocation of revenues since the 1950s that was diminishing the resilience of their economies.

2   These revenues are in effect rents. Natural resource rent is defined here as the residual revenue after deducting from total revenue all the costs of producing a commodity, including the risk-related return on investment. In theory, such rent can be extracted from the economic activity that generates it, say through taxation, without depressing production incentives – hence its description as a 'gift of Nature'. However, the definition identifies potential rent, which may be lost to the public good if dissipated through government corruption, monopoly profits and a wage aristocracy (all of which often occur with import substitution industry) and/or subsidies for goods services consumed overwhelmingly by the rich. Foreign aid can be conceived as a form of economic rent, which we can describe as geopolitical rent: a 'gift from outside the country' taking the form of a grant or low-interest loan, often tied in terms of its access and use to political and commercial interests, quality of governance or policy reforms. The critical destabilizing property of rent, whether natural resource or geopolitical, is its capacity to engender contests for its allocation that if mismanaged can undermine both the economy and the political state.

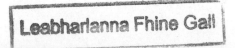

3   Independent inquiry committee into the UN Oil-for-Food programme, 'Report on programme manipulation', 27 October 2005, www.iic-offp.org/story27oct05.htm

4   Interim report of the independent inquiry into the UN Oil-for-Food programme, 2005, p4.

5   Interview with high-level UN official, New York, 2000.

6   See also Swanson et al (2003); Goldwyn (2004); Green (2005); Ballentine and Nitzschke (2005), and PWYP website www.publishwhatyoupay.org/english/

7   See www.gic-iag.org/ehome.htm

8   English translation of Law 001/PR/99, www.bicusa.org/bicusa/issues/Chad_Rev_Mgmt_Law.pdf.

9   UN Security Council, Resolution 1483, 21 May 2003, approved by all members except Syria (abstained).

10 English translation of Act, www.earthinstitute.columbia.edu/cgsd/STP/documents/oilrevenuemanagementlawgazetted_000.pdf

11 www.timorseaoffice.gov.tp/revmngtfacts.htm; and draft Act, www.timorseaoffice.gov.tp/PF-draftAct-eng.DOC

12 See www.eitransparency.org

13 See www.publishwhatyoupay.org/english/background.shtml

14 Investors' statement on transparency in the extractive sector (March 2005), www.publishwhatyoupay.org/english/pdf/relstatements/investors.pdf; PWYP, 'Norwegian oil major takes big stride forward on transparency by publishing payments to governments', press release, 14 April 2005, http://pwyp.gn.apc.org/english/media/mediapage.shtml?x=187021

15 A further potential loophole concerns the regulation of international brokers registered in offshore jurisdictions. Such brokers specialize in getting resource concessions through corrupt deals, before selling them on in a 'clean' manner to larger and complacent resource companies. Local 'sleeping partners' associated with the operations of resource companies, such as the board directors or parastatal companies in charge of some subcontracting operations, also act as agents for corruption by scooping large cash bonuses, commissions or profit shares.

16 Specific criteria have not been set in this respect, but EITI generally refers to 50 countries in which extractive industry revenue or export proceeds represent at least 25 per cent of fiscal revenues or total exports, respectively. See IMF (2005) and Boateng (2005).

17 Investments or trade by non-participants in participating countries, as well as by participants in non-participating countries, would be subject to a review and notification process through the designated authority of the participating party (see Schumacher (2004)); on review process, see Gagnon et al (2003).

References

Adams, R. H. and Page, J. (2001) *A Case of Pro-poor Growth? Poverty Trends in MENA 1970–2000*, Washington DC, World Bank Poverty Reduction Group

Aissaoui, A. (2001) *Algeria: The Political Economy of Oil and Gas*, Oxford, Oxford University Press

Alnaswari, A. (1994) *The Economy of Iraq: Oil, Wars, Destruction of Development and Prospects, 1950– 2010*, Westport, CT, Greenwood Press

Auty, R. M. (ed) (2001) *Resource Abundance and Economic Development*, Oxford, Oxford University Press

Auty, R. M. and Mikesell, R. F. (1998) *Sustainable Development in Mineral Economies*, Oxford, Clarendon Press

Ballentine, K. and Nitzschke, H. (2005) *Profiting from Peace: Managing the Resource Dimensions of Civil War*, Boulder, CO, Lynne Rienner

Bannon, I. and Collier, P. (eds) (2003) *Natural Resources and Violent Conflict: Options and Actions*, Washington DC, World Bank

Beaugé, F. (2005) 'L'Algérie va lancer un "plan Marshall" pour doper son économie', *Le Monde*, 25 June 2005, p2

Bell, J. C. and Faria, T. M. (2005) 'Sao Tome and Principe enacts oil revenue law, sets new transparency, accountability and governance standards', *Oil, Gas and Energy Law Intelligence*, vol 3, no 1, p1–8

Berdal, M. and Malone, D. (eds) (2000) *Greed and Grievance: Economic Agendas in Civil Wars*, Boulder, CO, Lynne Rienner

Bevan, D. I., Collier, P. and Gunning, J. W. (1987) 'Consequences of a commodity boom in a controlled economy: Accumulation and redistribution in Kenya', *World Bank Economic Review*, vol 1, pp489–513

Boateng, P. (2005) Closing Remarks, EITI London Conference, 17 March 2005

Boone, P. (1996) 'Politics and the effectiveness of foreign aid', *European Economic Review*, vol 89, no 1, pp22–46

Bruno, M. and Pleskovic, B. (1997) *Annual Bank Conference on Development Economics 1996*, Washington DC, World Bank

Burnside, C. and Dollar, D. (1997) 'Aid policies and growth', World Bank Research Working Paper 1777, Washington DC, World Bank

Cashin, P. and McDermott, C. J. (2002) 'The long-run behaviour of commodity prices: Small trends and big variability', *IMF Staff Papers*, vol 49, no 2, pp175–198

Chatterjee, P. (1994) 'Slush funds, corrupt consultants and bidding for bank business', http://multinationalmonitor.org/hyper/issues/1994/08/mm0894_09.html accessed in 2005

Collier, P. (2000) 'Doing well out of war', in Berdal, M. and Malone, D. M. (eds) *Greed and Grievance: Economic Agendas in Civil Wars*, London, Lynne Reinner, pp 91–111

Combes, J-L. and Guillaumont, P. (2002) 'Commodity price volatility, vulnerability and development', *Development Policy Review*, vol 20, no 1, pp25–39

Davis, J., Ossowski, R., Daniel, J. and Barnett, S. (2001) 'Stabilization and savings funds for nonrenewable resources: Experience and fiscal policy implications', IMF Occasional Paper No. 205, Washington DC, IMF

Deaton, A. (1999) 'Commodity prices and growth in Africa', *Journal of Economic Perspectives*, vol 13, no 93, pp23–40

Easterly, W. (2001) *The Elusive Quest for Growth*, Cambridge, MA, MIT Press

Economist (2003) 'After the war is over', *The Economist*, 8 March, pp27–29

Fasano, U. (2000) 'Review of the experience with oil stabilization and savings funds in selected countries', IMF Working Paper WP/00/112, Washington DC, IMF

Gagnon, G., Macklin, A. and Simons, P. (2003) 'Deconstructing engagement', *Public Law Research Paper No. 04-07*, University of Toronto, Faculty of Law

Gary, I. and Reisch, N. (2005) *Chad's Oil: Miracle or Mirage? Following the Money in Africa's Newest Petro-State*, Washington DC, Catholic Relief Services and Bank Information Center

Gelb, A. H. and associates (1988) *Oil Windfalls: Blessing or Curse?*, New York, Oxford University Press, pp262–288

Global Witness (2004) *Time for Transparency*, London, Global Witness

Global Witness (2005) *Making It Add Up: A Constructive Critique on the EITI Reporting Guidelines and Source Book*, London, Global Witness

Green, D. (2005) *Conspiracy of Silence: Old and New Directions on Commodities*, Oxford, Oxfam

Goldwyn, D. L. (2004) 'Extracting democracy', *Journal of International Affairs*, vol 5 (Winter/Spring), pp5–16

Goldwyn, D. L. and Morrison, J. S. (2004) *Promoting Transparency in the African Oil Sector. A Report of the CSIS Task Force on Rising US Energy Stakes in Africa*, Washington DC, CSIS

Horta, K. (1997) *Questions Concerning The World Bank and Chad/Cameroon Oil and Pipeline Project*, New York, Environmental Defense Fund

ICG (2004) 'Reconstructing Iraq', Middle East Report N°30, New York/Brussels, International Crisis Group

IMF (1998) 'Norway: Selected issues', IMF Staff Country Report 98/34, Washington DC, IMF

IMF (2005) *Guide on Resource Revenue Transparency*, Washington DC, IMF

Krueger, A. O., Schiff, M. and Valdes, A. (1992) *Political Economy of Agricultural Pricing Policies*, Baltimore, MD, Johns Hopkins University Press

Laffont, J. J. (2005) *Regulation and Development*, Cambridge, Cambridge University Press

Le Billon, P. (2005a) 'Corruption, reconstruction and oil governance in Iraq', *Third World Quarterly*, vol 26, nos 4/5, pp685–703

Le Billon, P. (2005b) 'Fuelling war: Natural resources and armed conflicts', *Adelphi Paper no 373*, London, Routledge for IISS

Martin, W. (2002) 'Outgrowing resource dependence: Theory and evidence', Development Research Group, World Bank, http://info.worldbank.org/etools/docs/voddocs/210/409/outgrowing_resource_doc.pdf

Mokgothu, B. (2003) Draft statement by Mr B. Mokgothu, Hon. Minister of Minerals, Energy and Water Resources, Republic of Botswana, made at the Ministerial Conference on Extractive Industries Traansparency Initiative (EITI), London, 17 June, www2.dfid.gov.uk/pubs/files/eitidraftreportbotswana.pdf

Murshed, M. (2004) 'When does natural resource abundance lead to a resource curse?', Discussion Paper 04/01, London, International Institute for Environment and Development

Nashashibi, K. et al (1998) 'Algeria: Stabilization and transition to the market', IMF Occasional Paper 165, Washington DC, IMF

Palley, T. (2004) 'Oil and the case of Iraq', *Challenge*, vol 47, no 3, pp94–112

Rodrik, D. (1999) 'Where did all the growth go? External shocks, social conflict and growth collapses', *Journal of Economic Growth*, vol 4, pp385–412

Ross, M. L. (1999) 'The political economy of the resource curse', *World Politics*, vol 51, no 2, pp297–322

Ross, M. L. (2001) 'Does oil hinder democracy?', *World Politics*, vol 53, no 3, pp325–361

Save the Children (2005) *Beyond the Rhetoric: Measuring Revenue Transparency in the Oil and Gas Industries*, London, Save the Children

Schiavo-Campo, S. (2003) 'Financing and aid management arrangements in post-conflict situations', CPR Working Papers No. 6, Washington DC, World Bank

Schumacher, J. A. (2004) 'Introducing transparency into the oil industry: The quest for EITI', *Global Jurist Advances*, vol 4, no 3, article 2

Svensson, J. (2000) 'Foreign aid and rent seeking', *Journal of International Economics*, vol 51, pp437–461

Swanson, P., Oldgard, M. and Lunde, L. (2003) 'Who gets the money? Reporting resource revenues', in Bannon, I. and Collier, P. (eds) *Natural Resources and Violent Conflict: Options and Actions*, Washington DC, World Bank

Tan, C. (2002) 'Tackling the commodity price crisis should be WSSD's priority', *TWN briefings for WSSD No.14*, Penang, Third World Network

Tellnes, J. F. (2005) 'Dealing with petroleum issues in civil war negotiations: The case of Sudan', Paper presented at the 13th Annual National Political Science Conference at Hurdalsjøen, 5–7 January 2005

Treisman, D. (2002) 'Post-communist corruption', Working Paper, Los Angeles, Department of Political Science, UCLA

Tsalik, S. (2003) 'Caspian oil windfalls: Who will benefit?', *Caspian Revenue Watch*, New York, Open Society Institute

Van de Walle, N. (2005) *Overcoming Stagnation in Aid-Dependent Countries*, Washington DC, Center for Global Development

Westley, G. (1995) 'Economic volatility from natural resource endowments', *Development Policy*, Washington DC, Inter-American Development Bank

World Bank (2001) *World Development Report 2000/2001: Attacking Poverty*, Washington DC, World Bank

World Bank (2005) *World Development Indicators 2005*, Washington DC, World Bank

Conclusion: Prospects for Peace and Progress

Mark Halle

It is a truism to say that everything is interconnected, but the events of the past decades have driven this lesson firmly home. Or they should have.

On an intellectual level, most trade policy professionals acknowledge that trade liberalization can restrict development policy space, hinder economic diversification and undermine political stability. But, when the trade rules are being crafted and negotiated, it is the same old mercantilist game that predictably plays out. Lip service is paid to development needs, and trade deals are still largely forced on poor countries, wrapped in arguments that the resulting economic growth will allow them to address whatever development problems trade openness has generated. Trade theory argues that trade liberalization is good. But if the evidence suggests a more mixed picture, it is too often blamed on imperfect application of the theory, rather than any inherent fault the theory might contain.

We know that unless aid projects take into account the macroeconomic and political realities within which countries are forced to operate, the benefits they bring are often unsustainable – if not downright counterproductive. Yet aid policy is often the preserve of one ministry and economic policy of another. It is well known that pressing short-term foreign policy considerations often derail carefully crafted aid programmes aimed at poverty alleviation or rural development. What is less well known is how often the potential for aid success is sapped by parallel macroeconomic policies pursued by the same donor country directly, or through surrogates in the World Bank or the IMF. These same institutions and governments have commissioned countless studies that show how aid policy can be made more coherent and how it can reinforce other policies. Unfortunately, most of these studies remain on the shelf.

Worse still, we know that the benefits of both trade and aid can disappear rapidly in times of conflict, or even of heightened social tension. Yet we pay little attention to the possibility that aid and trade interventions might aggravate social tensions and make conflict more likely. We know that conflict is a failure of our systems of social and political relations, the consequences of which can set back development by years, if not decades. But our approaches to both do not consider the avoidance of conflict as a solid foundation without which nothing lasting can be built.

We have learned a great deal in the past decades, but too few of the lessons have been put into practice. We know the reasons; most professionals in the field of trade policy, development assistance and conflict management are hopelessly overworked, and struggle even to run through the simplest checklists when faced with a new and urgent challenge. In responding to the pressures they face, they tend to take solace in the community of their peers, with whom they share a culture, a vocabulary and a common understanding of the situation. Taking the time to cross the institutional borders and to explore the culture, vocabulary and world outlook of another knowledge community, to mine it for valuable lessons that can be taken back and applied, is a rare luxury.

I well remember some years ago, in the wake of a number of devastating hurricanes that swept across Central America, causing terrible destruction and loss of human life, bringing together experts from three fields – disaster response, environmental management and climate change. The disaster response experts had honed the art and science of meeting urgent humanitarian needs with skill and efficiency. However, the growing frequency of natural disasters and the realization that their impact is aggravated by avoidable human actions had eroded the motivation and confidence of this sterling group of professionals.

The environmental management community had studied in depth the link between healthy watershed forests, wetlands, coastal mangroves and coral reefs on the one hand, and the human impact of some natural disasters on the other, and were convinced that sound environmental management can go a long way to mitigate disaster. Yet once the humanitarian crisis receded, they were highly discouraged to see environmental management slip once again down the priority list to take its usual place as a marginal concern, even if the next disaster would prove that it was in fact the contrary. And the climate change community warned that natural disasters were likely to grow both more frequent and more intense but were also deeply frustrated by the lack of political will to tackle the roots of the problem.

Each community found in the other not only rich and relevant experience, but also insights, tools, approaches and practices that could greatly improve the impact of their own work within their own sectors. They realized that by coordinating the planning, and understanding the actions, of the different communities, their results would be greater than the sum of the individual interventions. And they realized that, in doing so, they were far less likely unwittingly to take action that might undermine the aims of the other community. The linkages between the different areas of endeavour proved interesting and relevant, and offered a new way of approaching common problems.

This is the central point – that sustainability requires a holistic view. Partial views may be compelling in their own terms, and they may achieve a clear short-term benefit, but through their isolation they carry with them the seeds of long-term failure.

This volume is about these linkages. We have sought to demonstrate the importance of the links that bind trade, aid and security and to underline where in the complex set of interactions the linkages are most significant. We have sought to show how the relationships play out, how they influence one another, and how benefits, in a situation where linkages are ignored, can not only come unstuck, but in fact also aggravate an already difficult situation. On a more positive note, we have tried to show that 'getting it right' is not only possible, it is also not necessarily difficult.

Trade, aid and security – locating the positive synergies

In examining the triangle that these three topics form, it is clear that there are two-way interactions along each axis. Trade policy and practice can reinforce security, just as it can destabilize countries and create conditions in which conflict thrives. Aid can be deployed – and the debate on aid-for-trade suggests that much of it soon will be – in ways that give countries a better chance of benefiting from trade openness. But it can also be used to promote policies that, in today's world, leave the country worse off than it was before, adding to social displacement and stirring together the ingredients for conflict.

We have not, in this volume, treated each of the axes with equal attention. We have tended to look, instead, at how both trade and aid policy, on their own or in combination, affect prospects for conflict. We have looked at conflict as an avoidable result of misguided policy and asked ourselves how better outcomes might, in future, be secured. We have, it is clear, looked at the linkages through a conflict lens, aiming both to understand how to avoid moving down the path towards conflict and, more positively, to look at the interventions that will lower social tensions and render conflictual outcomes ever less probable.

We have chosen this approach because behind the paradigm, the mechanics of which we are trying to understand, lays the overall goal of sustainable development. We regard security as a necessary precondition to sustainable development – indeed, its portal. Where security and stability exist, the cooperation, positive interactions, and investment necessary to put in place the conditions for sustainable development can be gathered. When social tensions mount, trust is undermined, interactions turn sour, cooperation becomes more difficult, and nobody is prepared to invest in a future in which benefits will be slow to materialize. Where armed conflict breaks out, positive interaction and cooperation is replaced by violence, and resentment often prevents trust from rebuilding, even long after the conflict has ended.

We have chosen to focus on aid and trade in relation to security because trade and aid interactions make up a significant proportion of the links that bind developed and developing countries. Avoiding and resolving conflict – in particular conflict that spills over national borders – has risen steadily up the foreign policy agenda of the rich aiding and trading countries. In dealing with these issues, beyond the soft option of diplomacy and short of the extreme hard option of military action, economic relations offer the most viable tool to address how these interests are defined and defended. Aid and trade shape those relations.

Trade relations have long been regarded as a tool for peace and for building mutual understanding, but they hold the potential for coercion – to punish a trading partner that has acted contrary to one's interests. Even today, trade and other sanctions are regarded as the tool of choice in the international community when the military option is unfeasible or undesirable. But it can also prove counterproductive: misuse of the 'trade tool' through ill-considered, mercantilist protectionism was one of the contributing factors in triggering the Great Depression and in sending the Western world down the path to extremism and, eventually, World War II.

To a lesser extent, aid has served as an arrow in the quiver of those countries seeking to defend their national interests in the poor world. It is not to impugn the motives behind overseas development assistance to point out that, over the years, there has been a disturbingly high correlation between national political and economic interests and the pattern of aid delivered. To a lesser extent than trade (but not by much when the entire multilateral lending mechanism is included) aid has served as a tool for foreign policy ends.

To use both aid and trade as instruments in pursuit of the national interest is not illegitimate as such. In its execution, however, it has too often stirred social tensions and, in the most extreme cases, contributed to conflict.

But the more we learn about the causes of conflict, the less excusable it is that we were not willing to address these seriously or in good time, preferring (at least by default) to pick up the pieces afterwards. While peacekeeping is a necessary response to shoring up a tenuous peace once a conflict has been concluded it is, in terms of the broader human goals, nevertheless a response to a failure. If peacekeeping is necessary, it is because the peace was not kept. If the peace was not kept we must conclude that the policies, institutions and mechanisms for early warning did not work or were ignored. The more we learn of the long-term negative consequences of conflict, how seriously it undermines sustainable development and how expensive it is in financial, political and social terms, the less we can accept that the linkages presented in this volume can be given a low priority until attention to them becomes unavoidable.

Security is a precondition for successful trade and aid, just as it is for sustainable development. Without security, aid is unlikely to have a lasting impact, and trade will favour the unscrupulous, the exploitative or the downright illegal. And effective aid and trade policies are essential for cementing a durable peace. Get these right and peace may ensue. Get them wrong, and it is a good bet that all three will suffer. The links are no longer in doubt – poor aid and trade policies contribute to conflict and instability. Illegal trade in natural resources, misuse of aid funds, mismanagement of revenues from both aid and trade, and poor business conduct in fragile states – all have contributed to growing political instability around the world, as examples from Cambodia to Liberia indicate.

Where things have gone wrong, there is often evidence of compartmentalized thinking – the aid experts concentrating only on the immediate concerns of aid delivery, the trade experts seeking to maximize short-term national interest, and both downplaying their potential to provoke or aggravate conflict. Conflict is something for others to worry about.

We urge the trade and aid policy communities to pay greater heed to the realistic, rather than theoretical, outcomes of what they are proposing, and to consider the range of approaches available to lessen the chance of conflict. Is it correct to exempt the country from a new trade obligation, such as lowering a tariff or eliminating a quota? Or phase it in more slowly? Should it be delayed while the capacity and institutions are put in place to allow the country to benefit from its application? And is aid available to put it in place? Or is it clear that a country's resistance to the trade obligation is little more than a misguided effort to protect an elite industry or the interests of some politically powerful constituent?

What if the priority were to be defined as the smoothest possible transition to an open economy? What would be the sequence of change and what measures would have to be designed and implemented? And would this process not essentially represent an ideal agenda for the aid community? If so, what are the roles to be played by the different actors in government, civil society and the private sector?

Where to from here?

There are several steps in changing any situation. The first is to understand its dimensions, extent and interactions. The second is to identify the actors whose participation is needed. And the third is to work out the specific decisions, initiatives or agreements needed to effect the change.

We hope that we have convinced the reader that the linkages between trade, aid and security are not simply casual, but that they are instead compelling and current. We have indicated that some of the problems besetting aid, trade and conflict cannot be addressed without reference to one or both of the other fields and that, indeed, there is much to be gained by seeking insights from other disciplines or bodies of experience. We are convinced that compartmentalized thinking, while reassuring within a given fraternity, is, in the end, dangerous.

We hope also to have indicated who needs to participate in the search for the solutions in some of the key areas of action identified. It is clear, for example, that much of the creative thinking on trade, and the future of trade policy, is not emerging from the trade negotiators but from the range of research centres, think tanks, NGOs or business associations that flank, support and criticize them; it is often those exploring the margins of an issue who can best illuminate both the problem and the solution.

Wolfgang Reinicke, in his seminal book *Global Public Policy – Governing without Governments*, posits that much of the significant progress we have seen in the international field comes about through the operation of non-traditional alliances of government bodies, civil society and the private sector coming together for a specific, doable and time-limited purpose. Sometimes, even, the role of the government sector is – as the title of the book suggests – negligible.

Reinicke looks at a range of cases in which a solid step forward was made in addressing a public policy challenge, and seeks to identify the common characteristics of success. He concludes a number of things that are of relevance to addressing the challenges of Trade, Aid and Security. In cases where a notable success was achieved:

- The challenges taken on were specific, limited and time-bound: in other words, success was not achieved in alleviating world hunger, or in stabilizing biodiversity, or in reducing atmospheric carbon. Where it was achieved, it was in providing mosquito nets to rural villages in Botswana, or creating the political momentum to conclude a land mines convention, or finding agreement among stakeholders on the building of a dam, or even agreeing on a certification scheme for sustainably harvested timber or fish.
- The alliance brought together was made up of specific players each of whom brought a piece of the puzzle to the table: the Marine Stewardship Council, which agreed on standards for responsible fishing, was made up of little more than the World Wildlife Fund (WWF), who enjoy broad public trust, and Unilever, the world's largest fish purchaser, who guaranteed a major impact in the market. In the case of the World Commission on Dams, nothing less than the full range of stakeholders would have done the trick, but they had to be brought together in a neutral and balanced format, and one in which each felt its voice was heard. The Landmines convention was the result of an alliance of governments backed by NGOs fighting to overcome the natural inertia in the system to anything new and radical.
- The alliances united parties each of whom had a stake in solving the problem at hand: the successful networks have not primarily been bargaining forums, but an attempt to create the most complete and most powerful community around the shared objective. That community then sought the best way to prevail over the opposition. The coalition supporting disciplines on fish subsidies in the WTO is made up of a group of countries – North and South – that would not normally come together in that configuration around any other single issue, backed by the patient analytical work of WWF and a range of other NGOs, and allied to the market power of large players like Unilever. The coalition has specific objectives and a clear framework – the WTO negotiations – within which to deploy their power.

Reinicke's analysis is much more complex than the characterization offered above, but the central message is clear. We cannot solve the challenges of trade liberalization with trade tools alone; we cannot tackle the dilemmas facing aid delivery with aid tools alone; and we cannot resolve conflict simply by focusing on peace-building techniques. Each requires resources, skills and outlooks that come from other knowledge communities. Each must put together the right combination of actors, set the right goals and act within just the right framework if they are to bring about lasting change.

This is the other message of this volume: we have demonstrated the links between trade and aid, aid and security, and trade and security. They are real, they are compelling, and they are complex. But the answer cannot be to meld the three communities into one happy family, sharing every aspect of every responsibility. This is neither realistic nor even desirable. Specialization and focus are assets in dealing with issues central to one discipline, culture or community. They are not, however, adequate for dealing with the increasing range of issues that lie at the confluence of the different communities and interests.

In seeking to apply some of the lessons learned, some trends are discouraging while others are encouraging. The ebb of multilateralism, the steady expansion of new security threats, and the propensity of the international community to react to crises rather than patiently laying the basis for preventive approaches certainly do not make the challenge any easier.

Other trends, though, are encouraging. There is renewed and quite creative attention being paid to conflict and to conflict prevention, as evidenced by the recent creation of the UN Peacebuilding Commission, improved donor coordination in DAC around conflict-related issues, and better streamlining among the many international organizations concerned with conflict. And there is a significant new openness to ideas in the WTO, coupled with an understanding that the old way of doing things can no longer work and that new approaches – such as aid for trade – are needed.

This volume has broken the trade–aid–security nexus into its essential components, around issues and communities. Each section contains a series of particular recommendations and, where possible, identifies a number of actions that could be taken relatively easily and that would begin to make a serious difference. Where possible, these recommendations are aimed at specific lead actors, and address either principles to be adopted or actions that might be undertaken.

However, our new understanding of the issues covered and of their inter-connections suggests that we must be creative and experimental in the solutions we design. Just as we must build bridges to other relevant bodies of knowledge, and seek new institutional means to address unfamiliar problems, so we need to be creative in finding the right combination of actors and resources to bring to bear. We have to look not at our own partisan and self-interested positions alone, but at the way in which we might muster the right coalition of actors around the right set of specific, doable objectives and operate within just the right institutional framework.

If we do this creatively, we can break down the walls that impede sustainable solutions. If we do not, nobody will forgive us for having successfully defended our narrow interests. Nobody will admire us for meeting the objectives of our aid programme if the programme ends in disarray as avoidable conflict engulfs our target country. Nobody will remember the victory we secured in trade negotiations through our consummate skill and negotiating prowess; instead they will remember the conflict that followed the imposition of an unfair trade deal on vulnerable countries.

General Electric used to issue its employees with a plaque carrying their favourite slogan: *There is a better way. Find it!* We, too, believe there are better ways to do trade and aid and to reinforce the base of security on which sustainable development must be built. We hope that this volume has indicated some of them.

Reference

Reinicke, W. (1998) *Global Public Policy – Governing without Governments*, Washington DC, The Brookings Institution

Index